CW00923071

# Wellbeing and Aspirational Culture

Kevin Moore

# Wellbeing and Aspirational Culture

Kevin Moore
Faculty of Environment, Society and Design
Lincoln University
Lincoln, New Zealand

ISBN 978-3-030-15642-8      ISBN 978-3-030-15643-5   (eBook)
https://doi.org/10.1007/978-3-030-15643-5

Library of Congress Control Number: 2019934754

This Palgrave Macmillan imprint is published by the registered company Springer Nature Switzerland AG
The registered company address is: Gewerbestrasse 11, 6330 Cham, Switzerland

*To my father, James Noel Moore who taught me the importance of simply being an ordinary person.*

*To Ludwig Wittgenstein who, through his philosophy has made me understand* why *the ordinary, everyday world we live in is so extraordinary.*

# Acknowledgements

While the ideas behind this book have been coming together over several decades they came into much clearer focus during my study leave in 2017. I would like to thank Lincoln University for the financial support I received for that study leave. In many ways, however, the more important support I received was from my Head of Department, Roslyn Kerr, and the Dean of my Faculty, Greg Ryan. Both encouraged me to take leave and were fully supportive of me spending the time to develop these ideas into book form.

Ideas do not come from nowhere—and not even from one person's mind. I would like to acknowledge the very helpful conversations I have had with John Cromby, of the University of Leicester, and Will Davies, from Goldsmiths, University of London and for allowing me to take up some of their time when I was in the United Kingdom. I am especially grateful for the hospitality and opportunities provided by John Cromby during my short stay as a Visiting Scholar at Leicester.

The unobtrusive but always positive and supportive approach of the editorial team at Palgrave Macmillan, UK has also been much appreciated. From my first meeting with Grace Jackson at the British Psychological Society Conference in Brighton, to my contact via email with Joanna O'Neill and Kumaravel Senbagaraj the responses and advice I have received has been professional, prompt and always friendly.

Finally, I must do more than say 'Thank You!' to my wife Karyn and daughter Brianna. You have made the process so much easier for me by how you have understood the importance of this project to me, made space for me to work, put up with my evening and weekend absences, and never once made me feel like what I was doing was a problem for you. I know I did not always keep up with the work schedules you drew for me Brianna (sorry!) but having you do that for me said so much that was good about our relationship. When it comes to understanding the wellbeing of this person, you are both world experts.

# Contents

# 1

# Introduction: Wellbeing in an Aspirational World

## An Overview of the Argument

This book is about the difficulties involved in trying to experience wellbeing in today's world. I take as straightforward facts that people are having difficulty living well and that they are having these difficulties irrespective of claims by some that, on all sorts of dimensions, the human world is better than it has ever been. To put it at its starkest, there may well have been a reduction in all forms of physical violence (Pinker 2011) but, irrespective, that has not been matched by a reduction in psychological harm or pain. I argue that these difficulties are not like technical problems that require some kind of piecemeal technical solution. Instead, the explanation for what some see as a paradox (e.g., Easterbrook 2004) involves seeing that our wellbeing concerns are principally about persons—and being clear about just what a person is should therefore be central to understanding wellbeing. It is persons who are the enduring, identifiable subjects of experience and so they must also be the subjects of any experience of wellbeing. Yet, crucially, persons—perhaps unlike individual biological members of the human species—are intimately associated with the social and the cultural worlds that generate them. They are perhaps best expressed as

© The Author(s) 2019
K. Moore, *Wellbeing and Aspirational Culture*,
https://doi.org/10.1007/978-3-030-15643-5_1

'*doings*' in that world—rather than beings or entities (though I will refer to them as 'entities' and 'beings' for simplicity's sake). This connection to the sociocultural world is probably why psychology in general, and the psychology of wellbeing in particular, has had a deal of difficulty incorporating, or even acknowledging, persons in theory. Psychology is all about the person, but the person is nowhere to be seen in psychological theory (with some notable exceptions, as we will see).

Given these points, the way we are typically concerned with wellbeing cannot be understood without also understanding the kinds of cultures within which persons arise. And, to add some complexity, wellbeing also cannot be understood fully without some understanding of the typical *life tasks* (Cantor et al. 1987, 1991) a particular culture sets before the persons that it generates. The extent to which these tasks are mastered will determine the extent to which that person is found to be in good standing as a person in that culture. For a person, being in such good standing is a large part of living a good life; a life of wellbeing. But a person is not passive in these assessments of her standing. The skills we each develop and can draw upon to present ourselves—to both ourselves and others—as being in such good standing are crucial tools we bring both to achieving our life tasks and to our presentation of our success, or lack of success, at them.

The argument of this book is straightforward and has two parts. The first part is the claim that work on wellbeing—especially within psychology—has omitted from consideration a fundamentally important question: 'The wellbeing of what?' As already mentioned, I argue that the answer to that question is 'persons'. Much of the theoretical and conceptual importance of what follows therefore concerns understanding what persons are and why such curious entities came to be. That is, I make an argument for the basic functional features of persons and personhood and, hence, why and how persons evolved and also why they are one of the main targets of human development.

The second part follows from the first, though, in truth, the order in which these occurred to me was the reverse. Given that persons are principally "sociocultural artefacts"—to use Rom Harré (1983) phrasing—no understanding of (human) wellbeing is complete without consideration of the particular features of the culture within which persons emerge. Person's emerge as both a concept that concerns a fascinating form of life, and as an outcome of the development of individual human beings as they become, to one degree or another, persons. For several reasons I focus on what I call 'aspirational culture' to explain these links between personhood and wellbeing. The term is my own and I take it to mean that particular aspect of today's culture that most markedly informs the 'life project' of persons within it insofar as it bears on those persons' wellbeing. Our individual and collective 'project' is, at base, to aspire.

In one sense I am using the term 'aspirational culture' as a synonym for the equally imprecise term 'today's world'. That is, whatever 'aspirational culture' might be, it is also an increasingly pervasive and even dominant cultural form that is making its presence felt in more and more places on the planet. Globalisation would not be globalization in the form we have it if it did not also effectively 'aspirationalise' the economies, societies and people of the world. But there is another, more technical sense, in which I want to use the term 'aspirational culture'. Persons are the 'pivots'—or index points—for the navigation of multiple aspects of a (personal) life. Aspirational culture makes its presence felt in each of these aspects: the personal; the social; the political; and, the economic. These aspects have nested and overlapping features that, roughly and with some inevitable friction, maintain a culture of aspiration in a self-reinforcing and self-referencing manner.

One reason for focusing on cultures that are aspirational, in this sense, is that they appear to be spreading fast. A second reason is more substantive: Aspirational culture has a fascinating and complicated relationship with the wellbeing of people (persons). As I hope to show, that relationship provides especial insights into just what wellbeing is and what it involves. Third, there is a sense in which this notion of 'aspiration' is also not a recent feature of human cultures; it is baked into our culture because of the fateful turn to an agricultural way of life. It was only after that recent turn to agricultural production that the now familiar parade of various and sometimes vast societies, civilisations and even empires began. The tell-tale signs of this evolutionarily unusual form of human sociality include proliferation in the division of labour, increasingly focused specialisation of the skills and knowledge of individuals, and hierarchical social organisation. Wherever we look in human history (from about 12,000 years ago to the present) we find more of this form of society and culture and less of its egalitarian, socially 'flat', hunter-gatherer predecessor with its broadly skilled and knowledgeable members. Finally, aspirational cultures themselves seem to be the ones most responsible for generating the very interest in wellbeing that provides such a wide audience for books such as this. That interest, for my purposes, is a piece of data—a datum—used in evidence for my argument.

While it is not central to my argument, I also suggest that this 'aspirational' aspect of today's culture (certainly of the one I spend my time in) is pervasive and works as a structuring ideology. By 'structuring ideology' I mean that it has a direct 'channelling' influence at the level of personhood development and, therefore, in the lives people lead—in their material, social and psychological aspects—and in the wellbeing outcomes that attend those lives. Increasingly, it is being expressed throughout our social, political, legal, financial and economic institutions. It is the air we breathe. My conclusion with respect to such a culture is that it is—overall and despite common supposition—harmful to the wellbeing of the persons who are its constitutive entities. In other words, and far more simply, today's aspirational culture works against the wellbeing of the persons—and the notion of personhood—it helps constitute.

One only has to be passingly acquainted with the various streams of popular intellectual culture to realise that this conclusion is not original; but the theoretical explanation that leads to the conclusion is original, so far as I am aware. Further, I intend to show that the conclusion results from a well-integrated conceptual account of wellbeing that is informed by a range of disciplines including, to varying degrees, the philosophical, psychological, evolutionary, social, cultural and economic literatures. I should add that I also expect this conclusion to be provocative in the sense that many researchers may well feel a strong desire to oppose it on any number of grounds and so, hopefully, will do so. I also hope, however, that it is provocative in the sense that it provokes novel research and theoretical directions for those interested in understanding the processes of human wellbeing. The final chapter provides some of my own thoughts and suggestions about how we might begin to explore those novel directions.

This book, then, is about wellbeing. To that extent, it is in numerous–if not always 'good'—company. A fascinating feature of today's world is that when something becomes popular it often becomes *very* popular. 'Wellbeing' and its variants (e.g., 'wellness', 'living well') have undeniably become 'hot topics' and, evidenced by their increasing ubiquity, socially 'viral'. No doubt many wellbeing researchers have their own pet list of odd—or at least unexpected—domains in which the word 'wellbeing' has been rhetorically recruited (Who, for example, would have guessed that your local dental care outlet would also be one of your many guides for how to 'live well'?). For anyone living in the kinds of aspirational cultures on the march today, it would also be hard to miss the emergence of an industry almost entirely focused on delivering wellbeing options to individuals through the increasingly global 'marketplace' (and that notion of an *emergent* industry ignores older industries—such as the pharmaceutical industry—that have repositioned themselves as, at least to some extent, wellbeing providers).

The following is a brief overview of the basic argument to be developed in this book. The first point to note is that this book is not just a collation of what we know about our wellbeing (and what makes it 'tick' and how we might 'tick its boxes'). I summarise the rapidly increasing research work on wellbeing (in Chapter 3) in order to argue for a fundamental rethink of our approach to wellbeing. Most research in psychology on wellbeing has been about identifying the factors that seem to make people ('on average') 'flourish', 'thrive', be 'happy', be 'satisfied', or simply have more and better 'wellbeing'. It is this research that has, perhaps prematurely, developed a symbiotic relationship with those individuals, communities, organisations, nations (and even the entire planet) that have quickly acquired large appetites for such research.

This focus on the determinants and consequences of wellbeing, by both researchers and just about everybody else, is understandable. It almost seems a truism that much of our effort—from the individual to the global levels—*should* focus on the improvement of wellbeing. It then follows—again, almost as a truism—that whatever techniques or technology we can develop to enhance wellbeing *should* be produced and provided as rapidly as possible. Who could possibly argue against such an epidemic of virtuous intent? But as those who have investigated the notion of 'culture' have observed, culture, when operating effectively, is hardly noticed. It is akin to the aphorism about the fish and the water—invisible but utterly essential and pervasive. If 'truisms' are anything they are the all too familiar signposts that, paradoxically, hide in plain sight just those features of the world to which we should pay most attention. Instead of being uncritically assumed, these self-evident truisms are in need of investigation. The assumed value of our pursuit of wellbeing is the truism that is my target.

The argument that will be developed here makes a strong and, I would argue, conceptually defensible claim about the best way to understand and approach wellbeing. All concerns about the wellbeing of people I will claim, are subsumed within a much more fundamental concern: The nature of the conditions for generating and sustaining *persons* and *personhood*. The argument is straightforward: While we can be concerned about the wellbeing of all sorts of things (communities, planets, organisations, bodies, etc.) the prime focus of our wellbeing concerns are—and possibly *should be*—persons. And the concern for persons is primarily about the ways in which persons come to be and the ways in which personhood (the characteristics of being a person) is maintained or sustained. Therefore, to have a comprehensive theoretical account of wellbeing we need, first and foremost, a robust and carefully worked out understanding of what persons are, how they have been generated—both through evolution (*phylogeny*) and individual development (*ontogeny*)—and how they are sustained. Put another way, the wellbeing of persons is simply the condition of being a person and being able to maintain the state of being a person (personhood) in the relevant cultural milieu. In this sense, my claim amounts to a 'nature fulfillment' view of wellbeing (e.g., Haybron 2008)—but one unlike any other such view. Fulfilling the 'nature' of a person is not like fulfilling the nature of a cat, antelope or worm. Persons share some abstract features with living, biological beings (e.g., a focus on activity and its smooth enactment) but they are also complicated cultural inventions. Just how complicated will, I hope, become more than clear over the following pages. Persons are central to being the animals we are so, in that sense, we need to heed our 'nature' as an animal. But that 'nature' is constantly in need of construction through the cultural and discursive processes with which we are all so familiar. To use the same metaphor as previously, these processes are the sea in which we swim.

For psychologists—and, in fact, for all of us—wellbeing concerns begin, and in all practical senses, end with a concern for persons. There would be few people who would vote for a world in which every human body was optimally fit and healthy but, sadly, all the persons whose bodies they were, were miserable. It is also the wellbeing of *other persons* that can so predictably break our heart or, alternatively, fill it with joy—which is not to say that there are no other states of the world, or of parts of it, that can do the same. Our concerns are the concerns of persons and, so, our wellbeing concerns are concerns for the wellbeing of persons.

For those who like arguments to be stated more formally the same general point can be made in the following way. As a concept, the notion of a 'person' is *logically primitive* (Strawson 1959)—that is, it is logically prior to concepts such as 'body', 'self', 'subject', 'ego', 'individual consciousness' and the like. Therefore, states of a 'body', 'self', etc. are only ever of concern, in a wellbeing sense, to the extent that the 'body', 'self', etc. is that of a particular person and affects the wellbeing of that person. To put it nonsensically, the agony or the ecstasy that no person experiences (or will ever experience) is of no concern. For clarity, that is *not* to say that the experiences of a being that is not a person is also of no concern. A part of the analysis I will provide in this book assumes that, for example, the ability of persons to express and experience pain is based on natural expressions of pain that are common to many animals—and perhaps even plants. And we can definitely be moved by those natural expressions, enough sometimes to put our own lives on the line. But it is the experience of pain by persons that strikes us as tragically unique.

Reformulating wellbeing theory and research around the notion of the person is a central aim of this book. If I do that successfully, or even with partial success, I hope that you see the possibility for an understanding of wellbeing that speaks to you and your experiences in life— as, of course, a person.

# Wellbeing, Culture, and Persons

It is hard to be a person in the modern world. This is the paradox at the heart of wellbeing. We are frequently encouraged to believe that the world has never been better for people. At the same time, there is building evidence that people are struggling to maintain wellbeing in this same world. How can a world that is so good for people produce such experiences of psychological pain? It is a paradox that has been noted before (e.g., Easterbrook 2004), but attempts to resolve it have been more speculative than theoretically informed. Some have cited research on cognitive biases to suggest that we have an innate tendency to emphasise and better recollect negative rather than positive information, but even those attempts have usually been ad hoc suggestions recruited after the fact. In the following chapters, I aim to resolve this paradox and, as part of the same effort, reorient our understanding of wellbeing.

There are two omissions in current theories of individual wellbeing. The first is the deep nature of the connection between wellbeing and culture. When it comes to wellbeing, culture is more than simply one variable amongst many. It does not just influence personal experiences of wellbeing—as, for example, our physical health might influence how good we feel and how well our life goes. Culture certainly provides the normative contexts and practices necessary for the notion of wellbeing to make any particular sense. In the impossible case of the absence of culture, theories of human wellbeing would be very different beasts from those discussed today (in fact, there could be no such theories). The rich human psychological experience of life, for example, would shrivel to a much more rudimentary set of concerns around survival and preservation of bodily viability. But culture does something even more fundamental than providing the meanings and practices that allow us to identify, think about and discuss wellbeing: It also generates the entities that experience wellbeing. That is, culture makes people—and it is people that have experiences of wellbeing.

If you are still inclined to see culture as solely acting as a *context* rather than as a process that helps constitute human persons as we have come to know ourselves, there is a recent suggestion that might make you think again. In her book *Cognitive Gadgets: The Cultural Evolution of Thinking*, psychologist Cecilia Heyes has made the case for what is known as 'cultural evolutionary psychology' (Heyes 2012, 2018). Simply, the approach shares with 'high church' evolutionary psychology the view that there are evolved, genetically-based cognitive mechanisms. But, unlike this 'standard evolutionary psychology model' (SEPM—or 'high church evolutionary psychology' as Heyes 2012 calls it), these mechanisms are seen as quite basic and domain general rather than finely honed to solve particular problems in the Environment of Evolutionary Adaptedness (EEA) (see Barkow et al. 1992 for the early statement of the SEPM). They represent broad, 'instinctive' abilities such as being more socially tolerant ('friendly') and socially motivated than other primates. By contrast, most of what makes us human, such as language, theory of mind, metacognition, causal reasoning, episodic memory, imitation, and morality are not 'cognitive instincts' but 'cogni tive gadgets'. They are 'gadgets' in the sense that they are cognitive tools fashioned by culture—not by 'nature' or 'nurture' or even the combination of the two. Culture is a 'third source' and it is this source that is responsible for what makes us distinctively human in a neurocognitive sense. In contrast to nurture (which is the action of environmental experience on *innate* cognitive mechanisms), culture actively *creates* new, specific, and distinctive neurocognitive mechanisms through developmental processes, social interactions, and sometimes explicit training. Culture adds new bits to our cognitive architecture; it does not just alter the inputs into—and so the outputs of—a biologically pre-determined architecture. In Heyes' (2018) metaphor, culture does not just carry the 'grist of the mind' (beliefs and behaviour) but helps construct the mind's 'mill'. As the promotional blurb for the book puts it, "our malleable human minds can learn through culture not only what to think but how to think it". While inherited through social learning rather than via DNA, these gadgets are nevertheless still selected in the Darwinian sense, but this selection happens at the level of cultural evolution, not biological evolution. The inheritance of these gadgets, being cultural, can be within generations ('horizontal' inheritance) as much as between generations—and when it is between generations it can be between related ('direct' inheritance) or unrelated ('oblique' inheritance) individuals.

If something like this cultural evolutionary approach is correct, then culture constitutes people not just in some 'symbolic' realm of beliefs and behavioural norms that an individual may one day 'endorse' or 'internalise' but also in our material, neurocognitive capacities. We are neurologically as well as psychologically constituted by culture. Work on neurodevelopment over recent decades has made this possibility more than plausible. Areas of the pre-frontal cortex (PFC) closely associated with our abilities to plan, make judgments, exercise social intelligence and be self-conscious (so-called executive functions) are the last parts of the brain to develop to a relatively stable state, and this development continues into our third decade of life after birth. This means that the PFC is designed to be open to rich, primarily social, environmental stimuli to guide neurodevelopment (Keverne 2004). The interaction between the social world and neurodevelopment is especially crucial during adolescence. Each 'sculpts' the other in ways that can be fateful for our future susceptibility or resilience to mental health issues (Lamblin et al. 2017). Until our early 20s we are, in effect, occupying a 'social womb' that continues to determine our neural development. To the extent that social stimuli during this period carry fundamental cultural specifications for what it is to be a person and perform personhood, there is ample opportunity for culture to help design the neurocognitive tools, or 'gadgets' we then make use of to carry out the tasks that, in our culture, constitute us as persons. To state it as plainly as possible, when properly developed through social learning these cognitive gadgets—culturally inherited but themselves grounded in domain-general, biologically evolved cognitive mechanisms—allow each of us to perform, in a more or less coherent and continuous way, the life-time act of not only being *a* person but being the self-same person.

The second omission in work on wellbeing follows from the first. By neglecting the constitutive role of culture, we omit, as a direct conceptual consequence, the centrality of the notion of a *person* in understanding wellbeing. It has always seemed remarkable to me that the notion of a 'person' is absent from psychological theories of wellbeing. Instead, the default entity in most theories has been the 'self', not the person. In one way that is understandable: psychology, as a whole, defaults to the self (or 'ego' or 'mind') as the centre of experience. Psychological theories of wellbeing have simply inherited that default position. The reasons for that are historical, conceptual and ideological, but the consequence is that the meanings and practices that constitute the experiences and reports of wellbeing are nowhere to be seen.[1] The challenges people face in their lives as they struggle with day-to-day circumstances, cannot be represented in theories that exclude the entity—the 'person'—that can sensibly be said to encounter and have to deal with those challenges. These challenges only exist for persons, not for selves, egos, or minds. And they are a direct consequence of being a person and encountering the world (including other persons) in the particular ways that a person does. Delegating—or relegating—aspects of this experience of wellbeing to various features of bodies, minds, egos, cognitive mechanisms, or selves just adds to the confusion. A self—whatever it is—has no need for autonomy, for competence, or for relatedness (Ryan and Deci 2017); but persons do.

It may seem too obvious to state bluntly, but only persons experience wellbeing as *we*—persons—do. A body can perform what we call a stress response; but a body (including its brain) is unaware of the challenge to provide an urgent report for a superior at work before being able to get home to family. A person's brain is only 'blamed' for reneging on an obligation in rare cases (though there is a tendency to 'neurologise' our everyday failures as expressions such as 'brain fade' express); and, then, only metaphorically since the brain is not taken to be a person. A brain is not even properly understood as part of a person. At most it is a tool that a person is said to make use of to fulfill their commitments as a person. If we know that our physical bodies tire then we, as persons, are given the further responsibility of looking after them, not abusing them, and, therefore to have them available to be used in a state fit for the tasks and demands involved in being a person. Ultimately, the buck stops on the 'desk' of a person; nowhere else. This is what is neglected when both culture and persons are omitted from theories of wellbeing. Yet it is in this context of personal, felt obligations, judgments, and rewards that, so often, our wellbeing is created or destroyed. It is the person who must navigate their way through the numerous, competing and even conflicting demands that cultures impose. This is why cultures invented (evolved) persons in the first place.

To rectify these omissions, I investigate wellbeing in the context of what I call 'aspirational culture'—an important feature of the culture that is rapidly globalizing, albeit with many variations. That aspirational culture produces a certain kind of person and version of personhood. Seeing this connection between a kind of culture and a kind of person allows us to understand why, and how, wellbeing—and illbeing—is experienced in the particular ways it is being experienced today. And, by beginning with a focus on culture it becomes much clearer why we need to consider persons when understanding wellbeing. At the same time, emphasizing the aspirational nature of our current culture opens a way to resolving the paradox of wellbeing in today's world.

Understanding wellbeing as the wellbeing of persons, and therefore as based on an understanding of *personhood*, helps synthesise empirical findings on human wellbeing, from the biological to the cultural. As I will show, the notion of a person has been custom-made by our evolved sociocultural environment to cut across and, for better or worse, to attempt to integrate all aspects of the world—personal, social, economic, ecological—*within* its experience. This distinguishes the person from other candidates for our concerns with wellbeing (e.g., bodies, minds, egos, and selves).

In the rest of this chapter I will begin to add detail to this argument. I will consider some of the main observations cited as indications of a broad but patchy historical improvement in the human experience. These observations will be contrasted with some of the concerning trends in indicators of wellbeing and its related psychological factors. That is, I will present some of the most obvious facts and research that provide the data, or evidence, for the establishment of the apparent paradox. Previous attempts, or at least suggestions, have been made to resolve the paradox. I will argue that these suggestions, both individually and in aggregate, are incomplete, flawed or simply wrong.

I will also consider the role of 'culture'—broadly conceived—as the background to these paradoxical observations. Understood as an interlocking system of material concerns, practices, and collectively organized, meaningful acts, a culture is a self-generating and self-organising world. It achieves this self-generation and organization by populating itself, to varying degrees of success, with persons it fashions and who exhibit, from culture to culture, various broad forms of personhood. These persons are the primary experiencers of wellbeing. It is persons, that is, who experience, worry about, report, and sometimes seek wellbeing and it is in persons' lives that wellbeing finds its manifestation and expression.

## The Paradox of Wellbeing: The New Optimism

There has been something of a publishing genre established over recent decades in 'accentuating the positive' about the modern world, especially in its characteristics of liberal democracy, free markets, and prosperity. While such upbeat analyses of progress no doubt have a venerable history, the most recent trend in this genre began sometime in the mid to late 1990s. As cultural critics from both the political left and right began to highlight perceived flaws in this rapidly changing and developing post-World War II world—its claimed permissiveness, individualism, materialism, relativism, and fragmented, rootless nature—a counter-narrative emerged in popular non-fiction. In 1993, law professor Stephen Holmes published *An Anatomy of Antiliberalism* a book which vigorously defended what he saw as essential classical liberal, Enlightenment values against the post-Marxist cultural critiques of communitarianism, religious fundamentalism and 'ethnic particularism' (Holmes 1996). He argued against repeated charges from intellectuals and cultural critics—some historical, some contemporary—that the modern, increasingly global, liberal world was leading to cultural decay, a tearing apart of the 'social fabric' and a trampling of community and spiritual truths.

Taking much the same fight onto a less abstract field of play, in 1998 Virginia Postrel—one-time editor of the magazine *Reason* and variously described as 'libertarian' or 'classical liberal'—wrote a book titled *The Future and Its Enemies: The Growing Conflict Over Creativity, Enterprise, and Progress* (Postrel 1999), the title no doubt echoing Karl Popper's more famous tome *The Open Society and Its Enemies*. The theme was

that politics was being reconfigured around the parties of '*stasis*' ("a regulated, engineered world") and the parties of '*dynamism*' ("a world of
constant creation, discovery, and competition"), otherwise known as
the 'Party of Life' (Postrel 1999, p. xiv). Postrel defended technological change, competition, innovation, creativity and, as one reviewer
put it, "the free society, the free market, and even the *free person*" (my
emphasis). She presented the case in favour of the dynamism of contemporary society arguing that, despite its 'messiness', it was the 'one
best way' to create the future since it involved the proliferation of possible futures which would, in turn, be modified, changed or scrapped
as people demonstrated their preferences through their behaviour. The
case Postrel presented involved faith in a familiar process. It is a process found in the logic of the theory of evolution by natural selection
and, probably more relevantly, in the competitive logic of free markets:
Massive proliferation of novel options followed by an almost equally
massive, and immediate, process of culling of those options. Postrel's
targets—the 'enemies of the future'—were chosen because of what she
perceived as a pervading sense of, for her, misplaced pessimism about
the world's trajectory. Disconcertingly for Postrel, people were increasingly seeing the 'messiness' of the path that leads to the future as a continuous personal and social calamity rather than as the yellow-brick
road to freedom and fulfilment.

In similar vein, and at much the same time, economist Julian Simon
(posthumously) and Stephen Moore (a fellow at the libertarian think
tank 'The Cato Institute' and one of Simon's students) published the
statistically and graphically rich small book *It's Getting Better All the
Time: 100 Greatest Trends of the Last 100 Years* (Moore and Simon
2000). Whether presenting measures of material prosperity, changes
in social attitudes, or health and social indicators the point that was
repeatedly made was that these trends were—over the long view and
globally—'getting better all the time'.

By the turn of the millennium, optimism was clearly in the air
and even ready to challenge growing environmental concerns. Bjørn
Lomborg's book *The Skeptical Environmentalist: Measuring the Real State
of the World* was first published in Danish in 1997 then in English in
2001 (Lomborg 2001). In that latter edition he quotes—ahead of

the contents page and presumably approvingly given the book's contents—economist Julian Simon's (the same Julian Simon) "long-run forecast" that "material conditions will continue to get better for most people, in most countries, most of the time, indefinitely". The quotation also includes a 'speculation' that, despite this likely trend, "many people will continue to *think and say* that the conditions of life are getting worse". In his final chapter, Lomborg quotes another social scientist, Aaron Wildavsky (a political scientist who, amongst other achievements, argued against the precautionary principle in relation to new technologies and in favour of a principle based on 'trial and error') as saying "How extraordinary! The richest, longest lived, best protected, most resourceful civilization, with the highest degree of insight into its own technology, is on its way to becoming the most frightened" (cited in Lomborg 2001, p. 331).

In fact, that quotation from Wildavsky was, in turn, sourced by Lomborg from a publication by Paul Slovic, the famous researcher into the social psychology of public risk perceptions. Slovic's (1987) article in the journal *Science* on perceptions of risk was focused on the puzzlement and frustration of "industrialists and regulators" at general perceptions by the public that risks were greater 'today' (1987) than previously and that these "perceptions and the opposition to technology that accompanies them" was "hampering the nation's political and economic stability" (Slovic 1987, p. 280). These faulty perceptions may be the result of the news media "which rather thoroughly document mishaps and threats occurring throughout the world" (Slovic 1987, p. 280). Lomborg echoed, and elaborated, that evaluation when he stated that "[o]ur fear is due to a high degree to the fact that we are given ever more negative information by scientists, the organizations and the media. We are being made aware of things we had no idea we needed worry [sic] about" (Lomborg 2001, p. 331). That the population are being duped by 'naysayers' who find willing bedfellows in media devoted to the spectacular and disastrous is a repeated explanation for the wellbeing paradox and, in one form or another, it remains with us to the present day.

Overlaying this historical backdrop of published positivity about the modern world, a fresh wave of similarly motivated arguments has appeared more recently. Interestingly, this resurgence came after the eco-nomic crisis that began in 2008. Although pre-dated by Matt Ridley's (Ridley 2010) *The Rational Optimist: How Prosperity Evolves*, the intel-lectual stimulus seems to have been Steven Pinker's (2011) *The Better Angels of Our Nature: The Decline of Violence in History and Its Causes*. The book's argument is that there has never been a time during which people have enjoyed so little violence, of all forms and scales, as they do today. Violence is not only directly harmful—even fatal—for many peo-ple but it is also highly disruptive of personal and social activity, espe-cially those close to the victims of violence. That is, it adversely affects the lives and wellbeing of those not directly affected by it as individu-als, and often to the point of affecting people who are total strangers to the victim of a violent act (e.g., through spreading concerns over personal safety). As mentioned, prior to Pinker's *Better Angels*, in 2010 there was Matt Ridley's *The Rational Optimist: How Prosperity Evolves*, a book that combines evolutionary and economic logic to claim that the propensity to 'truck and barter'—noted by Adam Smith in *An Inquiry Into the Wealth of Nations*—has produced hugely beneficent effects, from reductions in violence and starvation to increases in happiness. In 2015, Michael Shermer's invigoratingly titled book *The Moral Arc: How Science and Reason Lead Humanity Toward Truth, Justice, and Freedom*, advanced the argument that humanity is now enjoying the most moral period in its long history, mostly as a result of the increasing influence of science and reason (Shermer 2015). And, in 2016, Johan Norberg—a Senior Fellow at the same Cato Institute associated with Julian Simon and Stephen Moore—released the book *Progress: Ten Reasons to Look Forward to the Future* (Norberg 2016) which echoes, even recapitu-lates, in updated form, Julian Simon's forecast and speculation (quoted by Lomborg in *The Skeptical Environmentalist*). For Norberg, "the great story of our era is that we are witnessing the greatest improvement in global living standards ever to take place. Poverty, malnutrition, illiter-acy, child labour and infant mortality are all falling faster than at any other time in human history" (Norberg 2016, p. 3). No doubt coin-cidentally, there are also apparently ten reasons why we get things wrong about the state of the world. In the 2018 book *Factfulness: Ten Reasons We're Wrong About the World—And Why Things Are Better Than*

*You Think*, Hans Rosling, Anna Rosling Rönnlund and Ola Rosling argue that there are ten 'instincts' that betray our efforts to understand the world factually (e.g., the 'instinct' that there is a 'gap' between the developed countries and developing countries when most occupy the 'middle-income country' group) (Rosling et al. 2018). And, finally, Pinker (2018) returned to the front-line of global optimism with his book *Enlightenment Now: The Case for Reason, Science, Humanism, and Progress*. The book reprises the now familiar theme of inexorable human progress but, this time, sheets the praise home to what Pinker claims are the Enlightenment ideals of reason, science and humanism.

This focus on optimism has become something of a semi-official movement with the establishment of 'The New Optimists' with their own website, 'newoptimists.com'. Some 81 scientists are listed as contributing to the book *The New Optimists: Scientists View Tomorrow's World and What It Means for Us*. Styled on the so-called 'New Atheists' (e.g., Richard Dawkins, Daniel Dennett and Sam Harris), the New Optimists wish both to counter what they see as a self-defeating general pessimism and promote a more positive view of the achievements of the type of society they see as responsible for these gains and for what should be our optimism about the future. It is no coincidence that it is scientists who are at the forefront of the movement as science is the poster-child of progress and collective aspiration for a better world. It is also no coincidence that the push for a more optimistic take on the state of the world comes at the same time as scientists are concerned that the reputation of science and the credibility of scientists is under attack.

While there is some variation in emphasis from author to author, the causes of such improvements are identified as property rights, free markets, trade, liberal democracy, science, rationalism, 'openness', the establishment of the nation state, human rights and other markers of the current globalizing world. By contrast, the causes most often identified for what these authors claim is unjustified pessimism about the current state of the human world and the prospects for the future are an unfortunate concatenation of the media, with its inherent bias towards negative events and catastrophes; opportunistic politicians who find it popular and useful to highlight fear; those—beyond the media and politicians—who have some material interest in emphasizing or even fabricating negative trends and features of the world (e.g., environmental organisations, some members of the 'helping professions' such as medicine and social work); and various supposed cognitive and affective biases that the human species has evolved which predispose people to focus on, and better remember, negative information and experiences.

It has to be emphasised that works such as those just cited are not mere polemics (or, at least, not solely). Official statistics, often now collected globally, support the trends most often referenced as evidence of progress and optimism for the future. For example, while extreme poverty (defined as less than US\$1.91 per day) still affects 767 million people (in 2013, when the latest reliable statistics were available) it has declined precipitously both in terms of rate–down from 35% of the world's population in 1990 to 10.7% in 2013—and in terms of absolute numbers of people (from 1.85 billion in 1990 to 767 million in 2013).[2] Similarly, life expectancy—the 'gold standard' measure of human wellness—has seemed to be on an incremental, and irreversible, upward trend, and not only in the wealthiest countries. Global life expectancy has increased from about 52 years in 1960 to over 72 years in 2016.[3] Further, all countries, regions and broad income groups have shown the same upward trend.

Over roughly the same period that these broad indicators of the human condition have shown improvement there has also been two other noticeable social trends. The first, as I will detail in a moment, is the rise in both reported human psychological suffering in a variety of forms and of population level increases in psychological traits and characteristics associated with such suffering. That is, beyond arguments over greater awareness of mental illness (and therefore increased reporting) and better diagnostic processes, more people are actually developing clinical symptoms sufficient for diagnosis of psychological disorders. In many developed economies, the population as a whole is scoring higher than ever on validated scales of various forms of psychopathology.

The second trend, and one that is inseparable from the first and is central to the overall paradox, is the rapid rise in efforts to understand and increase 'wellbeing'. This trend has two components. The first is an unprecedented research and policy interest in wellbeing. More governments are considering, developing or even implementing measures of wellbeing into their national accounts, a move advocated by Diener and Seligman (2004). It is no longer a surprise to find corporations and public sector organisations with wellbeing strategies, wellness programmes and even wellbeing managers or coordinators. Also unsurprising is that the topic of wellbeing took pride of place at a recent World Economic Forum meeting in Davos, Switzerland (see Cederström and Spicer 2015; Davies 2015). Politicians, corporate executives and owners, 'thought leaders' and 'influencers' not only attended presentations and read reports on wellbeing but also were encouraged to engage personally in wellbeing practices. Which brings us to the second component in the increased focus on wellbeing.

There has been a massive popularization of the individual pursuit of wellbeing as a personal priority. Through the now usual processes of fashion (e.g., new 'diets'), commodification (e.g., gym memberships) and cultural co-option (e.g., yoga), every aspect of one's self, relationships, home, work, play, spirituality, thoughts, attitudes, emotions—in short, every aspect of one's life—is now being mined and sold back to us in new 'wellbeing-optimised' versions. Better food, better relationships and ways of relating, better attitudes, better ways of thinking, better ways to work, better spiritualities, better emotional responses, better homes, and, of course, better bodies are now on offer via innumerable magazines, blogsites, short courses, online video courses, retreats and the ubiquitous self-help books. At the time of writing, the number one bestseller on Amazon was *Girl, Wash Your Face: Stop Believing the Lies About Who You Are so You Can Become Who You Were Meant to Be* by Rachel Hollis. Rachel is apparently "founder of the lifestyle website TheChicSite.com and CEO of her own media company" and has "developed an immense online community by sharing tips for better living while fearlessly revealing the messiness of her own life".[4] Simultaneously, at number two on the bestselling Amazon list was *Aware: The Science and Practice of Presence—The Groundbreaking Meditation Practice* by Dr. Daniel Siegel. In the book Siegel shows how the "Wheel of Awareness" can "focus attention, open awareness, and cultivate kind intention" to help you "grow a healthier brain", "reduce fear, anxiety, and stress in your life", "become more focused and present", and be "more energised and emotionally resilient".[5]

It would be easy to dismiss this focus on wellbeing, especially by individuals, as a mere 'first world problem'; the sort of preoccupation only possible once the more substantive and substantial problems of life—such as poverty, physical violence and disease—have been consigned to the 'dustbin of history'. That is, our wellbeing concerns (expressed by individuals, organisations, and governments) might themselves be seen as indicators of just how good human experience is in the modern world—even though it may well be experienced, felt and reported, as a lack that requires intervention. It is true that some psychologists of wellbeing (or 'well-being' as it is usually spelt in the psychological literature) have argued that positive psychology, wellbeing and 'flourishing' are all about making the 'ok' better rather than providing a cure for psychological distress (although, in practice, they have often been promoted as a defence against such ills). In his famous presidential address to the American Psychological Association in 1997, Martin Seligman promoted a psychology that investigated what factors generated human flourishing beyond the norm. For too long, he argued, psychologists had seen their job solely as the elimination of psychological pain and distress. That presentation of the research focus and approach to wellbeing could definitely be interpreted as an assumption that wellbeing concerns—in the sense of 'positive flourishing'—are reserved for those who have their more material and pressing circumstances in order. That is, it is for those already benefiting from the large-scale improvements in the human condition to add the final polish to the perfect life through cultivation of personal wellbeing.

The second aspect that is missed is that even if our individual concerns with wellbeing do involve an unnecessary, and ungrateful, focus on our selves rather than our unprecedentedly positive global circumstances (i.e., that it is little other than 'self-indulgence'), that focus is itself in need of explanation. And the best explanation may not simply be that it is an incidental side-effect (an 'unintended consequence') of the 'good life' when combined with 'human nature'; it may, as I will argue, be an effect, or even a crucial feature, of the changes that have been responsible for the deterioration in people's ability to cope with life in the first place. That is, these two aspects of our concerns over wellbeing are intertwined. Exploring and dissecting that entangled relationship leads to the overall argument of this book, which is that the difficulties that people have in today's world is a function, first, of changes in the kinds of persons and selves our world now generates; and, second, of the demands involved in the kinds of tasks increasingly required of such persons and selves in order to sustain personhood. Constructing this argument will involve combining an examination of the features of that world (in Chapter 2) with a revised conceptualization of the psychology of wellbeing that directly and explicitly incorporates personhood (in Chapters 3–5).

# The Paradox of Wellbeing: The New Suffering

There is another interpretation of these dual trends in psychological suffering and wellbeing concerns. There is now significant and building evidence that people are having serious problems coping in today's world and, further, these problems are being broadly replicated in each country that 'develops' through embarking on a trajectory towards a 'first world' life. The most obvious—and most rapidly implemented—example of this developmental trajectory is China. Between 1990 and 2015 China's GDP "multiplied over five times" yet "well-being today [2017] is probably less than it was in 1990" (Easterlin et al. 2017, p. 49). Over part of that same period in China there was also a rapid rise in diagnoses of depression (Parker et al. 2001).

For those aware of the social and economic circumstances that have dominated global and, in many cases, national attention in the first decades of the twenty-first century—the 2008 economic crisis, the increasing impact of climate change, inequalities in income and wealth, wars, terrorism, electoral polarization—it will seem unsurprising that, in many places, though by no means all, population measures of health and wellbeing are showing worrying trends. The *World Happiness Report 2018* (Helliwell et al. 2018), for example, focuses on the highly topical issue of wellbeing and migration and immigration. Since the turn of the millennium, migrant and refugee flows have burgeoned for many reasons with the wars in Iraq, Afghanistan and Syria being prominent causes. Those flows have impacted global politics, social cohesion and economics, and contributed to much-debated events such as the election of Donald Trump as United States president in 2016; the vote for 'Brexit' (exit from the European Union) in the United Kingdom also in 2016; and the increased popularity of far right political parties in many countries in Europe (including France, Hungary, the Netherlands, Sweden, and Poland), South America (where Jair Bolsorano has recently been voted President of Brazil), and Asia (including the election of Rodrigo Duterte as President of the Philippines in 2016). While such events are not the immediate concern of this book, they demonstrate the uncertain, even unstable, nature of a world that is the context for human wellbeing. They also demonstrate vividly and starkly the way in which the outcomes of a now global 'aspirational culture' have a dramatic effect on the prospects for that same wellbeing.

But beyond the focus on migration, one chapter in the report focuses on a startling fact. Over successive years, the United States has now seen a reduction in population life expectancy (Sachs 2018). In each of the years from 2014 to 2015 and 2015 to 2016 life expectancy reduced by 0.1 years. As Sachs (2018, p. 152) reports, this "reversal in the upward trend of life expectancy is shocking and almost unprecedented for a rich country in recent decades." The United States is not alone in this reversal. In 2012, eight countries in the European Union had declines in life expectancy while, in 2015, 19 countries experienced a decline including France, Germany, Italy and the United Kingdom.

Indeed, it is hard to overstate the significance of this reversal of the trend of increasing life expectancy. Beyond the locally explicable, and often temporary, departures (e.g., declines in Sub-Saharan African countries because of HIV/Aids; a decline of six years in male life expectancy in the former Soviet Union between 1989 and 2005[6]), there has been a seemingly unstoppable, steady increase in human life-expectancy over time (and similarly positive changes in related measures such as Health Adjusted Life Years (HALEs), Disability Adjusted Life Years (DALYs), and Potential Years of Life Lost (PYLLs)). These trends have been presented as near-irrefutable proof in support of a story of progress in the human condition during the modern period. Whatever the trends in other social, economic or psychological indicators of wellbeing may have shown, the brute fact of longer and longer (average) lives—in both so-called developed and developing economies—appeared final arbiter in any debate over the problems generated by modern life.

Sachs (2018, p. 148) argues that the causes of these declines in U.S. life expectancy may go some way to explaining why "income per capita has more than doubled since 1972 while happiness (or subjective well-being, SWB) has remained roughly unchanged or has even declined". He suggests that "certain non-income determinants of happiness are worsening" alongside increases in per capita income and, thus, the "gains in SWB that would *normally arise with economic growth*" are being more than off-set by other factors (Sachs 2018, p. 148, emphasis added). These non-income determinants are, firstly, "declines in social capital" of various forms (trust in institutions, social support networks, perceptions of corruption in politics and business)—discussed in the *World Happiness Report 2017*—and, secondly, "three serious epidemics: obesity, substance abuse, and depression" (p. 149), highlighted in the 2018 World Happiness Report. These two broad factors (declines in social capital along with three health epidemics) he describes as "complementary" explanations of the stubborn lack of improvement in SWB measures during a period of growth in GDP per capita income.

The statistics about these three epidemics are stark. According to the U.S. Centers for Disease Control, deaths from drug overdoses, for example, rose from a rate of 6.1 per 100,000 in 1999 to 19.8 per 100,000 in 2016 (cited in Sachs 2018, p. 152). Opioids were the major drugs involved. While there was a substantial increase in heroin overdoses there were also big changes in deaths from prescription opioids such as Oxycontin (introduced in the 1990s) and the powerful synthetic opioids such as Fentanyl such that these opioids contributed more to the increase than did heroin overdoses. Sachs (2018, p. 154) has no doubt that "because the U.S. is the epicenter of opioid drug manufacturing and prescription, it is also the epicenter of the global opioid epidemic". Similarly, obesity rates in the United States rose precipitously between 1976 and 1980 (around 15% of the adult population) and 1999–2000 (over 30%). Since 2000, it has risen steadily to reach 38.2% in 2015. Mexico, which borders the United States comes in second in OECD countries at 32.4% with four of the next five countries being the English-speaking Canada, United Kingdom, Australia and New Zealand which have "close business and advertising linkages with the U.S." (Sachs 2018, p. 159).

While hugely valuable in identifying the various factors associated with decreases in life expectancy, the analytic approach taken by Sachs obscures two possibilities while, perhaps, hinting at both. The first is that the 'complementary' explanations may in fact be intimately interconnected. That is, declines in social capital and the emergence of the three epidemics may be part of the same, single, phenomenon. The second possible explanation is that declines in social capital and the emergence of the three epidemics (the "non-income determinants of happiness") are, in fact, partly caused by the *same processes* that have helped produce the GDP per capita income gains. That would mean that, far from pushing towards gains in SWB, the particular way that GDP per capita income gains have been generated has also been the cause—or one of the causes—of the stagnation in SWB. That is, from a wellbeing perspective, the broad economic, social, and cultural arrangements that allow for gains in GDP may also be behind the opioid, obesity and depression epidemics. One possible candidate that would fit such a broad explanatory role is the notion of an increasingly pervasive aspirational culture which expresses itself economically, socially, and psychologically and at multiple scales of personal and social organisation.

Global data such as that presented in the various *World Happiness Reports* and other surveys of global wellbeing provide a useful macro-level picture of human wellbeing. Research at a finer grain, however, provides a level of detail that sharpens concerns over the state of people's wellbeing in the modern world. It is a sign of the times that there is now a surfeit of literature supporting a less optimistic story of human life than that presented in the previous section. A small selection of findings, however, can provide a sufficiently suggestive account.

About 1 in 10 Americans aged 12 years and over were using anti-depressant medication in 2008, an increase of about 400% since the 1988–1994 period (Pratt et al. 2011). Some 322 million people around the world were estimated to have depression in 2015, an increase of 18.4% since 2005 which reflected both population increase and changing demographics towards greater representation of older age groups that have disproportionately high rates (Depression and other common mental disorders: Global health estimates 2017). Suicide rates in the United States increased on average by 30% between 1999 and 2016, with significant increases in 45 states and a greater than 30% increase in 25 states (Stone et al. 2018). Up until recently, it was becoming commonplace to assume that—in developed economies and especially in the Anglophone west—rates of lifetime prevalence for mental illness hovered somewhere around 40–50% while, at any one time, something like 20% would be suffering over the course of a year. Recent findings from the world-leading Dunedin Study in New Zealand which has followed 1037 individuals since 1972–1973 (with a 96% retention rate) suggest that lifetime prevalence rates may be considerably higher (Moffitt et al. 2010). They focused specifically on the period between a participant being between 15 and 32 years of age. The prevalence rate they found overall is twice as high as the rates from retrospective studies (which ask people to remember episodes over their lifetime). Specifically, "prospective measurement yielded lifetime estimates that suggest the experience of certain DSM-defined disorders by age 32 may be very common indeed: anxiety disorder (49.5%), depression (41.4%), alcohol dependence (31.8%) and cannabis dependence (18.0%)" (Moffitt et al. 2010, p. 904).

If young people are the canaries in the coal mine of wellbeing, recent trends from major meta-analyses reveal increasingly toxic conditions. In one startling finding, the average American child in the 1980s had anxiety levels as high as child psychiatric patients in the 1950s, and college students and children had shifted a full standard deviation higher on anxiety scales between 1952 and 1993 (Twenge 2000). These increases in anxiety were correlated with decreases in social connections. Another birth cohort meta-analysis found young people becoming more convinced that their lives were not under their control, with the average college student in 2002 having a more external 'locus of control' (i.e., the location—either internal or external to them—of control over what happens to them) than 80% of similar students in the early 1960s (Twenge et al. 2004).

In fact, the scores for young people in the United States on a range of psychopathology measures have been trending upwards. Again, it has been the work of Jean Twenge that has provided the most detail on these trends. Her research team tracked college students' scores on the psychopathology scales of the 'industry standard' Minnesota Multiphasic Personality Inventory (MMPI) and MMPI-2 (from 1938 to 2007) and high school students' scores on the MMPI-A (from 1951 to 2002) (Twenge et al. 2010). Particular scales were those for depression, psychopathic deviation, paranoia, and 'hypomania'. The latter is an interesting category. It describes a state that is just below mania and one that, interestingly, can often be adaptive in today's society in terms of an individual's success but is less desirable in its effects on interactions with others. Twenge et al. (2010) found that the (then) current generation were scoring around one standard deviation higher on these scales than the earlier cohorts to the point that five times as many were scoring above clinical level scores than previously. For the hypomania scale, at the end of the study period a full 40% of young people were scoring above the clinical cut-off.

It may be that young people were increasingly coming to realise through cultural signals that a focused, 'high energy' mode of operating in the world was a prerequisite for survival. Richard Eckersley, an Australian epidemiologist seems to think so (Eckersley 2004). He discussed the paradox that young Australians were, on the one hand, reporting high levels of wellbeing in many surveys and were highly positive about their personal prospects (while quite negative about the world in general) but, on the other hand, as a group were suffering greater and greater incidence of mental health issues. His tentative explanation for the paradox was that young people were acutely aware of the need, today, to 'skate on thin ice' given the uncertainty and ever-shifting nature of the modern world. In response, they therefore subscribe to the kinds of values and behaviours they believed would see them through. Those values include an outward optimism and positivity and the imperative to 'back yourself'. But acting in this way constantly also requires enormous effort and brings with it associated stress and a sense of disconnection—hence the declining mental health statistics. For Eckersley, young people were developing so-called 'Separate

Selves' combined with 'Tribal Ties' amongst their peers to help them navigate an uncertain world.

It is in this curious mix of progress, optimism, anxiety, depression and suicide that the paradox of modern wellbeing arises. Something is happening. When it is happening on such a scale and seems so contradictory it suggests that we need to look closely at both our culture and ourselves for some integrated understanding of how our wellbeing is created in an aspirational culture. It is that culture I examine in the next chapter.

# Notes

1. Thomas Pettigrew (2018) has recently argued that social psychology may, at last, be starting to fulfil its promise to situate human psychological experience in its social context. He calls this 'Contextual Social Psychology'. This is definitely a promising development, but my intention is to take this development to its limit with the claim that the entity that has the psychological experiences of concern to psychologists is not itself a psychological entity: it is a sociocultural entity. That is, it is a person. But, despite not being a psychological entity, the person is a crucial construct for psychological theories, including theories of wellbeing.
2. World Bank (2018a). Accessed on 14 September 2018 from http://www.worldbank.org/en/topic/poverty/overview.
3. World Bank (2018b). Accessed on 14 September 2018 from https://data.worldbank.org/indicator/SP.DYN.LE00.IN.
4. Accessed on 28 August 2018 NZST from https://www.amazon.com/Girl-Wash-Your-Face-Believing/dp/1400201659/ref=zg_bs_books_1?_encoding=UTF8&psc=1&refRID=XPWA414HVJ5A6TCJM26D.
5. Accessed on 28 August 2018 from https://www.amazon.com/Aware-Practice-Presence-Groundbreaking-Meditation/dp/1101993049/ref=zg_bs_books_2?_encoding=UTF8&psc=1&refRID=XP-WA414HVJ5A6TCJM26D.
6. Downloaded on 2 September 2018 from https://www.thelancet.com/action/showPdf?pii=S0140-6736%2818%2931485-5. Published online 30 August 2018 http://dx.doi.org/10.1016/S0140-6736(18)31485-5.

# References

Barkow, J. H., Cosmides, L., & Tooby, J. (Eds.). (1992). *The adapted mind: Evolutionary psychology and the generation of culture*. New York: Oxford University Press.

Cantor, N., Norem, J. K., Langston, C. A., Zirkel, S., Fleeson, W., & Cook-Flannagan, C. (1991). Life tasks and daily life experience. *Journal of Personality, 59*(3), 425–451.

Cantor, N., Norem, J. K., Niedenthal, P. M., Langston, C. A., & Brower, A. M. (1987). Life tasks, self-concept ideals, and cognitive strategies in a life transition. *Journal of Personality and Social Psychology, 53*(6), 1178–1191. https://doi.org/10.1037/0022-3514.53.6.1178.

Cederström, C., & Spicer, A. (2015). *The wellness syndrome*. Cambridge: Polity.

Davies, W. (2015). *The happiness industry: How the government and big business sold us well-being*. London: Verso.

Depression and other common mental disorders: Global health estimates. (2017). (p. 22). Geneva: World Health Organization.

Diener, E., & Seligman, M. E. P. (2004). Beyond money: Toward an economy of well-being. *Psychological Science in the Public Interest, 5*(1), 1–31. https://doi.org/10.1111/j.0963-7214.2004.00501001.x.

Easterbrook, G. (2004). *The progress paradox: How life gets better while people feel worse*. New York: Random House.

Easterlin, R., Wang, F., & Wang, S. (2017). Growth and happiness in China, 1990–2015, ch. 3. In J. Helliwell, R. Layard, & J. Sachs (Eds.), *World happiness report* (pp. 48–83). New York, NY: Sustainable Development Solutions Network.

Eckersley, R. (2004). Separate selves, tribal ties, and other stories: Making sense of different accounts of youth. *Family Matters, 68*(Winter), 36–42.

Harré, R. (1983). *Personal being: A theory for individual psychology*. Oxford: Blackwell.

Haybron, D. M. (2008). *The pursuit of unhappiness: The elusive psychology of well-being*. Oxford: Oxford University Press.

Helliwell, J. F., Layard, R., & Sachs, J. D. (2018). *World happiness report*. New York: Sustainable Development Solutions Network.

Heyes, C. (2012). New thinking: The evolution of human cognition. *Philosophical Transactions of the Royal Society B-Biological Sciences, 367,* 2091–2096. https://doi.org/10.1098/rstb.2012.0111.

Heyes, C. (2018). *Cultural gadgets: The cultural evolution of thinking*. Cambridge, MA: Harvard University Press.

Holmes, S. (1996). *The anatomy of antiliberalism*. Cambridge, MA: Harvard University Press.
Keverne, E. B. (2004, September 29). Understanding well-being in the evolutionary context of brain development. *Philosophical Transactions of the Royal Society of London B. Biological Sciences, 359*(1449), 1349–1358.
Lamblin, M., Murawski, C., Whittle, S., & Fornito, A. (2017). Social connectedness, mental health and the adolescent brain. *Neuroscience and Biobehavioral Review, 80,* 57–68.
Lomborg, B. (2001). *The skeptical environmentalist: Measuring the real state of the world*. Cambridge, UK: Cambridge University Press.
Moffitt, T. E., Caspi, A., Taylor, A., Kokaua, J., Milne, B. J., Polanczyk, G., et al. (2010). How common are common mental disorders? Evidence that lifetime prevalence rates are doubled by prospective versus retrospective ascertainment. *Psychological Medicine, 40*(6), 899–909.
Moore, S., & Simon, J. L. (2000). *It's getting better all the time: 100 greatest trends of the last 100 years*. Washington, DC: Cato Institute.
Norberg, J. (2016). *Progress: Ten reasons to look forward to the future*. London: Oneworld Publications.
Parker, G., Cheah, Y. C., & Roy, K. (2001). Do the Chinese somatize depression? A cross-cultural study. *Social Psychiatry and Psychiatric Epidemiology, 36*(6), 287–293. https://doi.org/10.1007/s001270170046.
Pettigrew, T. F. (2018). The emergence of contextual social psychology. *Personality and Social Psychology Bulletin, 44*(7), 963–971. https://doi.org/10.1177/0146167218756033.
Pinker, S. (2011). *The better angels of our nature: The decline of violence in history and its causes*. London: Penguin Books.
Pinker, S. (2018). *Enlightenment now: The case for reason, science, humanism, and progress*. New York: Viking.
Postrel, V. (1999). *The future and its enemies: The growing conflict over creativity, enterprise, and progress*. New York: Touchstone.
Pratt, L. A., Brody, D. J., & Gu, Q. (2011). Antidepressant use in persons aged 12 and over: United States, 2005–2008. In *NCHS Data Brief* (Vol. 76). Hyattsville, MD: National Centre for Health Statistics.
Ridley, M. (2010). *The rational optimist: How prosperity evolves*. New York: HarperCollins.
Rosling, H., Rosling, O., & Rönnlund, R. (2018). *Factfulness: Ten reasons we're wrong about the world—And why things are better than you think*. New York: Flatiron Books.

Ryan, R. M., & Deci, E. L. (2017). *Self-determination theory: Basic psychological needs in motvation, development, and wellness.* New York: Guilford Press.

Sachs, J. D. (2018). America's health crisis and the Easterlin paradox. In J. F. Helliwell, R. Layard, & J. D. Sachs (Eds.), *World happiness report* (pp. 146–159). New York: United Nations Sustainable Development Solutions Network.

Shermer, M. (2015). *The moral arc: How science and reason lead humanity toward truth, justice, and freedom.* New York: Henry Holt and Company.

Slovic, P. (1987). Perception of risk. *Science, 236*(4799), 280–285.

Stone, D. M., Simon, T. R., Fowler, K. A., Kegler, S. R., Yuan, K., Holland, K. M., et al. (2018). Vital signs: Trends in state suicide rates—United States, 1999–2016 an circumstances contributing to suicide—27 States, 2015 (N. C. f. I. P. a. C. Division of Violence Prevention, Trans.). *Morbidity and Mortality Weekly Report, 67,* 617–624.

Strawson, P. F. (1959). *Individuals: An essay in descriptive metaphysics.* London: Methuen.

Twenge, J. M. (2000). The age of anxiety? Birth cohort change in anxiety and neuroticism, 1952–1993. *Journal of Personality and Social Psychology, 79*(6), 1007–1021. https://doi.org/10.1037//0022-3514.79.6.1007.

Twenge, J. M., Gentile, B., DeWall, C. N., Ma, D., Lacefield, K., & Schurtz, D. R. (2010). Birth cohort increases in psychopathology among young Americans, 1938–2007: A cross-temporal meta-analysis of the MMPI. *Clinical Psychology Review, 30,* 145–154. https://doi.org/10.1016/j.cpr.2009.10.005.

Twenge, J. M., Zhang, L., & Im, C. (2004). It's beyond my control: A cross-temporal meta-analysis of increasing externality in Locus of Control, 1960–2002. *Personality and Social Psychology Review, 8*(3), 308–319.

# 2

# Understanding Aspirational Culture—Its Foundations and Development

## Aspirational Culture in Daily Life

A lot can be learnt about a culture from the kinds of stories it tells its children. The myths, fairy tales, nursery rhymes, songs and stories of a culture reveal many things: the nature of moral virtue and the righteous life; typical social and moral predicaments that will be encountered in life; the pitfalls that await the hasty, lazy, selfish or presumptuous; the journey to self-control, wisdom and discernment. They also provide cultural models for both interpreting life and living life. That is, they provide some blunt and general, but deeply etched and developmentally embedded, notions and practices that comprise what it is to be a person in a particular culture.

In this sense, sitting down to watch a contemporary self-labelled 'family film' (often animated) is a lesson in the imperatives and life-jlessons that are part of today's aspirational culture and a window into what kinds of persons are valued. Whether it is *The Incredibles*, *A Bug's Life*, *Happy Feet*, *The Lion King*, *Brave*, *How to Train Your Dragon*, or *Tinkerbell*, invariably the message of the story is about the importance of being the individual that you are. It is by no means an entirely

© The Author(s) 2019
K. Moore, *Wellbeing and Aspirational Culture*,
https://doi.org/10.1007/978-3-030-15643-5_2

novel theme. Previous—but still recent—generations were similarly drenched in the imperative to be who they really were. The life lessons that could be drawn from *Mary Poppins*, for example, are strikingly similar to those available in today's offerings.

In these family-friendly films, the main character's individuality and unique talents are initially unrecognized, under-valued or even actively discouraged by the oppressively conformist and, often, timid—and sometimes intimidated—surrounding society (usually the main character's peers or family). But, through adversity and crisis, that same society eventually comes to adulate the central character and his or her special and unique talents since they invariably are the means by which some crisis is averted or some enemy repelled. Not only does this lead to the fulfillment of the protagonist's personal 'dream', or achievement of personal goals, but also those talents—and that character—become seen as vital to the salvation of the society itself.

So much would, at least today, be taken as unabashedly positive, inspirational and even 'life-affirming'. But this personal aspirational (and anti-anti-aspirational) message can have a darker side, as a closer look at one of these films reveals. In the society that forms the backdrop for the highly popular animated film *The Incredibles*—an interesting mix of dated 1950s tropes and futuristic technology, but still recognizably 'our own'—there is a class of people with extraordinary talents (the 'supers'). But there is also an official clampdown on such people by the bureaucratic and political class who respond to public concern over the damaging 'side-effects' of the supers' actions. This clampdown has forced the supers into hiding and, as a consequence, into full-time adoption of their 'secret identities' (in effect, socially-required disguises that obscure their 'true selves').

The blonde-haired oldest son in the central family (Mum, Dad and three children) is called 'Dash'—named after his ability to run incredibly fast. At one telling point, Dash is called into the Principal's office at his school after being suspected by his teacher of pulling a prank by using his special ability. Afterwards, he bemoans to his mother ('Elasti-Girl') how unfair it is that he is not allowed to use his 'special' talents in public. She counters with an immediately recognizable trope from our own cultural milieu: 'everyone is special!' In response, Dash sinks into an even deeper, frowning sulk as he quietly mutters, 'If everyone's special, then no-one is!'. To hammer the point home, there's a further fascinating recurrence in the film of almost the same line. The arch-villain (explicitly psychopathologized through his name, 'Syndrome') is driven by malicious envy born of his lack of superpowers. Not only is he a 'wanna-be super' but he also has a plan to help *everyone* have superpowers through selling his inventions (that mimic those powers). Echoing Dash's previous comment, and at a critical moment in the film, he reveals his devious plot with a mouth twisted into a tell-tale smirk: "When everyone is super, *no-one will be super!*"

These lines of dialogue are stark in their promotion of a crucial element of what I term 'aspirational culture': That those who aspire, and who have the ability to succeed in their aspirations, *should be distinguished from those who do not*, on either or both counts. That is, aspiration comes in tandem with distinction; and distinction, through aspiration, is both the immediate and the final goal of life (whether that be of an individual or a society, or 'civilisation'). As Stuart Ewen (1988, p. 58) put it, "[t]his highly individuated notion of personal distinction … stands at the heart of the 'American Dream'"—a dream which is now the 'Global Dream'. In an aspirational culture, aspiration is constituted as a competitive sport in which 'playing the game', while obviously necessary as a precursor, is done principally to sort and rank individuals on their relative success; to generate distinction. Further, any attempt to obscure that distinction—and remove its competitive aspects—is depicted as a flawed and invidious act that not only frustrates those gifted with special talents but also denies society the benefits of those talents. If 'everyone is special' then—like all ubiquitous commodities—there is no value in that specialness: Hence, 'no-one is special'. Thorough-going aspirational cultures attempt to organise society just in order to generate, and justify, exclusivity—but, crucially, on an array of rapidly proliferating dimensions.

It may seem that this kind of competitive filter would not appeal to the majority since, by definition, only a small minority are likely to aspire successfully. However, since 'distinction' can be on *any and all* dimensions the imperative is transformed into a tantalizing hope: That through some act of self-innovation one should be able to find a dimension, a version of distinction, that would demonstrate one's 'unique talents' (or 'special powers'). In a paradoxical twist, aspirational culture makes itself acceptable to the majority by oxymoronically promising—at least in principle—the potential for *ubiquitous exclusivity* through the notion of ever-expanding variety and diversity (and, its psychological bedfellow, 'choice'). The putatively anti-aspirational mantra that 'everyone is special', that is, may appear opposed to aspiration but is merely its more democratic and liberal dancing partner in the thoroughly embedded aspirational cultural ideal that only one person can be the best. (If you've ever wondered why super heroes have different and diverse 'special powers', there's your cultural explanation.)

Following this analysis, the currently prevalent pursuit of uniqueness and originality in forms of 'self-expression'—often affirmed as exploration of one's 'true self' buried beneath an adopted *persona* ('secret identity')—is best understood as the exploration of 'market niches' for selves seeking distinction or a unique 'identity'. It is an inventive way of making exclusivity inclusive of all people—and so to reinforce the aspirational project as fundamental to *all* human lives. It is no coincidence that this process of personalized exclusivity is also a guarantee that each individual's life trajectory has—and is subjectively experienced as having—unique patterns of '(self)interest' to the point at which 'common interest' fades into the background. The point of living is not only to be different, but to excel in that (self-chosen) difference. The cultural embrace of diversity—whether diversity in personal preferences (as in consumerism), ideas (as in the liberal intellectual ideal of free speech and debate), knowledge (in its expression as relativism or, more traditionally, skepticism), skills (as in the 'portfolio career' and curriculum vitae aligned with precarious work conditions) and, of course, experiences (as in leisure travel to authentic and exotic destinations and participation in 'events')—thus becomes the pathway not only to personal distinction but also to a life well-lived. Your wellbeing, in effect, becomes defined by how successful you have been in whichever eclectic combination of values and pursuits you have chosen to establish your unique being. This more or less conscious production of individuation and singularity has deep roots that, in this book, will lead us to ask what, exactly, are we? As I will argue, the answer to this question goes beyond our biological 'nature'—though it depends upon it—and even beyond our malleable experiences of socialisation.

In an aspirational culture, a life that is not an expression of the constant frothing found in the cauldron of diversity, choice and change, in all its forms, barely qualifies as life at all. Absent such unceasing dynamism, life is presented as empty of the very vitality (and excitement) that defines being alive—it amounts to 'marking time' and 'treading water'. The expression 'You haven't lived until …' neatly encapsulates this imperative as does the refrain 'I was so envious when I heard/saw …'.

I have only sketched the barest bones that fit together as the elements of an aspirational culture, the kind of culture within which humanity increasingly manufactures its experiences. The foundations of this culture, however, are both deep within our species' past and laid down extensively in current social institutions and daily practices. The rest of this chapter is devoted to excavating those foundations or, to return to the metaphor that began this paragraph, putting flesh on those bones.

Aspirational culture is baked into the bedrock of human civilization. That means it is as old as history—though not older. In fact, it is the reason we have what we call history. For vast stretches of the evolutionary history of *Homo sapiens* (about 300,000 years), humans were a precarious species often coming close to extinction. Up until very recently (about 10,000–20,000 years ago) any propensity or capacity this species had to 'aspire' to the point of dominating and totally transforming the planet was extremely well hidden. In any primordial vote on the 'species most likely to rule the world', *Homo sapiens* would have barely made it onto the ballot. How, then, did an expansionary, 'aspirational' momentum enter into the history of our species? How did aspiration get baked into human culture?

First, I need to explain why understanding human wellbeing requires us to understand culture. That means prefiguring my main theoretical point—that our wellbeing concerns are about the wellbeing of *persons* and, therefore, persons must enter explicitly into our theories of wellbeing. In turn, that means we need a good account of what persons are and how they differ from psychological subjects, selves, minds and a host of other candidates for our wellbeing concerns. Focusing

on persons implies focusing on culture because persons are, principally, sociocultural entities. But the concept of a person is also a largely
ignored synthesis of what—in its absence—we see as our distinct biological and social 'natures'. Crucially, a 'person' is our biology recruited
to sociocultural action. At some point in our evolutionary past this
recruitment began in earnest and provided *Homo sapiens* with a distinctive, though untried, tool to employ in the evolutionary project.

Second, I need to make it clear that aspiration can be seen in all parts
of the human world: In our ecology, economy, society, politics, cultural narratives, and personal lives. The way aspiration manifests in each
of these parts of our world and experience is what makes aspirational
culture self-supporting. Like the lodge poles that form the structure
for a traditional tipi of the Great Plains tribes of North America, each
'pole'—each aspect of our human world—leans against the others. The
point at which they converge we can think of as the 'burning point' of
the daily life of the individual person. And at this point are the 'ropes',
tied tightly, that hold the structure together—that hold the lives of persons together.[1] To end my use of this metaphor; arguably those binding
ropes—the lives of persons—have now frayed and loosened to the point
where, for many people, the twisted structure has either collapsed or is
exerting huge strain on those lives and, so, on those individuals.

Each one of us lives our life at the point of this cultural convergence.
Because of that, our wellbeing as persons is a complicated function of
culture. These close links between wellbeing and culture are more fundamental and pervasive than is often acknowledged. Culture is not just
one factor or variable that exerts its influence on wellbeing (e.g., as in
research that compares how wellbeing is experienced in collectivist versus individualist cultures). For a start, any judgment of being or living
'well' depends not only on a specific set of cultural values and meanings but also on the economic, legal, political and social institutions and
practices that hinge together to form contemporary cultural contexts.
But, even more importantly, culture does not just provide the *contexts*
(of institutions, practices and meanings) within which wellbeing can be
attained, sustained and judged. It also creates the *entities* whose wellbeing is of concern: Culture, as just emphasised, creates *persons*. The reasons why persons should be seen as the proper target of our wellbeing

concerns will be outlined in Chapter 4. In this chapter I take those reasons as given and move directly to an explanation of 'aspirational culture' and the kinds of persons it creates.

But why talk of culture? Why not just focus on 'aspirational society' or 'aspirational personality'? The point I want to emphasise with the notion of an aspirational *culture* is that aspiration acts as a pervasive organizing principle rather than simply as a social or psychological propensity or trait. It can be found in the form of our economic activities (and how they connect—or not—to ecological settings), in overtly symbolic practices (myths, rituals, legends, stories), and in the manifest and latent functions of social institutions (such as political systems, education, childcare, the legal and judicial systems). Finally, and importantly for wellbeing, it is expressed in the daily activities of persons. These activities are not entirely arbitrary, idiosyncratic or self-chosen. They reflect and reproduce broader economic, symbolic, and social arrangements that support aspirational imperatives, albeit in diverse ways from person to person. It is what persons do—and what they see themselves as doing or trying to do—that simultaneously expresses, reinforces and reproduces any culture. Aspiration is 'cultural' in this sense that it is present in all parts of a way of life and these 'parts' structure the daily activities of the kinds of persons that an aspirational culture also creates. The term 'aspirational culture' is an attempt to capture this pervasiveness. It also denotes an 'ideal form', though I accept that no 'ideal forms' ever exist. While aspiration is not (yet) a totalizing influence on human experience, the concept expresses a trajectory that, like the track of a particle in a cloud chamber, can be made clear when viewed in the right conditions. Today's world provides those conditions.

As a cultural imperative, aspiration invites a rationale and a de facto set of guidelines for how the various components of a way of life should be structured and arranged: economies should grow; lives should be lengthened; educational qualifications and careers should form ladders or staircases (and ones that, today, unpredictably shift and rotate like those in Hogwarts School and so lead to ever-changing destinations); lifestyles should evolve and be diverse, fluid and experimental; selves should 'actualise', 'grow', and 'realise'; persons should 'become'. In short, in an aspirational culture nothing is understood as already being what it *should* be. To 're'-produce something (in the same or similar state) is always inferior to, and of a lower priority than, producing something in some novel, improved, form. This applies not just to economic production but also to the production of our lives and selves, to our interactions with nature, and to our social and political institutions. Promotion of the value of 'life-long learning', for example, is not just about a personal imperative for constant improvement and 'self-actualisation' but is also a pre-requisite for the acceleration of economic growth, social mobility (and status), and risk management (at the personal, social, and species levels). Reproduction, by contrast, is treated as *mere* maintenance, as 'treading water'—useful only to the extent that it might give rise to more (novel) production at some future point. Production naturally trumps reproduction; growth (whether economic or psychological) trumps sustainability; dynamism trumps stability; novel innovation and speed trumps consolidation and arduous crafting.

American anthropologist Ruth Benedict's view of culture was famously described by Margaret Mead as 'personality writ large'. Just as Benedict spoke of 'Apollonian' cultures of restraint and 'Dionysian' cultures of abandonment, there is a sense in which 'aspirational culture' aims for a sweeping characterization. But no actual culture could be summed up in one word and no cultural tendency is entirely dominant. So, why use the label 'aspirational culture'? As I said, I want to highlight particular similarities in different domains (e.g., economic, ecological, social, psychological) that might otherwise go undetected. But I also argue that there exists a mutually supportive 'logic' or 'ideology' in the organizing principles that underpin these diverse domains. Today's culture may not be *all* about aspiration; but aspiration forms a large part of its guiding ideology. Over time, that logic of aspiration comes to inform more and more of the activities that go into our cultural performances. The attempt to understand wellbeing in today's world therefore cannot succeed without understanding that 'ideo-logic' and the attempts made to navigate it.

Aspiration, viewed in this way, is simultaneously expressed in ecology, economics, social institutions, and psychological experience. This breadth of expression implies the adoption of a similarly broad definition of 'culture'. Such a broad meaning, in anthropology, goes back to theorists like Edward Tylor whose evolutionary approach saw culture as a broad-ranging set of acquired beliefs, institutions and practices. His definition in his book *Primitive Culture* (1871) described culture as a "complex whole which includes knowledge, belief, art, morals, law, custom, and any other capabilities and habits acquired by [a person] as a member of society". A culture is a complex 'whole' because its parts cohere. In aspirational cultures, the 'glue' that produces that coherence is the notion of aspiration.

By contrast, anthropologists such as Benedict, Alfred Kroeber, Clyde Kluckhohn and Clifford Geertz tended to see culture 'cognitively' as a set of meanings, symbolically expressed, and passed down from generation to generation through communication and learning. This approach sometimes assumes that individual members of a culture share a *similar set of mental concepts* about the lives they live together. For reasons that will become obvious, this assumption that culture stems from individuals who possess similar mental concepts does not align well with the overall argument of this book. But even within this cognitive view, meanings still ultimately are 'cashed out' in the social world—rather than in the individual's mind—and, so, culture is still best seen as a collective performance. Geertz's approach, for example,—inspired in part by the philosophy of Ludwig Wittgenstein—depicts culture as 'semiotic' and symbolic in a way that emphasises the public and social nature of a culture.

Whichever definition of culture is preferred, I use the term 'aspirational culture' to highlight the convergence in daily life of institutional arrangements in the political, legal and economic spheres as well as any habitual practices and moral orders that are widespread enough to be recognised by individuals as 'the way things are done'—even if some individuals fail to follow or even reject, eschew or oppose such practices. For example, buying or renting a separate house from one's family after getting married or when embarking upon an independent life connects economic systems (such as markets for property), personal 'desires' (such as the goal to have one's own home), social institutions (such as the family), political and legal systems (such as systems of property rights and law), local moral orders (such as the responsibility, as an adult, to 'stand on your own two feet') and ecological relationships (such as modern urban or suburban development and the resource use required to sustain them). Put bluntly, culture 'hits home' in our daily practices. And this is where—and how—aspirational culture comes to constitute our experiences and our wellbeing.

It is in these everyday practices that people integrate—or at least attempt to integrate—the physical, biological, ecological, economic, moral and social orders that dominate in a given time and place. Human beings have to survive (or even 'flourish') in relation to all of these contexts more or less simultaneously. And these contexts affect each other. For example, getting a job 50 kilometers away from your home, successfully driving your car to work, emitting $CO_2$, obeying the road rules, resisting 'road rage', and self-regulating your morning routine to get to work on time along with performing successful psychological transitions between home, commute and work are everyday practices that reflect and reproduce the broader arrangements that pass for normal in an increasing number of cultures. It is, then, in the life of a person that cultural sites of aspiration converge. But these sites should not be understood simply as the *context* within which we live. Ultimately, their convergence and interaction *are* our lives—and are us. If this complex daily life is the contemporary culmination of aspirational culture the first question to address concerns what it was that set our species on this course in the first place?

## Aspirational Ecology/Economy

Humans are animals. Like all other animals we have made an accommodation with the physical world and the world of other living things. This accommodation is our ecological niche. In the last 10,000 years or so that niche has become particularly interesting, and problematic. Ecological economists John Gowdy and Lisi Krall (2013, 2014, 2016) describe our species as ecologically and economically similar to several *ultrasocial*[2] animal species, such as termites and ants. We are, of course, genetically distant from ants and termites, but our common ultrasociality, they argue, is a result of 'convergent evolution'. Dolphins (mammals) and sharks (cartilaginous fishes) look remarkably similar yet do not share a common ancestor. What they do share is a common selective environment (as did the extinct icthyosaurs that had a similar body form). Sharks and dolphins are both large animals that live in the open ocean and hunt good-sized fishes. That niche similarity led to selection for similar body size, form, and fin placement to allow for effective hunting speeds, power and agility.

In the same way, convergent evolution between ants, termites and humans has led to selection of similar social arrangements: An advanced division of labour; economic specialization (often involving non-food producing members); the sharing of information about danger and food sources; and even self-sacrifice for collective defence. With some termite species this leads, through evolution, to marked differences in size between members of the same species and sometimes enlarged development of body parts. In humans, apart from the basic sex-based division of labour, this is not the case: Accountants, cleaners, and marketers are not (yet) identifiable and distinguishable at birth by a quick inspection of the body. But humans do now have an unprecedented *division of labour* and *specialization* to the point that fewer and fewer people are directly involved in activity connected to food production. We also have a radical form of *interdependence*, again in common with other ultrasocial species. In fact, this (principally economic) interdependence is often seen as a positive feature of our social world and even one of the reasons for reductions in the occurrence of violence and war (Pinker 2011). So why did these same social features develop in such markedly different species? What 'niche' provided such similar selection pressures?

Ultrasocial arrangements, according to Gowdy and Krall, evolved as a direct consequence of the discovery and widespread adoption of agriculture. Some species of termites, for example, cultivate fungi as a food source. In fact, this has only occurred twice amongst social insects. Old World termites are so renowned for this cultivation that the fungus genus they specialize in cultivating is named after them—*Termitomyces*. Over evolutionary time, the efforts of all individual members of these species became selected to ensure the success of the agricultural enterprise.

Ever since the agricultural revolution around 10,000 years ago, humans have, similarly but more elaborately, domesticated and cultivated a huge array of plant and animal species. That revolution had immediate and impressive consequences: "the human population exploded from around 6 million to over 200 million by the beginning of the Common Era (CE) 2000 years ago" (Gowdy and Krall 2014, p. 180). Today the human population is around 7.7 billion people. Following the same trajectory, ultrasocial termite and ant colonies transform their environments to support food production. Recently, parts of an area of "fully deciduous, semiarid, thorny- scrub *caatinga* forests" scrub in Brazil has been cleared to reveal 200 million termite mounds from a still active population of termites (Martin et al. 2018, p. R1292). The mounds were the waste from a vast tunnel network created to take advantage of the episodic availability of leaf litter in the forest (used to grow fungi) and, through an over-dispersed pattern, covered an area of 230,000 km², about the size of Great Britain. Because of this ability to transform their environments, and despite comprising only about 20,000 of the one million plus species of insects, ants and termites contribute half of the planet's insect biomass.

Humans have been just as impressive in their effects on planetary biomass and functioning to the point of now having a geological period named after them—the 'Anthropocene'. We have successfully transformed the planet to support ourselves and to flourish, at least in raw numbers. While huge biodiversity loss is a current concern, humans and some other species—notably those that we use for food production—have multiplied spectacularly. Bar-On, Phillips and Milo (2018) have estimated current human biomass at 0.06 gigatonnes of carbon (Gt C), livestock at about 0.1 Gt C and *all wild mammals* at 0.007 Gt C. That is, humans and their livestock tip the scales at almost 23 times the biomass of all other mammals combined. The biomass of domesticated poultry at 0.005 Gt C is about three times greater than all wild birds, estimated at 0.002 Gt C. While cultivated crops are only estimated at 10 Gt C (about 2% of total plant biomass) Bar-On et al. (2018) note estimates that total plant biomass has *declined* approximately twofold since the onset of human civilisation. Given that plant biomass is so massive in planetary terms that it is, in effect, a proxy for *total* biomass, a two-fold reduction in plant biomass is an astonishing human impact over such a short time. This dynamic towards environmental dominance is characteristic of ultrasociality. That dynamic is not itself 'aspirational' in any purposive sense but it is not hard to argue that it lays deep foundations that invite, and even select for, aspirational activity at social and individual levels. The impetus to exploit and expand is inherent in ultrasociality and provides a powerful selective environment for social organisation and individual behaviour.

According to Gowdy and Krall, this ability to generate—and control the generation of—food surpluses is an economic innovation of such a magnitude that it qualitatively alters the evolutionary dynamic for any species that happens upon it. Unlike most other animal species, ultrasocial animals do not depend on hunting and gathering food in order to survive. Nature's bounty is not a (directly) limiting factor. Ultrasocial species not only convert plant and animal matter into their own biomass (e.g., through digestion and, ultimately, increased reproductive rates), but they also re-engineer surrounding biomass and physical resources to produce their food and, in the case of recent human history, many other 'goods'.

This radical innovation leads to two notable consequences. The first is the one already noted: the ability to generate food surpluses allows such species to dominate ecosystems. That domination is through a spiral of ever larger populations and increasing conversion of ecosystems and environments into the economic machinery that generates the food surpluses. The environment becomes an 'input' into the social and economic system rather than being the system *within which* a species operates. It is therefore less a 'habitat' and more a site for systematic exploitation—not directly of food, but of the raw materials for the production of food via the agricultural system. Feedback processes from the broader ecosystem therefore no longer exert immediate pressure on the species. So long as sufficient raw materials for the agricultural process are available, disruptions to other ecosystem processes have limited immediate effect on the activity of ultrasocial species. This means that the ecological-economic system that is created becomes insular and *self-referential*. Crucially, all the incentives for activity by members of that species are 'internal' to the food production system and the culture and social organization that develops around that. ('Innovations' in this context are, in effect, attempts to maintain this economic system as a process independent of the surrounding ecosystem.) At the same time, incentives to adjust activity in response to alterations in the broader environment (that now is 'external' to the self-referential system) are weak, attenuated and delayed. For their individual survival, members of the species are effectively 'locked-in' to activities required by the ecological-economic system, irrespective of the impacts those activities might have on the environment beyond. The evolutionary record for ultrasocial termites and ants shows just how 'locked-in' this form of economic production is: "No secondary reversals to the ancestral life style are known in either group, which suggests that the transitions to farming were as drastically innovative and irreversible as when humans made this step about 10,000 years ago" (Aanen and Boomsma 2006, p. R1014).

The second consequence follows from this behavioural 'lock-in': *Individual autonomy in ultrasocial species is subordinated to the dynamics and 'needs' of the system.* In Gowdy and Krall's (2016, p. 1) words, adoption of agricultural economies by ultrasocial species results in "the suppression of individual autonomy as the group itself became the focus of economic organization". The challenge is to explain how subordination of individual autonomy evolved since this seems to defy gene-centric readings of evolution by natural selection. How could cooperation with unrelated others—to the point of sacrificing individual autonomy—have arisen? The massive material and energetic advantages of an agricultural system are obvious, but these accrue to the group not the individual. Gowdy and Krall argue that it is through a form of group selection that those advantages favoured groups that adopted agricultural practices. They make use of Multi-Level Selection theory to explain how the central dynamic of ultrasociality—managed exploitation of environments that then leads to food surpluses and group expansion—was able to evolve. This economic rearrangement increasingly drove the ultrasocial mode at both social and individual levels (i.e., division of labour, specialization, interdependence, self-sacrifice).

The reduction in individual autonomy partly results from the greater proportion of time that individual members of the species need to devote to cooperative (agricultural) production. But reduced autonomy also stems from the more limited range of tasks carried out by individuals, with each member only being required to provide a sub-set of the overall tasks involved in production. For humans, that also means a reduced breadth in knowledge and skills required for survival. By contrast, individual hunter gatherers had vast and detailed knowledge of their environment and the skills needed to hunt and gather. The exceptional brain to body ratio in humans in large part may well have been a result of the need for each individual to acquire extensive ecological knowledge. While there is a broad correlation between brain (or neo-cortex) size and *social* demands (e.g., Dunbar 2014; Shultz and Dunbar 2006), there is also evidence that strong *ecological* challenges and demands—rather than between-individual competition or social cooperation—led to the evolutionary surge in human brain growth (prior to the last 10,000–20,000 years, over which period there has been a *reduction* in brain size). From analyses that challenge the social hypothesis as the dominant explanation for increased brain size, González-Forero and Gardner (2018, p. 556) found, for brain and body size, that a "near-perfect adult fit" occurs with a mix of cognitive challenges that are about 60% ecological, 30% cooperative (often in relation to ecological challenges), 10% between-group competitive challenges (which probably includes some within-group or 'within-alliance' cooperative challenges) and "an approximately complete absence of between-individual competitive challenges (around 0%)". (The latter 0% estimate suggests that we did not evolve large cortices in order to become more Machiavellian, which will surprise some evolutionary psychologists.) That is, encephalisation—the evolution of an increase in brain size and relative increase in cortical versus non-cortical functions—may have been driven principally by the ecological demands that followed from a hunter gatherer subsistence with a much reduced, but still present, role for sociality as the driver. The intensive, interdependent forms of cooperation that are so much a part of ultrasocial existence may even have led to a *reduction* in brain size: "In this eco-social scenario, between-individual competition is unimportant, as it does not lead to human-sized brains and bodies … [and] [c]ooperation decreases brain size, because it allows individuals to rely on their partners' skills and thus decrease their own investment into costly brains (cooperation invites cheating)" (González-Forero and Gardner 2018, p. 556). (As an aside, the bracketed reference to cheating in this quotation suggests that the kind of culturally-induced ultrasociality that occurs in human history has likely increased the opportunities to cheat and therefore—over the last 10,000 years—increased our concerns about cheating. Provocatively, the refined 'cheater detection' module of cognitive evolutionary psychology fame may, in fact, be quite a recent, culturally-organised neurocognitive capacity.)

In summary, by reducing individual autonomy, ultrasociality has led to, or hastened, the de facto domestication of humans. As with all domestication, it has meant that, individually, our repertoire of knowledge and behaviours has shrunk. The reduction in brain size over the past 10,000–20,000 years may partly be explained by this domestication and the associated reduction in the range of knowledge and skills individuals needed to master. For similar reasons, domesticated animals have smaller brains than their wild counterparts.[3] To the modern mind that might seem odd. Aren't we far more knowledgeable today? Can't humans carry out far more complex behaviours than they ever could? Collectively that may be true; but, individually, our abilities and skills may well have narrowed significantly (though changed in content quite dramatically). Greater specialisation and division of labour gave rise to the rapid development of cooperative interdependency which, in turn, has meant that individuals have had progressively less to do and think about.

In human societies, that same interdependency also led to the embedding of hierarchical social classes and castes that have been endemic to, and ubiquitous in, human civilisations of the last 10,000 years. Despite agriculture being discovered many times in human history in different places, cultures, and eras, the social systems that resulted were remarkably similar. Gowdy and Krall (2016) quote a passage from Ronald Wright's book *A Short History of Progress* to make the point. The encounter between the Old World and the New in the sixteenth century—"two cultural experiments, running in isolation for 15,000 years"—revealed staggering similarities such that Cortés, on arriving in Mexico, could find "roads, canals, cities, palaces, schools, law courts, markets, irrigation works, kings, priests, temples, peasants, artisans, armies, astronomers, merchants, sports, theatre, art, music, and books" (Wright 2004, pp. 50–51). Ultrasociality, that is, not only shows its structuring role in the convergent evolution of ants, termites and humans but also in independent and parallel instances of its convergent *cultural* evolution in humans. To support these now very familiar features of civilisation, individual members of the group had to, in effect, become 'cogs' necessary for the function of the ecological-economic ultrasocial system. On an evolutionary scale, our existence as autonomous—but cooperating—individual human beings was brought to an abrupt halt with the cultural adoption of agriculture and, therefore, ultrasociality.

Subordination of individual autonomy to the imperative of food production is obvious in the extreme bodily differences in some termite species where members have been subject to genetic changes that fitted them to their social and economic roles. For humans, however, the adoption of ultrasociality and the consequential subordination of individual autonomy differed in an important respect. Agricultural activity—and its associated division of labour, specialization, social hierarchies, and interdependence—is a *newcomer* in human evolutionary history. It emerged only about 10,000 years ago and—at the historical scale—took time to spread. That recency implies that, in the human case, ultrasociality has been organized through cultural rather than biological evolution.

Prior to agriculture, human social life was generally egalitarian (e.g., Rogers et al. 2011; Dyble et al. 2015) with almost flat or non-existent social hierarchies and minimal division of labour. Interpersonal status differences presumably existed but there were few institutionalized differences in status between different groups. Yet, this distinctive human social tendency for egalitarianism is anomalous amongst primate species, most of which tend to form varieties of hierarchies even in quite small groups. Why, then, did humans initially adopt and evolve egalitarianism?

Boehm (1993) provided one well known answer. He argued that egalitarianism depended upon the development of a 'reverse dominance hierarchy'. Previously, many specific explanations of egalitarianism were based on what he called 'automatic', external factors—material and structural features of a wide variety of ways of life (e.g., the presence of

nomadism, fluid group membership, economic vagaries of cattle ownership, natural cycles of 'big man' leadership). These structural features,
their proponents argued, mitigated against the possibility and viability
of hierarchies. But, despite identifying these many specific structural
factors, what was missing, Boehm claimed, was a *general* account of
egalitarianism. The striking fact was that *no* society had stratification
beyond a rudimentary level. Boehm claimed that a flat society was not
simply a structural result of the (sometimes) cooperative hunting, fish-
ing, gathering, horticultural and herding forms of subsistence—though
that is part of the explanation (they certainly support egalitarianism).
Instead, hunter gatherers and other traditionally egalitarian societies
*actively and intentionally prevented* formation of hierarchies. They did
this via 'followers' dominating 'leaders', especially if they demonstrated
any hint of what he called 'bossiness'. This inverted domination is what
Beohm called the 'reverse dominance hierarchy'.

The way Boehm characterized this intentional effort is crucial.
Citing some of his own previous work, he noted that "egalitarian political styles developed *only after the emergence of the human capacity for
purposeful, moralistic sanctioning*" (Boehm 1993, p. 228, emphasis
added). To be blunt, the capacity for moral sanction—and, therefore,
why humans could for so long maintain an egalitarian social organization—is something new under the sun. It is not only an interesting
explanation of the otherwise anomalous emergence of egalitarianism
in primate societies, but it is also a clue to the emergence of a new
kind of 'being' or entity. That new kind of being is susceptible to just
this kind of moral sanction (and is also a being that is inclined, and
able, to inflict it). Trying to shame or ridicule a tiger, or even a human
baby, is a lost cause.[4] Trying to shame a *person*, however, is remarkably
easy—especially if you are, yourself, a person. Tellingly, at very young
ages—around two years old—we can experience shame and guilt. Moral
sanction would be entirely ineffective without this susceptibility. This is
also roughly the same age that our capacities with language are rapidly
improving, with our 'receptive' vocabularies—what we can 'receive' in
a meaningful way—initially out-running our 'productive' vocabularies—the utterances we can perform with meaning or 'intent'. Not coin-
cidentally, it is also about the time we start to see ourselves as a 'social

actor' in the world (McAdams 2013)—and perhaps also start seeing ourselves as a being that can be *acted upon* (regulated) by others. It may only be in mid- to late-childhood that we have a sense of ourselves as an 'agent' and then, later still, as an 'autobiographical author' of our lives (McAdams 2013). If the evolutionary arrival of personhood explains the human disposition for egalitarianism, then the subsequent and very late cultural evolution of agricultural ultrasociality—with its decidedly non-egalitarian generation of social hierarchies—is likely to have had, at best, ambivalent and, at worst, punishing effects on this new kind of being (a person).

It is worth emphasizing that, as well as widespread egalitarianism, there was also minimal division of labour in most prehistoric social groups, beyond that based on sex differences. No doubt this allowed for a high level of individual autonomy as the norm. Most adults had the knowledge and capability to support themselves (and perhaps some children) but living cooperatively in small groups enhanced longer-term survival and demographic stability. Experiences may not be found in fossils, but the weight of evidence, and opinion, suggests that the human pre-agricultural way of life is best characterized as 'autonomous cooperation' within an egalitarian political climate. That basic independence meant social regulation could only have been relatively light, beyond expectations of food sharing, participation in cooperative hunting and gathering, and, necessarily, enforced reciprocal commitments to egalitarianism.

There is debate over how much biological (genetic) evolution has occurred in humans over the last 10,000–15,000 years but, irrespective, there has been nothing like the amount of evolutionary time that has allowed termites and ants to be morphologically selected for an ultrasocial existence. For humans, the economics of agriculture is still the driver of ultrasociality, but the evolutionary mechanism has been cultural rather than biological (Gowdy and Krall 2016). As mentioned, a form of group selection may well have led to the unrelenting spread and dominance of ultrasocial groups. One explanation for the group selection advantage is that division of labour and specialization led to surpluses which allowed them to out-compete egalitarian hunter gatherer groups, perhaps through higher population levels. But there is another, complementary, explanation that might seem paradoxical: Regardless of the kind of subsistence (e.g., hunter gatherer versus agricultural), hierarchical societies may be inherently unstable (Rogers et al. 2011) *and this social instability itself causes such societies to spread.* In stable environments, stratified societies can experience wild fluctuations in population because of the unequal distribution of resources (especially food). According to Rogers et al. (2011), higher classes (in the hierarchy) typically survive these fluctuations but lower classes cyclically suffer or experience high mortality. This then leads to migration in search of new resources which also means it leads to the spatial and demographic expansion of stratified societies. Members who migrate 'carry' the cultural norms of stratification both directly as norms enforced through interpersonal expectations and indirectly through the practices involved in the manner by which they are used to pursuing their means of subsistence.

Whatever the cause of the origins, spread and dominance of stratified human societies, they represent a departure from a much more egalitarian evolutionary experience. In turn, that egalitarianism was an evolutionary departure from the various forms of hierarchy present in other primate social groups. The upshot of this rapid turn to an ultrasocial form of existence over the last 10,000 years is twofold. First, social organization (and stratification) has increasingly been about how to generate food (and associated production and wealth) rather than how to generate wellbeing for members of those societies. That is, since embarking on an ultrasocial trajectory, the material foundation of human social existence has been an economic and social disposition for accelerated growth, demographic expansion and intensified division of labour. Surplus food (essentially, calories) fueled this growth in much the same way that coal, then oil, has fueled spectacular economic and population growth over the last century and more.

As ultrasociality became more embedded, previously 'autonomous' but cooperative human beings became domesticated—mainly by cultural means—into the service of that growth and expansion. Crucially, only pre-existing entities like persons could have precipitated such a rapid social and economic shift. To use evolutionary terms, the cultural artefact of a person may well have been 'preadapted' to be 'exapted'[5] for ultrasociality. Gowdy and Krall (2013) make the same point in relation to cooperation. While it is common to see human cooperation in positive terms, it also has a "dark side" that can be understood through its relationship to the evolution of ultrasociality: "Beginning with the agricultural revolution, the human propensity to cooperate was *co-opted by a bioeconomic evolutionary force* as several large-scale hierarchical societies emerged" (Gowdy and Krall 2013, p. 140, emphasis added). That is, while persons first evolved to operate in cooperative egalitarian social conditions, their susceptibility to social regulation (a feature initially designed to allow egalitarianism to be *maintained*) could later be used to organise them into non-egalitarian, hierarchical relations with each other, once agriculture spread. As I will discuss in Chapter 4, persons are sociocultural creations and therefore eminently suited to the normative and moral regulation and subordination necessary for ultrasocial arrangements. The kinds of gene-based, morphological specialisations of ants and termites were therefore not needed for humans, though genetic changes might now be playing 'catch-up' over the longer term.

There is a second consequence of the shift from autonomous existence in a cooperative, egalitarian social group to individual persons occupying varied 'positions' within increasingly complicated hierarchical arrangements. Once ultrasociality takes a firm hold over everyday life, the path to wellbeing potentially splits in two. A person's *material* wellbeing can part company with their wellbeing *as a person*. The latter, with all its associated experiences of autonomy, enjoyment, happiness, meaning, purpose, connection and fluid vitality, ceases to be inherent in living. Instead, it becomes something experienced in the interstices of the everyday; achieved through effort and expressed as a (personal) goal that must be pursued, worked at, and 'stolen' from a process not designed to generate it. Even more worryingly, the social relationships and normative judgments so necessary for the wellbeing of persons become determined by the increasingly pervasive, and novel, forms of social and economic hierarchies rather than being generated from a society of equals. In short, a person's contribution to the ultrasocial form of socioeconomic arrangements and their experience of wellbeing each become the elusive target of personal aspirational effort. In Biblical terms, Eden has been lost, and, after the Fall, the wearying drudgery has begun. Or, as the more secular saying goes, after agriculture 'the rest is history'.

## Aspirational Society

As that history proceeded, the features that are characteristic of ultra-sociality became, in human societies that followed this path, ever more elaborate. An agricultural economic form of life cemented the need to guarantee not only continued production but, as the human population grew (in fits and starts), *increased* production. That ultrasocial dynamic helped embed the precursors for a full-blown aspirational culture. Societies developed advanced division of labour, specialization and complicated social hierarchies. The primary life-task of individuals in these societies was to find a way to play a viable role in that differentiated and—almost always—hierarchical social system. In one sense, the establishment of often quite rigid social classes and castes made fulfilling that task easy, even automatic, since everyone had a place in a social hierarchy. But the life that followed was often far from easy. It is perhaps too tempting to over-emphasise how hard and powerless life for the majority of people in such societies was (and is), but Hobbes' famous description of life as 'solitary, poor, nasty, brutish, and short' can be reinterpreted as a depiction of the extreme subordination of individual autonomy (and hence wellbeing) to the 'locked-in' ultrasocial 'superorganism' that emerged after the adoption of agriculture. Enjoyment and pleasure were by no means absent from the life of the masses and in some ways the communal events, celebrations, and, in Europe, non-work 'holy-days' that peppered day-to-day life may have provided a form of wellbeing in short supply today (see Ehrenreich 2007). The overall trend, though, was to increased marginalization, regulation and even prohibition of these remaining potential sources of wellbeing since they have also often been seen as potential *threats* to the functioning—and flourishing—of the social system.

It is no surprise to find critiques of the modern world in sociology.[6] (But see Veenhoven 2010—a prolific author in wellbeing research—for a contrarian view.) Sociology arose at the time of the massive social transformations in nineteenth century Europe. But—like North American psychology which burgeoned in the late nineteenth century (see Chapter 3 and Leahey 2000; Hergenhahn 2005)—it was motivated as much by the *optimistic* view that the challenges of the rapidly urbanising era of industrial capitalism could be met by an equally new (aspirational) science of human behaviour and society as by a thorough-going pessimism about the modern world. In fact, that original optimism may be undergoing a twenty-first century resurrection (Holmes 2016) as part of what seems to be a partial 'turn to optimism' (also see Chapter 1).

Optimistic or pessimistic, sociologists were confronting major social change. One of the most distinctive of these has been the creation of the middle classes. Whether in today's so-called emerging economies of China or India, amongst African Americans over the past few decades or, historically, in the urbanising centres of Britain and North America in the nineteenth and early twentieth centuries, it would be hard to overstate the significance of the rise of this class. It now demographically dominates many countries and is perhaps even more dominant when it comes to self-identified class (the class to which people report they belong). When Hadley Cantril surveyed the American population in 1943, he found that the majority self-identified as 'middle class', both socially and economically (Cantril 1943). Even low income groups tended to identify themselves, socially, as middle class consistent with a broader tendency to view one's social class as higher than one's economic class (which itself is evidence of the pervasiveness and cultural embeddedness of aspiration). In fact, Cantril found that the distance between social and economic identification increased going *up* the social scale and *down* the economic scale. That is, the lower the income the—relatively—higher the evaluation of social class; the higher the self-rated social class, the—relatively—lower the income. That dual trend could be characterised as either delusional or, of course, 'aspirational' depending on whether a person's social and economic positions are seen as largely static or mobile.

Stuart Ewen's book *All Consuming Images: The Politics of Style in Contemporary Culture* is an analysis of the shift—economically, socially, and culturally—from the concrete immovability of substance to the dynamic, ever-shifting presentations of style, symbol, and imagery. While the 'middling classes' had, from Medieval times, been considered to be a more or less static band of the population hovering somewhere between poverty and wealth, industrial capitalism transformed them into fully-fledged, restless aspirers after the dream—a dream that, today, "has left its imprint on the aspirations and discontents of people and cultures around the globe" (Ewen 1988, p. 59). The ability of industrial capitalism to produce "styled goods" that provided "a spectacle of upward mobility" meant that an emerging middle class could be populated by two quite different groups. Not only were there the truly prosperous merchants who could afford expensive homes, furniture and entertainment but there were also the white-collar workers who, reports Ewen—quoting the historian Alan Dawley—, lived on "subsistence salaries", "called their condition 'genteel poverty'" but could afford cheap versions of the luxury items enjoyed by the truly prosperous, and so possess the "symbolic accoutrements of status" (p. 59). Ewen quotes from an 1847 issue of the magazine *Scientific American* that applauded factory industrialism as the path to a new consumption-based democracy, "one 'which invites every man [sic] to enhance his own comfort and status'" and which, through mass production, was "providing 'the vehicle for the pursuit of happiness'" (p. 60). It was here, in the building of a consumption pathway to happiness, that another 'vehicle' developed: a widespread, socially institutionalised vehicle for materialistic values. These same values have now come into clear focus in much work on subjective well-being, mostly because of their detrimental effects.

Both wealth and poverty were increasing as industrial capitalism gathered momentum. This reflected the poor wages of those in the burgeoning factories and, at the same time, the increased profits of industrialists. These radically divergent consequences created concerns about the accumulation of the new wealth in fewer and fewer hands, in a way similar to recent criticisms of our modern economy. Through the lens of *consumption*, the symbolic trappings of wealth and status hung alluringly close in the expectations of more and more people. Yet, through the lens of industrial factory *production*, "widespread immiserization [sic]" simultaneously became the lot of more and more people.

It was this 'double-aspect' of industrialisation that led to "two distinct ways of apprehending the very question of *status* and *class*" (Ewen 1988, p. 60, original emphasis). In one way, class can be understood in terms of the "social relations of power" involved in *production*. The second way involves defining class by patterns of *consumption*. Viewed from the former perspective, work based on craft and small-scale production was being eviscerated and its refugees had, as their only remaining survival option, the work generated in the same factories that had brought their way of life to an end. This means that class identity "was not a matter of individual choice, but of the position one inhabits in relation to the forces of production" (Ewen 1988, p. 62). But in a world in which, courtesy of industrial mass production, the *image* of the class one aspired to could be bought, these 'objective relations' in the process of production could be ignored. In its place the consumptive idea of class could arise, stripped of notions of social power- and "highlighting individual, above common, identity" and so herald the "idea of an American 'middle class,' constructed out of images, attitudes, acquisitions, and style" (p. 62). In the process, an entire class could now aspire to at least emulate the 'civilised' and refined life that had first emerged as the etiquette, manners, and appropriate forms of self-presentation and behaviour in the medieval courts of Europe (see Elias 2000 for the classic account of this 'civilising process'). Social aspiration could start to be prised loose from economic destiny.

But not entirely. In increasing numbers, the upper strata of the new middle classes took to the opportunities for professional upward mobility. The 1890s saw the rise of professionalisation across the American economy (with the American Psychological Association being founded in 1892): "Leading lawyers, engineers, teachers, social workers, and members of other professions said the same thing: expertise should confer autonomy, social status, and economic security on those who possessed it, and they alone should regulate and restrict the members of their calling" (Diner 1998, p. 176 cited in Leahey 2000, p. 359). As a result, the "new middle class desire to advance oneself by acquiring professional expertise lead [sic] to a huge increase in the number of college students from 238,000 in 1900 to 598,000 in 1920" (Leahey 2000, p. 359). It was the role of these professionals to coordinate and manage the new form of society emerging as a result of industrialisation and urbanisation (see Chapter 3 and the discussion of the rise of applied and professional psychology as part of that coordinating system).

Fast forward to today and we see the worked out version of the now global phenomenon of the rapid growth of a consumer middle class as a marker of a country's entrance into the modern world. Today's middle class is different from, and more widespread than, the middle class that Ewen argued began to emerge in America in the mid-nineteenth century, but it retains one central innovation from those origins. The 'middle class' is no longer believed to be simply a position in a static social order—it is an *escalator* that embodies 'social mobility'. The dynamic is usually understood as *upward* social mobility though is as likely—if not more likely at certain times—to involve *downward* mobility. But the vital observation is that the whole point of this new consumption-based middle class is to emphasise (social) aspiration as much as, and often more than, (economic) attainment. Being 'middle class' in this way involves seeing one's current social, economic, occupational and, increasingly, geographic location fundamentally as a 'way station'—perhaps for one's children rather than oneself. That location is not a place to settle but, instead, is like the landing on a staircase or the crest of a foothill—all the better for viewing the vista of ascending stairs or mountain peaks stretching upward and ahead to the horizon. Not to realise the aspirational nature of your membership of this middle class is not, in the final measure, to be one of its members. Objective location in the social and economic order now matters less—in terms of middle class group membership ('identity')—than does embracing this aspirational orientation and ethic. All of which goes a long way to explaining Cantril's (1943) findings, a mere century after this form of a middle class began to emerge.

Social change has by no means halted since the establishment of the middle classes. Over the past few decades a social order has emerged which almost defies the term 'order'. In the wake of the global social and economic jolts associated with the so-called neoliberal reforms in the 1980s and 1990s (Harvey 2005) tendencies which had been present for some time became much stronger. Modernity has transformed into a 'risk society', a 'new modernity': "Just as modernization dissolved the structure of feudal society in the nineteenth century and produced the industrial society, modernization today is dissolving industrial society and another modernity is coming into being" (Beck 1992, p. 10). The risks that modern societies and people face are not simply natural or 'external' ones but are, instead, directly a product of the modernisation process itself. There is an acceleration in the dynamism of change— whether technological, economic, or social (or an interlinked mix)— which spills over into the daily lives of everyone. This new modernity is "vastly more dynamic than any previous type of social order" and has formed a society that "unlike any preceding culture lives in the future rather than the past" (Giddens and Pierson 1998, p. 94). But these modern institutions not only "undercut traditional habits and customs" and have "global impact" but their world "radically alters the nature of day-to-day life and affects the most personal aspects of our experience" (Giddens 1991, p. 1).

This picture of a 'radically altered' world is echoed in Zygmunt Bauman's book *Liquid Modernity* (Bauman 2000). Preceded by 'concrete modernity', 'liquid modernity' is a process of constant shape-shifting. Social forms are changing so rapidly that there is little chance that they can "serve as frames of reference for human actions and long-term life strategies because of their short life expectation" (Bauman 2007, p. 1). In *Liquid Times: Living in an Age of Uncertainty*, Bauman (2007, p. 94) voices the everyday fear we have about what life can, and does, throw our way: "As long as dangers remain eminently free-floating, freakish and frivolous, we are their sitting targets—there is pretty little we can do, if anything at all, to prevent them. Such hopelessness is frightening. Uncertainty means fear." Prior to this 'liquid' modernity was the modernity of 'utopias' and progress towards them. As part of that more concrete version of modernity these utopias were assumed to be the endpoint of progressive efforts and, in that way, to provide a point to that effort. But "utopias were born together with modernity and only in the modern atmosphere were they able to breathe" (Bauman 2007, p. 97). In liquid modernity it ceased to make sense to idealise an endpoint to our aspirations.

To make this shift plain, Bauman made use of the metaphors of the gardener and the hunter. In fact, before the gardener was the 'gamekeeper' whose job was to prevent any tinkering with the natural order. This was the conservative impulse of theocratic society. But the first moderns were 'gardeners' who "assumes that there would be no order in the world at all (or at least in the small part of that world entrusted to his wardenship) were it not for his constant attention and effort" (Bauman 2007, p. 98). Gardeners plan their garden; select plants to plant and remove weeds. They actively construct the desired end—the utopia—as a progressive project. To do all of this they need control and stability. Like the gamekeepers who preceded them, the gardeners are also conservative, but of their own plans and efforts rather than of the 'natural order' or of 'God's creation'.

The 'hunter' is different: "The sole task hunters pursue is another 'kill', big enough to fill their game-bags to capacity" (Bauman 2007, p. 100). They are the denizens of liquid modernity. They move ceaselessly from one exploitative possibility to the next. But 'they' are all of us: "We are all hunters now, or told to be hunters and called or compelled to act as hunters do, on penalty of eviction from hunting, if not (perish the thought!) of relegation to the ranks of the game" (Bauman 2007, p. 100). This poetic invocation of a new type of 'aspiration' sets the scene for the world within which the person of today is asked to be concerned about their wellbeing, and the wellbeing of others. The 'forces of globalisation' "favour hunting and hunters" (p. 101) and therefore the idea of progress "is no longer thought about in the context of an urge to rush ahead, but in connection with a desperate effort to stay in the race" (p. 103). The restlessness of today's aspirations, given Bauman's analysis, looks more like the expressive activity of an age of anxiety than of an age of optimistic, unbounded achievement.

This aspirational anxiety—as we saw in Chapter 1—is now easily detectable at the population level in major surveys and meta-analyses. It also finds an expression in the changes occurring in the daily experiences of our economic lives. As Richard Sennett (2006, p. 2) has observed, migration is the "icon of the global age, moving on rather than settling in" with workplaces "more resembling train stations than villages". The challenges of these new arrangements are multiple. They include the challenge of managing "short-term relationships, and oneself, while migrating from task to task, job to job, place to place" which may require an individual "to improvise his or her life-narrative, or even do without any sustained sense of self", the question of "how to develop new skills … as reality's demands shift" when the world "militates against the ideal of craftsmanship", and, finally, the vital skill of knowing "how to let go of the past" which requires a "peculiar trait" that "discounts the experiences a human being has already had" (Sennett 2006, pp. 4–5). This last challenge—to let go of the past—will be shown to have a direct resonance with the argument of this book. The person (and their person-hood) adopts, as part of its function and form, a 'diachronic' approach to life—that is, persons value occurrences in their lives irrespective of whether they are in the past the future or the present (Stokes 2017). A 'self', by contrast, is 'temporally asymmetric' and tends to discount the past and be mostly concerned about the present and immediate future. If Sennett is correct, then the fragmentation of the world of institutions that he describes is likely pushing persons to see themselves more and more as selves and less and less as persons—purely in order to survive.

The experience of aspiration at the personal level in this way comes into focus. How are individuals experiencing, and responding to, this new environment of 'liquid aspiration'? My answer, for now and in the following section, is more an impressionistic sketch than a fully-formed account. The remaining chapters will provide colour for the sketch.

## Aspiration at the Personal Level

Aspiration, as understood here, is primarily cultural. It is not some-thing that just pops up within individuals and that can be measured by, for example, the Aspiration Index (developed by Tim Kasser and colleagues—e.g., Kasser and Ryan 1996; Grouzet et al. 2005; Sheldon and Kasser 2008). In an aspirational culture the daily practices of peo-ple are subject to the assumption that—potentially if not practically—they can be improved or optimized. Often this optimization has to be done in the context of multiple, nested, competing and even contradic-tory culturally-mediated demands. The choice of which car to buy for commuting purposes, for example, could be 'optimized' in many ways: social status; cost; ecological footprint; practicality; horse power or other technical specifications concerning performance or convenience. But that is not the end of the task. The choice of which dimension should dominate in that optimization process implies a further question about the best ('optimal') set of values upon which to make that choice (e.g., should one value environmental impact over convenience?). The choice of this set of values, in turn, raises questions about the type of person one is, or should be: 'successful', 'rational', 'concerned', 'cooperative', 'devil-may-care'.

It is in this way that an aspirational culture transforms our activity as individuals into a continuous test of how successful we are at aspiring (which is now taken as a synonym for 'living') and, crucially, in defending the aspirational efforts we demonstrate. For individuals in an aspirational culture, judgment of the worth of what one has done—or will do—and the worth of what one 'is' becomes a pressing pre-occupation. Daily activities increasingly are seen—and, we accept, *should* be seen—as outcomes of 'choices' and 'decisions' that (should) optimise and improve ourselves and our lives. There is less opportunity for actions to be seen simply as the outcome of fate, fortune or circumstance. Since they are seen in this way, our activities increasingly present as legitimate targets for judgment, by others and, often pre-emptively, by ourselves. Evaluation and judgment necessarily become ubiquitous in an aspirational culture since, as the management aphorism says, 'what you can't measure [i.e., evaluate or judge], you can't manage'. To close the circle, the rhetorically claimed point of management, in an aspirational culture, is to improve and optimize what is being managed. Life comes to be seen as fundamentally about project management and continuous improvement. Living is, in effect, work. And constant work is always hard.

The ubiquity, and types, of ways that people are thought to aspire is made clear by Kasser and colleagues' Aspirational Index (AI), mentioned above. Originally, the AI examined four domains: self-acceptance (sometimes called 'personal growth'); financial success (wealth); community feeling; affiliation (meaningful relationships). By 2005 it had expanded to an examination of 11 domains. Added to the original four domains were image, popularity (fame), physical health, spirituality, conformity, safety/security and hedonism. It has been broadly validated, including cross-culturally, with the 11 domains found to be statistically distinct. The general finding is that those who score higher on *extrin-sic* goals (e.g., financial success, popularity, image) tend to score lower on various measures of wellbeing. By contrast, those who score higher on *intrinsic* goals (e.g., community feeling or contributions, affiliation, self-acceptance/personal growth) tend to score higher on wellbeing measures.

But there is a more revealing feature of the AI: The index *assumes* that people are goal-seeking and so are motivated by a system of goals, whether those be mostly extrinsic or intrinsic. What is assumed is that all people aspire (perhaps most of the time) and that the only difference between them is the nature of their aspirational goals. This is particularly clear when we think about the so-called intrinsic goals, though the same point could be made about extrinsic goals. Affiliation, for example, is not seen simply as a natural part of living as a social animal—a birthright. To be experienced, affiliation must be a 'goal' or a 'choice'. The implication is that affiliation is something that the individual must, and should, work on so that it will be attained or improved, or simply sustained. The modern mantra is that we must 'work on our relationships', an idea that would have seemed odd to most humans who have, or still do, live in far less aspirational cultures. The possibility that affiliation might, by contrast, be a constitutive feature of a human form of life—of being a person—does not enter into consideration. (If it did come into consideration attention may well turn to the form of culture that is either reducing or preventing affiliation from arising or which seeks to present it as primarily a result of personal inclination and effort.) As with so many other features of life in an aspirational culture, affiliation is increasingly seen as a 'preference' and, so, subject to and determined by personal choice. Indeed, the notion of choice is vital for the legitimation of the obligation to aspire.

The same is true of self-acceptance as is true of affiliation. When we take a step back, there is something odd about seeing 'self-acceptance' as a goal rather than as an inherent state of affairs for individuals. To be fair, the AI also asks about the extent to which each goal has been attained and so incorporates a measure of current experience. But, again, this still assumes that the goal is just that, an endpoint of aspirational activity. In this case, it is simply that the tick box for that goal has already been checked. By phrasing these experiences (e.g., of self-acceptance, community feeling, and affiliation) as goals it obscures the possibility that they may be 'attained' (i.e., present) in a person's life without any personal goal-seeking efforts at all. That is, it is conceivable that, at least in some cultural arrangements, these 'intrinsic goals' are inherently present in life. The AI—along with assumptions central to psychology—reinforces and reproduces aspirational culture by simply assuming it; and it does so especially in how we see ourselves. The imperative of personal aspiration is not challenged but supported. All that is left for the individual is the choice of aspirational goals and the consequent effort needed to achieve them. With that base assumption, life devoid of aspiration becomes unthinkable.

Aspirational culture, then, is expressed in all aspects of our reality—ecological, social, economic and personal. How persons integrate these multiple aspects of reality into their lives, and over the course of their lives, will go a long way to determining their experience of wellbeing. The question of whether aspirational cultures make it more or less likely that people can successfully integrate these aspects of life is a substantial part of the focus of this book. What, then, are the elements of aspirational cultures?

In an aspirational culture life is all about progress. It is typically hard-won progress and, for individuals, always requires conscious effort and self-discipline in order to persevere through obstacles and even failure. The over-riding principle is to become more and better, and to do so in more and more dimensions of life. The dominant question is 'How well am I doing?'

In one form or another, aspiration's founding myth is of Prometheus, the Greek Titan who defied Zeus to make 'man' and provide him with fire and, hence, the gift of progress and civilization. In ancient Greek, 'Prometheus' means 'forethought'. The price paid by Prometheus—extracted by Zeus—was to be permanently chained to a rock (until finally freed by Heracles, a demi-god who, famously, performed a number of 'labours' as part of his own aspirational quest). Enchained in this way, Prometheus would have his liver (the seat of emotions) eaten by an eagle (Zeus' typical symbol) before regenerating only to be eaten once again the following day.

The same 'defiance' or hubris and the same consequence of eternal torture—that are the usual hallmarks of aspiration and progress in mythology—is also found in the (even darker) twin of the Prometheus legend. Aspirational culture's Jungian 'shadow' to the Promethean myth is the myth of Sisyphus. Zeus—yet again—punished King Sisyphus for his hubristic cleverness by having him endlessly push a boulder up a hill in Hades. Each time that Sisyphus would almost reach the summit the boulder would roll back down. Sisyphus' toil involves constant, goal-directed labour without ever making substantive progress—the definition of an eternal nightmare in an aspirational culture.[7]

Aspiration always has this sense of the forbidden and the hubristic. Sometimes that is cast as heroic, or at least inevitable. Like the fall from the garden of Eden, it is both an original moral error but also the inherent fate of humanity and an irreplaceable feature of God's plan. It also, *always*, has a price. Whether being cast out of the garden and into a life of laborious toil or having your liver ('emotions') endlessly eaten, aspiring is hardly ever pictured as an entirely fun adventure (though, today, some come close to describing it in that way). Many cultural optimists see progress and aspiration as a positive force working like the home-help doggedly tidying up the mess that we inadvertently make through our lack of forethought. By contrast, throughout history aspiration has most often been seen not as some life-giving compensatory impulse in an otherwise harsh existence but as the *responsible source* of many of the world's woes. That is, aspiration—and whatever its claimed benefits may be—is not a free lunch. We might be compelled by our nature to aspire, but the usual take-home message is that it also condemns us to lives of pain and toil. The truly aspirational are even meant to embrace the cost and the pain as somehow being worth it and so see aspiration as the essence of a meaningful life. Pain and work are valorized and characterized as a reflection of our fundamental humanity.

Yet, myths—like those of Prometheus and Sisyphus—are less guides to universal truths than they are signs of what a culture has to justify, and cast as natural or ideal, if it is to be sustained. Myths are multi-layered narrative devices to reconcile persons to the prevailing material, social and political realities of their culture. Aspirational culture is distinguished by its promotion—and justification—of movement, change, novelty, growth and progress. While conceptually distinct, notions such as these are linked by their dynamic qualities. Temperamentally, an aspirational culture tends to the side of the early Greek empiricists such as Heraclitus. Reality is—of ideological necessity for an aspirational culture—a matter of constant change. Not only can one never step into the same river twice, but one cannot even claim to be using the same foot when taking each step.

This focus on dynamism has now reached a crescendo, a point at which the irresistible clarion call of change has encountered the immovable requirement for unity, coherence and continuity at the heart of the cultural invention of personhood (as I will explain in Chapters 4 and 5). Human culture's most curious artefact is the person. Yet, aspirational culture has now ballooned to the point that the unity, coherence and continuity of personhood itself has been weighed in the balance of aspirational culture and found wanting. Being a unified, coherent and continuous person is no longer good enough; it is a cultural mismatch; a tool that can no longer do the work that the culture demands. Yet it is a tool made by that self-same culture and that culture still, paradoxically, uses the demand for personal unity as one of the ways it leverages its other demand for constant change, flexibility and adaptation. It is the *same* 'you' who last year worked in a factory, this year works as a courier driver and next year will work as a door canvassing marketer for a local power company: And in all three jobs you are immediately to act as if you have always been each of those workers; skilled at repetitive factory work; unfailing at high-pressure, on-time package delivery; and, unrelentingly personable and persuasive. That one person should be obliged to excel, or even just perform competently, at such a wide range of cultural tasks is, itself, a novel expectation. The logically primitive unity, the lifetime continuity, and the active processes of coherence-making that are fundamental to personhood are potential impediments to the kind of personal aspiration needed to sustain such chameleon-like, repeated metamorphoses. It is not just that the centre *cannot* hold; it is that, if the centre *does* manage to hold, it will generate psychological pain as we try our best to make these rapid, dislocative changes.

It is in these sorts of everyday cultural forms that the intertwined story of the individual person (or 'self'), on the one hand, and their life understood as an aspirational project, courageously pursued, on the other, is provided as a dual model. That is, stories involve both 'characters' (characterisations of what it is to be a person) and 'plots' (in this case, hinged on motifs of personal aspiration). Like all cultural mythologies, its appeal to members of the culture is partly a result of how individuals are constituted by that very culture. That is, a creation—a 'creature'—of a culture is inevitably going to resonate and be aligned with at least some of the values of that same culture.

But the appeal also comes from the fact that cultural mythologies, if they are to gain purchase, must reflect some general aspect of being a person or, at least, of being a human being. Specifically, aspirational cultures leverage a simple fact about persons: That persons are progressive creations of a culture. It takes time for a culture to generate personhood and there is no guarantee that the process will be completely fulfilled in any particular case. In that sense, personhood is itself an achievement or an 'aspiration'. But, crucially, that achievement ('aspiration') is of the culture, not the individual. To aspire as an individual person, that is, echoes the cultural process involved in becoming a person; but it does so as if this process is the responsibility of the entity (the person) that is also the *product* of these efforts. That is, aspiration, as a personal project, is not just about external achievement and success but is also supposedly about becoming the person that you already are and doing so as an act of self-creation for which, inevitably, you are responsible—and, so, will be judged. Your ability to execute this project successfully becomes the primary criterion used to judge the value of what, it turns out as a result of your own efforts, you *are*. The 'journey' that constitutes living is characterized as at once circular—ending at the origin, 'you'—and yet also dynamic and progressive; never ending, just the repeated opportunity to reflexively reinvent oneself as a closer and closer approximation of what one truly is. This unendingly reflexive and paradoxical project is not likely to end happily in every case—or in many cases. Life and living, presented as an elusive and deep philosophical conundrum, becomes a source of fundamental uncertainty and anxiety. Despite the prevailing assertion of the ubiquity of change we are, as persons, subject to *increasing* levels of judgment, evaluation, monitoring and accountability (by ourselves and others) that aims to measure our 'success' and worth on any number of dimensions. It is difficult to imagine a better mechanism for generating the kind of illbeing that, uniquely, is able to be experienced by persons.

# Notes

1. As I understand it, the tipi's structure is representational of spiritual and sacred insights into the human experience of life and the world. Specifically, the tipi reproduces the various circles or hoops of existence and the poles reflect features of the world such as sacred sites. In some traditions, the vortex of the structure (the point where the poles are tied together) is the point that connects the individual and the tribe to the spirit world—the inflected meeting point of the material and spiritual. In light of Strawson's account of the concept of the 'person' to be discussed in Chapter 4, this might be a fortuitous, parallel meaning if we take that convergent point as the 'site' of the person. For Strawson, the concept of a person refers to a unique entity that has ascribed to it *both* the kinds of predicates we might make of material objects *and* what we call psychological predicates (e.g., beliefs, thoughts, feelings) that we typically do not ascribe to a material object. The material and the psychological 'meet' each other at the site of a person. In much the way, the material and spiritual meet each other at the vortex of the tipi.

2. As Gowdy and Krall (2016) discuss, the word 'ultrasocial' is used by biologists in several different ways. They—and I—use it to refer to the groups of social insects (species of New World ants and Old-World termites) that use some form of agriculture for their subsistence. The term *eusocial* is reserved for social insects that do not use managed agriculture (e.g., honey bees).

3. There are other explanations for reduced brain size. It may partly be a result of reduced body size that has also occurred over that period (smaller brains and nervous systems are needed to coordinate smaller bodies). Reduced body size may have resulted from the post-Ice Age warming that occurred at the time since larger bodies can conserve heat better than smaller ones. Alternatively, smaller bodies may have also resulted from a less nutrient rich diet after—or leading up to—adoption of agriculture as the dominant food source that produced a diet rich in calories but not as varied, and so less nutrient rich, as diets based on hunting and gathering.

4. There may be other animals that could have some of the requisites for personhood. In a recent thought piece, behavioural economist Don Ross has suggested that, perhaps, elephants may have—or could one day have—some of the capacities that, under a broadened understanding of personhood, would suffice for ascribing personhood to them. See https://aeon.co/essays/if-elephants-arent-persons-yet-could-they-be-one-day.

5. An exaptation is a trait that has gained an adaptive function for which it was not originally selected. Feathers, for example, may have been originally selected for warmth but became co-opted to serve for flight (a capacity that became highly adaptive in its own right). The word was introduced by biologists Stephen Jay Gould and Elisabeth Vrba (1982) specifically to highlight cases where non-adapted traits are later co-opted for adaptive purposes but it turns out that there are many permutations of this general scenario. As Gould and Vrba (1982) argued, there are traits that may not have originally been selected at all or traits that were selected for one purpose but became adapted to some other (as with feathers). Because personhood is essentially a sociocultural artefact its 'exaptation' is a cultural rather than biological process; but that may eventually lead to processes of natural selection on the biology underpinning personhood capacities.

6. But see Veenhoven (2008)—a prolific author in wellbeing research—for a determinedly contrarian view.

7. In Albert Camus' book *The Myth of Sisyphus*, the character is analysed not only as a representation of the absurdity of life but also as symbolizing its heroic aspect. For Camus, "one must imagine Sisyphus as happy" since "the struggle towards the heights is enough to fill a man's heart". Aspiration is its own reward. It never seemed to occur to Camus that it is not life itself that is absurd but simply the view of life as fundamentally an aspirational project.

# References

Aanen, D. K., & Boomsma, J. J. (2006). Social-insect fungus farming [mini-review]. *Current Biology, 16*(24), R1014–R1016.

Bar-On, Y. M., Phillips, R., & Milo, R. (2018). The biomass distribution on Earth. *Proceedings of the National Academy of Sciences, 115*(25), 6506–6511.

Bauman, Z. (2000). *Liquid modernity.* Cambridge, UK: Polity Press.

Bauman, Z. (2007). *Liquid times: Living in an age of uncertainty.* Cambridge, UK: Polity Press.

Beck, U. (1992). *Risk society: Towards a new modernity.* London: Sage.

Boehm, C. (1993). Egalitarian behavior and reverse dominance hierarchy. *Current Anthropology, 34*(3), 227–254.

Cantril, H. (1943). Identification with social and economic class. *The Journal of Abnormal and Social Psychology, 38*(1), 74–80.

Dunbar, R. I. M. (2014). The social brain: Psychological underpinnings and implications for the structure of organizations. *Current Directions in Psychological Science, 23*(2), 109–114. https://doi. org/10.1177/0963721413517118.

Dyble, M., Salali, G. D., Chaudhary, N., Page, A., Smith, D., Thompson, J., et al. (2015). Sex equality can explain the unique social structure of hunter-gatherer bands. *Science, 348*(6236), 796. https://doi.org/10.1126/science.aaa5139.

Ehrenreich, B. (2007). *Dancing in the streets: A history of collective joy.* New York: Metropolitan Books.

Elias, N. (2000). *The civilizing process: Sociogenetic and psychogenetic investigations* (2nd ed.). Oxford: Wiley-Blackwell.

Ewen, S. (1988). *All consuming images: The politics of style in contemporary cultures* (1st ed.). New York: Basic Books.

Giddens, A. (1991). *Modernity and self-identity: Self and society in the late modern age.* Stanford: Stanford University Press.

Giddens, A., & Pierson, C. (1998). *Conversations with Anthony Giddens: Making sense of modernity.* Stanford, CA: Stanford University Press.

González-Forero, M., & Gardner, A. (2018). Inference of ecological and social drivers of human brain-size evolution. *Nature, 557*(7706), 554–557. https://doi.org/10.1038/s41586-018-0127-x.

Gould, S. J., & Vrba, E. (1982). Exaptation—A missing term in the science of form. *Paleobiology, 8*(1), 4–15.

Gowdy, J., & Krall, L. (2013). The ultrasocial origins of the Anthropocene. *Ecological Economics, 95,* 137–147.

Gowdy, J., & Krall, L. (2014). Agriculture as a major evolutionary transition to human ultrasociality. *Journal of Bioeconomics, 16,* 179–202.

Gowdy, J., & Krall, L. (2016). The economic origins of ultrasociality. *Behavioral and Brain Sciences, 39,* E92. https://doi.org/10.1017/S0140525X1500059X.

Grouzet, F., Kasser, T., Ahuvia, A. C., Dols, J., Kim, Y., Lau, S., et al. (2005). The structure of goal contents across 15 cultures. *Journal of Personality and Social Psychology, 89,* 800–816.

Harvey, D. (2005). *A brief history of neoliberalism.* Oxford: Oxford University Press.

Hergenhahn, B. R. (2005). *An introduction to the history of psychology.* Belmont, CA: Thomson/Wadsworth.

Holmes, M. (2016). *Sociology for optimists.* London: Sage.

Kasser, T., & Ryan, R. M. (1996). Further examining the American dream: Differential correlates of intrinsic and extrinsic goals. *Personality and Social Psychology Bulletin, 22,* 280–287.

Leahey, T. H. (2000). *A history of psychology: Main currents in psychological thought* (5th ed.). Upper Saddle River, NJ: Prentice Hall.

Martin, S. J., Funch, R. R., Hanson, P. R., & Eun-Hye, Y. (2018). A vast 4000-year-old spatial pattern of termite mounds. *Current Biology, 28,* R1283–R1295.

McAdams, D. P. (2013). The psychological self as actor, agent, and author. *Perspectives on Psychological Science, 8*(3), 272–295. https://doi.org/10.1177/1745691612464657.

Pinker, S. (2011). *The better angels of our nature: The decline of violence in history and its causes.* London: Penguin Books.

Rogers, D. S., Deshpande, O., & Feldman, M. W. (2011). *The spread of inequality: PLOS One, 6*(9), e24683. https://doi.org/10.1371/journal.pone.0024683.

Sennett, R. (Ed.). (2006). *The culture of the new capitalism.* New Haven: Yale University Press. Retrieved from https://ebookcentral.proquest.com.

Sheldon, K. M., & Kasser, T. (2008). Psychological threat and extrinsic goal striving. *Motivation and Emotion, 32,* 37–45.

Shultz, S., & Dunbar, R. I. M. (2006). Both social and ecological factors predict ungulate brain size. *Proceedings: Biological Sciences, 273*(1583), 207–215. https://doi.org/10.1098/rspb.2005.3283.

Stokes, P. (2017). Temporal asymmetry and the self/person split. *Journal of Value Inquiry, 51,* 203–219. https://doi.org/10.1007/s10790-016-9563-8.

Veenhoven, R. (2010). Life is getting better: Societal evolution and fit with human nature. *Social Indicators Research, 97*(1), 105–122.

Wright, R. (2004). *A short history of progress.* Toronto: House of Anansi Press.

# 3

# Understanding Wellbeing

At the sharp end, human wellbeing[1] is about individual people. But to do justice to wellbeing we need to think well beyond the individual person. Our explanation must straddle the biology of our bodies and their development, the evolution and ecology of our species, the social and cultural worlds we have created (past and present) and how these all tie together in our lives and experiences as persons (see Huppert and Baylis 2004; Huppert et al. 2004). If I am correct about taking this comprehensive approach, the obvious question is 'Where to start?'

In fact, I do not think it matters too much where we start. As a psychologist, I often start with the individual and, therefore, I begin with the psychological research on wellbeing. But 'all roads lead to Rome'. As I have already mentioned and will argue in more detail in the next chapter, wherever we begin our inquiry into human wellbeing there are good reasons to direct our efforts, ultimately, towards a single target: The person. And persons are not just psychological beings. To put it better: A person's psychology does not happen *within* the individual; it happens in that person's life. It is what happens in our life—which includes the happenings we usually call thinking and feeling about ourselves and our life—that determines our wellbeing.

© The Author(s) 2019
K. Moore, *Wellbeing and Aspirational Culture*,
https://doi.org/10.1007/978-3-030-15643-5_3

Despite this acknowledgment that the attempt to understand wellbeing inevitably draws into its orbit all aspects of the world that make us, and our lives, what we are, the study of wellbeing is today dominated by the discipline of psychology. Psychology may not have had 'first dibs' on the field but it certainly has 'current dibs'. If only for that reason—and putting disciplinary loyalty or rivalry to one side—it makes sense to begin with the story of how psychologists became interested in wellbeing—and why they have successfully planted their flag at the heart of the field.

## Understanding Wellbeing by Understanding Psychology

When the modern discipline of psychology arrived on the scene it did so in Germany, the vigorous intellectual and scientific heartland of Europe. The nominal founder was Wilhelm Wundt, a prodigious and prolific academic who could claim to be a physician, philosopher and physiologist as well as being the first person to call himself a 'psychologist'. Wundt—with his two PhDs, the requirement for university posts in Germany at the time—was steeped in both the German philosophical tradition and the new biological and physiological sciences. He studied under Johannes Muller and at one time was an assistant for the legendary physiologist Herman von Helmholtz. By the time he established the first psychology laboratory in 1879 at the University of Leipzig he was working alongside two other renowned German physiologists, Ernst Weber and Gustav Fechner who pioneered the study of psychophysics. Given its origins, and in an alternative universe, psychology would, sensibly, have developed and thrived principally as a German or European discipline. That would likely have led to a quite different set of psychological terms, areas of research focus and theoretical understanding of human psychology.

But an important aspect of Wundt's prolific output was his Ph.D. graduates, some of whom were American and established psychology in the United States (e.g., G. Stanley Hall, first president of Clark

University and the American Psychological Association (APA); James Cattell, a Professor of Psychology at the University of Pennsylvania and Columbia University and APA President in 1885; Frank Angell, who established psychological laboratories at Cornell and Stanford Universities). The origins and nature of the United States were to have a marked effect on how the discipline of psychology was put to use. This restless, unstable, expansionary society and psychology expressed a form of aspirational individualism and egoism that political theorist and historian Alexis de Tocqueville highlighted—and criticized—in a prescient and precise manner. When he wrote, in 1835, of the recently minted democracy in the United States he incisively observed the nature of this first, modern, aspirational culture: "In the United States, a man will carefully construct a home in which to spend his old age and sell it before the roof is on … He will settle in one place only to go off elsewhere shortly afterwards with a new set of desires" (Tocqueville 1835/2003, p. 623 cited in Oishi 2010, p. 8). As the vast American frontier expanded, in its wake it deposited a rainstorm of settlements or "island communities" (a phrase used by Robert Wiebe) sprinkled across the continental expanse. Relatively small, isolated, tightly knit, and independent, these semi-rural towns enabled the exploitation of the country and dispossession of Native American tribes. But they also provided the economic impetus that would lead to their own downfall as they helped fuel the rapid industrialization and urbanization of America. Economic and population expansion led to the development of the telegraph, the railroad, and, ultimately, the electric grid in the 1880s all of which started to connect these communities to the urban cities in the east and to the wider world. In the last part of the nineteenth century, Chicago (in the Mid-West) was the fastest growing city in the world as it processed the natural resources flooding in from the Western frontier. In 1850 only about 15% of the country's population lived in urban centres. By 1900 that proportion had increased to almost 40% and had stimulated the rapid emergence of the American middle class (see Ewen 1988, and Chapter 2).

When Wundt's Ph.D. students returned home, then, it was to a United States undergoing major social upheaval and transformation. It was also to an America that was developing its own form of

philosophy—the Pragmatism of its philosophers, scientists, mathe-
maticians, and psychologists such as Charles Peirce, William James,
Chauncey Wright, John Dewey and George Herbert Mead. In the sim-
plest terms, philosophical pragmatism understands thought, knowledge,
meaning, belief, language and the entire host of psychological concepts
(and any other concepts) primarily in terms of their practical consequences and, hence, function and success. Most dramatically, this view
has an especially practical consequence for the notion of 'truth'. For
James at least, the truth of a proposition like 'God exists' does not follow from whether the words in some way correspond to some feature of
the world (the presence of a being called 'God') but by its practical consequences, particularly for the person who believes it. If the proposition
promotes adaptive function, it makes sense to call it 'true' (it is a 'successful' instrument for operating in the world). Nevertheless, under the
influence of Charles Darwin's theory of evolution by natural selection,
pragmatists treated "mind as part of nature, not a gift from God" and
therefore, as Wright argued, "a person's beliefs evolve just as species do",
an idea that, with the substitution of 'behaviours' for 'beliefs', "states
the central thesis of B.F. Skinner's radical behaviorism" (Leahey 2000,
p. 339). The mind and consciousness, in this view, are to be understood
as means of getting on in the world in a practical manner rather than
as complex processes that endow the ability to represent or picture the
world.

This historically specific mix of social upheaval, philosophical pragmatism, the new theory of evolution by Charles Darwin, and the first
generation of American psychologists minted in Wundt's laboratory was
a fateful one. As the new, scientific psychology arose it quickly morphed
into, and became dominated by, William James' 'functionalism'—a psychology of consciousness imbued with a philosophical Pragmatism that
emphasized the functionality of consciousness as a 'stream' of 'adjustment' to the world. That world was, of course, going through the social
revolutions of urbanization and industrialization so, as the discipline
quickly professionalized, its focus—and its 'selling point' to the broader
society—was the contribution it could make both to increasing the effi-
ciency of the new social arrangements and, in tandem, helping individuals adjust to their new roles and lives in that society. Immigration to

the rapidly growing urban centres either from overseas or from domestic rural areas brought with it "psychological changes and demands for new psychological skills" and the rapid shift from 'island communities' to the nation state brought with it a transformation in everyday life by generating "a constant flow of change with which people must keep up" (Leahey 2000, p. 359).

In this context, psychology, according to James, should work towards prediction and control, so that it can be "a practical psychology that tells people how to act, that makes a difference to life" (Leahey 2000, p. 345). He suggested that consciousness itself would not exist in humans unless it made a difference and was of practical use to people. It was for this reason, and with this mission, that the new American psychology went out into the field and generated the early forms of its professional specialisations. Functionalists studied child development, mental testing, educational practices and gender differences rather than sensation and perception. For example, Leta Hollingworth, one of the earliest women psychologists, studied mental retardation and 'gifted children' (her term). (She also debunked popular gender-based theories such as the idea that women had performance decrements at certain phases of the menstrual cycle.) One of William James' students was another woman psychologist called Mary Calkins. She founded one of the first dozen psychological laboratories in the United States and was primarily interested in memory. Hugo Münsterberg, a German student of Wundt's who ended up at Harvard University, pioneered industrial psychology and developed the Motor Theory of Consciousness—the latter being a theoretical step on the way to the emergence of Behaviourism in the early twentieth century.

This pragmatic (and Pragmatist) psychology of adjustment to the modern world reached its purest expression in the study by Bryan and Harter (1897) of learning in telegraph operators. Eschewing discussion of consciousness entirely, it measured error rates of the operators over a training period and came up with the classic learning curve that would become the staple of behaviourist approaches in the twentieth century. Strikingly, it did so in an occupation that could not have been better aligned with the social, technological and workplace changes at the infrastructural heart of the modern, industrial economy. Factors that affected task performance could be isolated and predictions about speeding up training, improving accuracy and sustaining performance levels were now the socially useful output that psychologists could deliver. On the heels of the Bryan and Harter paper, and before the new century completed its first decade, the Yerkes-Dodson Law was proposed, uniting task performance with arousal levels. As APA President in 1917 Robert Yerkes actively lobbied to have the U.S. military instigate large-scale intelligence testing using his Alpha and Beta intelligence measures as part of his push to have psychology contribute to the war effort in World War I. Over a million soldiers were tested and, while his eugenicist sympathies became clear later, the immediate effect was to establish the profession of psychology at the heart of institutionalized efforts to select, manage and coordinate individuals at the mass population level (Leahey 2000, pp. 425–426).

Politically, many of these early, functionalist American psychologists were also members of, or aligned with, the Progressive movement of the late nineteenth and early twentieth centuries (Leahey 2000). While critical of the increase in corporate power Progressives were equally concerned about the "disorderly masses of urban immigrants" who they saw as "victims exploited by corrupt political machines, which traded votes for favors and indispensable services" and so in need of "disinterested, expert, professional government—that is, government by themselves" (Leahey 2000, p. 361). Psychologists who aligned with the Progressive movement no doubt saw their role as enhancing individual adaptation and adjustment to the world of progress but working class people "resisted Progressive reform, because it moved political influence from neighborhood citizen groups to distant professional, middle class, bureaucrats" (Leahey 2000, p. 361). As part of this bureaucratic and professional management of the daily lives of ordinary people, workplaces and schools would, through the research and professional efforts of psychologists, become more efficient in smoothing the individual's path into contributing to the increasingly complex social and economic system. John Dewey, a leading Progressive and psychologist, founded 'Progressive education', a response, first, to the new immigrants who were "perforce bringing with them alien customs and alien tongues" and "needed to be Americanized" and, second, rural migrants who needed to be "educated in the habits appropriate to industrial work" (Leahey 2000, p. 362). Further, the school was to be the new 'community' to replace the, now forever lost, "island communities" of the rural migrant and "home communities" of international migrants. The child's community was now the "school community" which would "reform the American community *through the adult it produced*" (Leahey 2000, p. 362, emphasis added). Dewey was explicit that, beginning with schools which would teach "the values of social growth and community solidarity"—values that would become "the values of every social institution"—psychology and psychologists "would inevitably be led to intervene in society at large" (Leahey 2000, p. 362).

It is hard to over-state the ambition of the new, American, psychology. Looking through the lens of Gowdy and Krall's (2016) economic account of the origins of ultrasociality (see Chapter 2), the role of this new psychology was as a novel mechanism to regulate citizens in the service of, and reconciliation with, the new productive machinery. Psychology had transformed into a conscious effort to 'adapt' individuals to a world that was running hot on economic aspiration, technological innovation in a hurtling path towards a Progressive utopia. Dewey even argued that psychology—with its applied and professional mission—was a "social analogue to consciousness" (Leahey 2000, p. 363). The functionalist focus on the adaptive origins and purpose of consciousness, that is, was being socially expressed through the applied discipline of psychology: Psychology was the adaptive consciousness of society. In hindsight, the 'German Mandarin' psychology of Wilhelm Wundt with its intellectually aristocratic and philosophically hegemonic ambitions can barely hold a candle to the much more material and practical ambitions of the socially and politically oriented psychology that developed in the New World. Progressives "were obsessed by social control, the imposing of order on the disordered mass of turn-of-the-century American citizens" (Leahey 2000, p. 363).

It is no surprise then, that the striking way in which psychology—and its rapidly multiplying professional specialisations—became socially embedded and institutionalized led to the twentieth century being termed "the century of psychology". But, partly via psychology, it was also the century in which aspirational culture evolved into its current form. In the new, functionalist-inspired psychology, the aspirational spirit was not merely implicit: "The process of growth, of improvement and progress … becomes the significant thing …. Not perfection as a final goal, but the ever-enduring process of perfecting, maturing, refining is the aim in living ….*Growth itself is the only moral end*" (Dewey 1920/1948/1957 cited in Leahey 2000, p. 364, emphasis added).

For decades, this socially-oriented version of the aspirational spirit was, in psychology, expressed through the behaviourist school that followed in natural sequence from the ambitions of functionalist psychologists (Leahey 2000; Hergenhahn 2005). Environmental control, it presumed, was the source of behaviour and therefore of the means of control necessary for the personal and social regulation understood to be vital to achieving progressivist goals. While the 'folk history' of psychology often depicts the behaviourism of psychologists such as John Watson and, then, Burrhus (B.F.) Skinner as a departure from the liberal, humanistic values that supposedly underpin the discipline's applied efforts, it was, in fact, an alternative rendering of the same aspirational project that continues today.

Along with its long-lost twin, Structuralism, the nineteenth century school of Functionalism now only gets formal mention in texts on the history of psychology. But, unlike Structuralism, that is not because the time has passed when it spoke to dominant social and economic currents. It no longer gets mentioned because, in the most important sense, in psychology 'we are all functionalists now': According to one account, "No happier fate could await any psychological point of view" as happened to functionalism as it was "absorbed into the mainstream psychology" (Chaplin and Krawiec 1979, cited in Hergenhahn 2005, p. 345). Put simply, "functionalism lost its distinctiveness as a school because most of its major tenets were assimilated into all forms of psychology" (Hergenhahn 2005, p. 347). Primary amongst those tenets was the assumed role of psychology in an unending, aspirational project of human adjustment, better phrased as human *improvement*. The same functionalist pragmatism that spurred the rise of behaviourism also gave rise to the focus on personal 'becoming', 'human potential', 'growth', and 'self-actualisation' within humanistic psychology, and to the engineering design perspective in (neuro)cognitive science that accounts for human experience and behaviour using the terminology of sub-personal 'modules', 'mechanisms' and 'information'. The functionalist—and 'progressivist'—spirit is as strong as ever in contemporary approaches in psychology. And that emphatically includes psychological work on wellbeing.

## Current Approaches to Wellbeing

Contemporary research on wellbeing is now vast and represents a multi-disciplinary, occasionally interdisciplinary, endeavour. In an introduction to a special issue on 'The Science of Well-Being' in 2004, Huppert et al. (2004, p. 1331) staked-out the scale of the ambition: To encourage a "scientific understanding of life going well … a life characterized by health and vitality, by happiness, creativity and fulfilment, and by the sorts of positive social relationships and civic institutions that harness and enhance these desirable characteristics." The definition of wellbeing used at the Discussion Meeting that informed the special issue was similarly broad: "a positive and sustainable state that allows individuals, groups or nations to thrive and flourish" (Huppert et al. 2004, p. 1331).

As broad as the area is, philosopher Daniel Haybron has categorised theories of wellbeing into five groups (Haybron 2008a). Building on Parfit's (1984) distinction between hedonistic, desire and objective list theories, Haybron (2008a, p. 22) adds "an important new approach" and "an ancient family of theories [that] has gained substantially in prominence". Haybron also coins the term 'prudential psychology' to include approaches that go well beyond that taken in Subjective Well-Being (SWB) research. The term, he argues, is one most people, from a variety of disciplines, could accept as describing their interests whereas more parochial theoretical terms (such as hedonic or eudaimonic) are not. Even those who study "misery and mental illness" can be gathered beneath the umbrella of prudential psychology since they are concerned with the psychology of wellbeing. Haybron's own attitude to our 'aptitude' for living a prudential life (and, hence, one with a good degree of happiness) is skeptical (Haybron 2008b), largely because of the well-documented accounts of the so-called biases and errors in our decisions and judgments. (See the classic work of Daniel Kahneman and Amos Tversky—much of which is summarised in Kahneman [2011]—and a good, concise review in Hsee and Hastie [2006].)

## Hedonistic Theories

'Hedonistic theories' owe their providence to what Gordon Allport (1985) termed the 'Simple and Sovereign' theory of psychological hedonism or, citing Jeremy Bentham, the 'Principle of Utility'. We are governed by our "sovereign masters" of pleasure and pain (or enjoyment and suffering); we are destined to pursue the former and avoid the latter. Pleasure, in this account, is often taken as a synonym for 'happiness' but, in contrast with the Aristotelian view of 'happiness' (*eudaimonia*), it is an understanding that emphasizes an inner mental state. Hedonistic approaches tend to focus on the hedonic quality of psychological or 'subjective' states, highlighting the role of so-called positive emotions and feelings ('affect') in generating momentary experiences of wellbeing.

There are huge differences between these positive states in both intensity and meaning. To enjoy the taste of a mouthful of ice cream is of both a different kind and degree as the enjoyment gained in a 'job well done', a sense of relief from successfully averting a crisis, or from the thrill of skydiving for the first time. How these differences are to be measured preoccupied Bentham and prompted him to devise an intricate 'hedonic calculus'. But that approach, in turn, ends up with counter-intuitive 'calculations'. Some pleasures—at least for humans—may just be better than others. If we accept that an oyster can have pleasant experiences and that it could live for a very long time would that make the life of an oyster preferable to the shorter life of someone like the composer Haydn (though presumably with higher quality hedonic experiences)? As Haybron (2008a, p. 23) adds, many philosophers "find it implausible that an oyster could be better off than Haydn". As we will see, exactly the same measurement issues remain today for researchers interested in affect as a component of wellbeing.

## Desire Theories

Hedonistic theories bear a strong relationship to 'desire theories' of wellbeing. (These theories are also sometimes called 'desire-satisfaction', 'desire-fulfillment' or 'preferentism' theories—see Heathwood 2016.) While notions of pleasure and pain are no doubt implicit, desire theories portray the good life as one in which people get what they want and, in doing so, achieve satisfaction of the desire that led them to want what they wanted. Sometimes 'actualist' desire theories are contrasted to 'idealist' desire theories. The former involves getting what you actually desire, and the latter involves getting what you would ideally desire if you were fully informed and had no inherent cognitive biases (Heathwood 2005). Desires are sometimes not satisfied by getting what we want. But this might simply be that what we wanted to do or have was instrumental to achieving our 'basic' desire and was not itself the fulfillment of our desire. This is one example of what have been called 'defective desires' which can include ill-informed desires, irrational desires, poorly cultivated desires, base desires, pointless desires, artificially aroused desires, and the desire to be badly off which are thought by some to be fatal flaws in the desire theory approach to wellbeing (but see Heathwood 2005).

Despite these various criticisms desire theory is "the theory to beat", largely because of its popularity with economists and philosophers (Haybron 2008a, p. 23). Individual (revealed) preferences form the neo-classical view of choice in consumer behaviour and are often linked to utility arising from consumption. More fundamentally, desire theories are connected to so-called Belief-Desire action explanations that are ubiquitous (along with their close relatives, belief-desire-reason models), especially in cognitive science "where it appears as folk psychology, economics, rational-choice sociology, and political science, and also appears everywhere decision theory and game theory are employed, as well as the field of philosophy of action" (Turner 2018, p. 291). Simply, Belief-Desire action explanations make a fundamental assumption about people and their psychology: That individuals act as a result of their desires and the associated beliefs they have about the world in relation to those desires. I enrol at university (I perform that *act*), for example, because I *desire* to be rich and of high status and I *believe* that becoming a medical specialist will help me fulfil ('satisfy') that desire. Despite being itself a pervasive set of beliefs, the Belief-Desire action explanation can be, and has been, criticised and alternatives proposed. When we give reasons for what we do are we simply reporting some inner mental state (i.e., 'of belief')? Are we even able to do this (i.e., is it conceptually coherent to claim that this is what we are doing)? Mercier and Sperber (2011) have argued that argumentation ('giving reasons') evolved to win arguments and not to report accurately on inner states and that, understood as a social activity, many so-called 'biases' in human reasoning can be explained parsimoniously in this view.

Even on their own terms desire theories have recently been extensively criticized. People can desire things that are irrelevant or even detrimental to their wellbeing and, yet, fudging that fact by talking about preferences based on 'perfect information' can abstract the theory too far from people's actual lives to be of any practical use. Then there is the important question of the so-called 'happy slave' problem (Haybron 2008a). A person living a life of slavery or who is treated especially poorly may adapt 'successfully' to that life—and even claim to be happy—by developing desires that have come to be constrained by that existence, but few would want to call it a happy or good life.

## Authentic Happiness Theories

Authentic happiness theories are those that try to deal with some of the difficulties with hedonistic and desire theories while preserving the emphasis on individual sovereignty and subjectivity (Haybron 2008a). The word 'authentic' is an attempt—only partially successful—to claim that it is possible for an individual to construct an 'informed' and 'autonomous' life. That life will supposedly correspond to the person's 'true' (inner?) values rather than values that have been imposed coercively or through social conditioning. As we will see in Chapter 4, Ryan and Deci's (2017) 'Self-Determination Theory' (SDT) relies heavily on the possibility of action that is motivated in just this authentic way.

But, as Haybron (2008a, p. 24) muses, why could not "passive couch potatoes or even slaves be authentically happy, having reflected on their values and decided to affirm [or 'endorse' (Ryan and Deci 2017)] their life just as it is?" The problem, and one that remains in today's science of wellbeing, is a problem for all subjective approaches to wellbeing. Giving the individual 'sovereignty' over judgments of their own psychological states may be compatible with a broader cultural ideology and make some sense as a rough guide to understanding wellbeing, but it can be hard to square with the facts about how people are enmeshed in the material and social world. The attempt to preserve some vestige of an initiating psychological subject or 'core being' will always have trouble dealing with the fact that ultimately there are normative or, better, relational foundations for any 'value', 'belief' or 'motive' individuals may feel they experience or 'endorse'.

## Eudaimonistic Theories

The fourth category of theories Haybron (2008a) mentions is 'eudaimonistic theories'. As diverse as these are, from the ideas of Ancient Greek philosophers to modern proponents of eudaimonic approaches to wellbeing (e.g., Ryan and Deci 2001; Deci and Ryan 2008), eudaimonistic theories share the idea of 'nature-fulfillment'. Wellbeing arises out of the fulfillment of one's nature, though there is still plenty of room for disagreement over just what that nature is like or the breadth it encompasses. If all humans have a similar 'human nature' then does a eudaimonistic theory simply highlight that common nature (as evolutionary psychologists might suggest—e.g., see King et al. 2018)? Or does it focus, instead, on the different 'natures' that each individual might be said to possess? Humanistic psychologists famously claimed to be interested in the 'uniquely human' aspects of our nature but, equally famously, also advocated the need for each individual to find their own unique process of 'actualisation', 'realisation', or 'becoming' (i.e., to realise their own, particular nature).

Once again, we are confronted with the possibility that there could be a conflict between the wellbeing of one's broader human nature (e.g., around bodily health) and that of the more particular, individual 'nature' (e.g., 'the artist who must paint'—to paraphrase Abraham Maslow—but who starves in the process). Whichever scale is thought most central the heart of eudaimonistic approaches is that wellbeing (and 'flourishing' and 'thriving') depend upon the full exercise of the capacities one possesses or could develop as a human being. For Aristotelians, one of the most important of those human capacities is 'virtue'. To live a virtuous life is integral to their conception of wellbeing. Yet does that always resonate with our concerns over wellbeing? When we think about our lives overall we might well emphasise virtues such as honesty, integrity, love, prudence and compassion. But joy and pleasure are not always only of peripheral concern, like mere fortunate by-products of a well-lived life. As Haybron (2008a, p. 26) insightfully notes, when we think of our children's wellbeing we really do think that 'happiness' (joy, pleasure, etc.) is "what really matters".

## List Theories

Finally, so-called 'list theories' of wellbeing, as the name suggests, provide a list of variables, factors or components that appear—through empirical research or careful consideration—to comprise wellbeing. They have the advantage of being able to include anything and everything that goes into a life of wellbeing. They have the disadvantage, because of this open inclusivity, of not providing much insight into why or how all the listed factors 'go together' or constitute the nature of wellbeing.

## Specific Theories of Wellbeing

Specific psychological theories of wellbeing can be seen as falling under one or more of Haybron's broad umbrella categories of theories of wellbeing. The evolving work of Martin Seligman (the founder of Positive Psychology, a development to be discussed shortly) is a good illustrative example since it has clearly engaged, at different times, with hedonistic, eudaimonistic, authentic happiness, and even list approaches to wellbeing. Seligman's earlier 'Authentic Happiness' theory (Seligman 2002) centered 'happiness' at the heart of positive psychology, as its name indicates. But it was also an attempt to go beyond a sole focus on 'happiness'. What we prefer (or 'choose') is not only positive emotion but also what he called 'engagement' (discussed mainly in terms of Mihalyi Csikszentmihalyi's concept of 'flow'—see Csikszentmihalyi 1990) and 'meaning'. The pursuit of positive emotions—such as feelings of pleasure, joy, warmth and rapture—will, if successful, lead to what he termed a 'pleasant life'. Pursuit of the other two elements, if successful, leads to an 'engaged life' and a 'meaningful life', respectively. While the centering of positive emotions aligns directly with hedonistic approaches to wellbeing and the name 'authentic happiness' directly invokes Haybron's identically titled category of authentic happiness theories, engagement, meaningfulness and purpose in life are more obviously eudaimonic in focus. A decade later, Seligman (2011) added two more elements—relationships and accomplishment—to develop his five-component model of wellbeing that usually goes by its acronym 'PERMA' (for 'Positive emotion', 'Engagement', 'Relationships', 'Meaning and purpose', and 'Accomplishment'). Unlike authentic happiness, PERMA is explicitly about wellbeing, rather than happiness, with no one element taking priority. In effect, PERMA is also a 'list theory'—though not an exhaustive one—of the most important components of wellbeing. This move to a more 'democratic' account of the components of wellbeing was because of Seligman's insistence that his theory provide practical guidance for 'building' wellbeing (see Seligman 2018; Goodman et al. 2018). Both authentic happiness and PERMA are also underpinned by so-called 'character strengths' in an explicit acknowledgment of the virtues and values associated with eudaimonic wellbeing in the account most often associated with Aristotle. Just as virtues in practice were, for Aristotle, the guarantee of a 'happy' (eudaimonic) life, so too, for Seligman, Chris Peterson and their colleagues, 'values' or 'character strengths' are essential for achieving a life of pleasure, meaning, and engagement (Park et al. 2006; Peterson et al. 2007; Peterson and Seligman 2004). Successfully deploying your character strengths in your daily life—whether at work, at leisure, or in relationships—generates the full range of wellbeing components that PERMA conceptually corrals.

The inclusion of 'accomplishment' in PERMA is especially relevant given my focus on the links between wellbeing and aspiration. One of Seligman's students—Senia Maymin a high achieving student who ran her own hedge fund—made a comment during one of his courses that inspired him to broaden his approach. She told him that his authentic happiness theory could not be correct because it made no mention of success and mastery and that people often try to achieve just for the sake of winning. It would be hard to imagine a sparser description of the centrality of aspiration in today's world. Mastery over—and competence in—the world is a feature of several wellbeing theories. Edward Deci and Richard Ryan's SDT, for example, claims that humans have a universal need for competence (see Chapter 4 for more discussion of this theory). And later in this chapter, Carol Ryff's theory of Psychological Well-Being (PWB), which includes the dimension of 'environmental mastery', will be outlined.

To this point, we have seen that psychology, as a discipline, has been historically predisposed to see itself as the means for the adjustment, adaptation, improvement and perfection of individuals in the modern world. We have also considered the 'lay of the wellbeing land' by reviewing broad categories of theories of wellbeing (leaning heavily on Haybron 2008a). It is time to bring these two together and see in more detail how psychologists have applied their 'historic mission' to understanding and improving wellbeing.

## The Positive Psychology and Subjective Well-Being

There are two contemporary strands in the psychological study of wellbeing, both of which have maintained and even reinvigorated the original 'Progressivist' tradition that motivated the establishment of psychology as a discipline and profession in nineteenth century America. The more recent strand, but also the more general, began with a proclamation by Martin Seligman in his Presidential address to the American Psychological Association in 1998 (Seligman 1998).[2] In one sense, the address echoed, decades later, what the humanistic psychologist Abraham Maslow had regretfully opined: "The science of psychology has been far more successful on the negative than on the positive side. It has revealed to us much about man's [sic] shortcomings, his illness, his sins, but little about his potentialities, his virtues, his achievable aspirations, or his full psychological height" (Maslow 1954, p. 354 cited in Linley et al. 2006, p. 5). Provocatively,—if only because much preceding psychological research and theory would, by implication, become 'Negative Psychology'—Seligman called for the establishment of 'Positive Psychology'. According to Seligman, the discipline of psychology had "largely neglected the latter two of its three pre-World War II missions: curing mental illness, helping all people to lead more productive and fulfilling lives, and identifying and nurturing high talent" (Linley et al. 2006, p. 4). From Freud to modern neuropsychology most of psychologists' time, effort and research money had been directed towards understanding psychological *mal*function. At least since World War II, psychology had concentrated on "repairing damage within a disease model of human functioning …[but that this] … almost exclusive attention to pathology neglects the *fulfilled individual* and the *thriving community*" (Seligman and Csikszentmihalyi 2000, p. 5, emphasis added). The aim was to change the focus from "repairing the worst things in life" to "building positive qualities" (Seligman and Csikszentmihalyi 2000, p. 5). Advocacy for Positive Psychology has, as much as anything else, been an attempt to reclaim the optimism of the discipline's American origins as part of the Progressive movement; psychology's role would, once again, not simply be to maintain and sustain people in the modern world but, more ambitiously, to fulfill Dewey's hope—quoted previously—that psychology would be pivotal in "the ever-enduring process of perfecting, maturing, [and] refining" humanity. Psychology, that is, could return to its mission and belief that simply helping people to live is not nearly enough. Living ever-better must be the goal.

For positive psychologists, the psychological capacities involved in thriving and flourishing had been under-valued and under-researched.

While not denying the importance of understanding and tending to those who suffer, positive psychologists believed that the absence of suffering could not be taken as the measure of a fully—or optimally—functioning person. Yet, despite this claimed imbalance, 15 years before Seligman's Presidential address to the APA there was already a clearly demarcated area of research into just those factors that contributed to human happiness, flourishing and wellbeing.

The area of SWB is typically dated to Ed Diener's 1984 paper in the journal *Psychological Bulletin* (Diener 1984) but, as a review paper, it naturally referred to previous research. Diener (1984, p. 542) spoke of work "[i]n the last decade" (prior to 1984) with the 1973 inclusion of 'happiness' as an index term in *Psychological Abstracts International* and the establishment of the journal *Social Indicators Research* in 1974 noted as important institutional markers of that work. According to Diener (1984, p. 542), such research "is concerned with how and why people experience their lives in positive ways, including both cognitive judgments and affective reactions". As well as chiming with the yet to be declared approach of 'Positive Psychology' (which Ed Diener helped initiate), this seemingly innocuous formulation sets SWB research apart from other enquiries into wellbeing. The most obvious way it does this is through its focus on the measurement of 'personal experience' or 'subjective experience'. Individuals, it is presumed, experience wellbeing directly as a particular type of psychological state or condition. It can be directly known, felt and, hence, reported. That leads to a tempting, but debatable (e.g., Haybron 2008b), proposition: It is the individual who is best able to judge, and so report on, their state of wellbeing. In support, Diener quotes Marcus Aurelius as stating that "no man [sic] is happy who does not think himself so". It would be perverse to claim that people who believe themselves unhappy are, in fact, happy. And, at least as a first approximation, we should take someone's claim that they are, indeed, happy as preliminary evidence that that is the case.[3] But there are other possibilities: We can be objectively 'happy' or 'unhappy' (i.e., be in a state of wellbeing discoverable by others) during times when we are not reporting upon, or even thinking about, that experience as one of happiness or unhappiness. At least some people (e.g., Aristotle) have argued that 'happiness' (or the 'good life') might arise as an incidental by-product of other activity (e.g., acting virtuously) that is our attentional focus. And the experience of 'flow' (Csikszentmihalyi 1990) may leave little or no room for such awareness. More strongly, we could also be *objectively* happy or unhappy but claim that we are the opposite (or neither happy nor unhappy). Wellbeing researchers (e.g., Ryan and Deci 2017, pp. 266–271) are now familiar with the fact that we differ in our ability to be 'self-aware' and that that difference affects our wellbeing.[4] It is also well-known that self-reports of SWB have likely inadequacies such as denial (e.g., of being unhappy), the various biases associated with any cognitive judgments (e.g., memory retrieval differences, mood effects, etc.), and the forces at play in any communicative act (see Diener 1994, for a review of these inadequacies and his recommendations both to broaden the range of methods used and to make greater use of multiple methods). Presumably, any lack in self-awareness or tendency to succumb to these inadequacies will affect our (reported) sense of our own wellbeing.

This corrigibility in our self-reports of our own wellbeing is compounded when we consider time. It is a common enough experience to revisit a previous time in one's life and realise (i.e., *now* claim) that one was not actually happy then, despite professing at that time that one was happy (or vice versa). Kahneman's (2011) famous work on two distinct selves (the 'experiencing self' and the 'remembering self') is a further cautionary tale about the role of time in our understandings of our 'subjective' experiences. At the very least, this distinction implies that how we understand our 'happiness' depends in part upon whether we are concerned with immediate experience or with reflecting upon and judging our experiences of happiness or unhappiness retrospectively—or, indeed, prospectively (Lyubomirsky 2013). It is also a distinction that maps onto the contrast I draw between selves and persons in Chapter 4.

Partly in response to these many and varied problems, self-reports are not (now) the only method used to measure aspects of SWB—though they remain overwhelmingly popular. More research studies involve methods such as the Experience Sampling Method, Day Reconstruction Method, facial and physiological measures, and peer reports (judgments of others who know us, such as friends, family members, and work colleagues). Also more common are longitudinal methods at the population level using 'waves' of large datasets (e.g., the World Values Survey, various general social surveys, regular Gallup polling) and, in more targeted studies, tracking the effectiveness of particular positive psychology interventions over months, or even a year or more, often using randomized clinical trials (e.g., see Sin and Lyubomirsky 2009; Hendriks et al. 2018; Meyers et al. 2013). There has also been an increase in the use of multiple methods in the same study, as advocated by Diener (1994) and, more recently, Pavot (2008).

Despite these innovative approaches, cross-sectional, single measure, correlational, and survey-based self-reports still provide the bulk of data in the SWB literature. This leaves almost completely intact Pavot's (2008, p. 133) decade-old criticisms that concerned three features of an "empirical shortfall", or 'gap', between the techniques potentially available and the research designs used: An overly narrow and incomplete assessment of SWB; preponderance of single-method, cross-sectional designs; and, "the lack of a programmatic effort to refine subjective well-being assessment".

Another distinctive feature of Diener's formulation of SWB is that the relevant self-reports about wellbeing focus on two broad, summative aspects of each person's experience—a cognitive judgment about one's life and an assessment of affective reactions and experiences over some period of time. The first is a cognitive evaluation of satisfaction with life as a whole or, in the case of Cantril's Ladder, an evaluation of how similar one's life is to the best possible life. The second is an assessment of the overall positive or negative quality of experienced affect ('affect' covers a diverse set of concepts such as 'emotion', 'mood', and 'feelings'). In its most familiar terms, SWB has been understood as a composite measure of overall life satisfaction (LS) and the degree (or proportion) of experienced positive affect (PA) and negative affect (NA). Early work established an independence between PA and NA (Diener and Emmons 1985) which led to the conclusion that the hedonic component of SWB was a function of the relative proportions of the two broad types of affect rather than simply the experience of PA. Self-report scales have been developed that have reasonable validity and reliability as measures of LS, PA and NA. The most common include, for LS, the Satisfaction

With Life Scale (SWLS) (Diener et al. 1985) and Temporal Satisfaction With Life Scale (TSWLS) (Pavot et al. 1998), and, for PA and NA, the Affect Balance Scale (Bradburn 1969) and Positive and Negative Affect Schedule (PANAS) (Watson et al. 1988).

Measures of life satisfaction and affect have remained blunt instruments—an example of the lack of refinement in SWB assessment noted by Pavot (2008). The simple categorization of affective states into 'positive' and 'negative', for example, has been forcefully criticized by the prominent emotion researcher Richard Lazarus (2003). For Lazarus, 'positive' and 'negative'—whether used to describe emotions or types of 'psychology'—are simply "two sides of the same coin of life, like structure and process, stability and change, stress and coping, and so-called positive and negative emotions" and, "above all" the positive and negative "should not be regarded as separable" (Lazarus 2003, p. 94). He goes on to detail how any emotion (e.g., joy or happiness, anger, hope, love, pride) can be experienced sometimes as positive but, at other times, as negative since emotions have "relational meaning". That is, emotions have meanings—both for those who have them and for others—*in relation to* the events within which they arise. Different contexts can change the experienced and instrumental valence of just about any emotion. The experience of *unrequited* love, for example, is not unambiguously positive while an expression of anger can be experienced positively and have positive consequences for oneself and others (e.g., 'righteous anger').

Lumping together certain emotions and moods into either 'positive' or 'negative' valence categories based on surface meanings of emotion words not only misses the way affect is weaved into, and transformed by, our activity and life but it also slips in a spurious assumption 'under the radar'. Perhaps unintentionally, the science of SWB—and the more ambitious Positive Psychology project—has conspired to promote a neo-Benthamite utilitarian calculus of personal happiness, a weighing in the scales of the positive and negative aspects of our emotional lives. The temptation to understand wellbeing in this way has, in fact, been explicitly embraced (or succumbed to). The mathematical underpinning of the so-called 'positivity ratio' championed by prominent SWB researcher Barbara Fredrickson (Fredrickson and Losada 2005) has recently been emphatically debunked by Brown et al. (2013) leading to a published correction and withdrawal of the mathematical model (Fredrickson and Losada 2013). The extraordinarily precise calculation of a 'tipping point' at which the preponderance of PA over NA catapults individuals into a virtuous cycle of 'flourishing' (a ratio of 2.9013 to 1) was widely promoted and applied in a broad range of organizational, educational and personal settings (see Friedman and Brown [2018] for an overview of the practical impact of the work). Even after the criticism of the mathematical modelling, a response from Barbara Fredrickson (2013) continued to promote the value of the idea of a positivity ratio (now promoted less precisely but still around 3:1). This broader claim was itself criticized (Brown, Sokal et al. 2014) as was the reasoning behind the very idea that there might exist a quantifiable ratio between the categories of 'positive' and 'negative' affective experiences (Friedman and Brown 2018). As Friedman and Brown (2018, p. 243) argued, the implication that affective experiences have similar magnitude and duration—even if filtered through validated subjective scales and measures—seems hard to believe: "If someone laughs at a joke on TV, eats an ice-cream, sees their dog get run over, and watches a nice sunset, are they at a 3 to 1 ratio of positive to negative emotions and flourishing?"[5]

Disputes over measures of affect and wellbeing such as these highlight a tension that has existed in the literature for a long time. When Seligman and Csikszentmihalyi (2000) formally introduced positive psychology they explicitly contrasted it to previous work in humanistic psychology based on the theories of psychologists like Carl Rogers, Abraham Maslow, Rollo May, and James Bugental. They criticized humanistic psychology for its inability to "attract much of a cumulative empirical base" while it had "spawned myriad therapeutic self-help movements" and ensured that the 'psychology section' in large bookstores "contains at least 10 shelves on crystal healing, aromatherapy, and reaching the inner child for every shelf of books that tries to uphold some scholarly standard" (Seligman and Csikszentmihalyi 2000, p. 7). This scholarly disdain may well have been one reason why there was a special issue in the *Journal of Humanistic Psychology* on the implications for humanistic psychology of debunking the 'positivity ratio', as just discussed (Friedman and Brown 2018).

## The Eudaimonistic Challenge

The neglect of prior work on optimal human functioning in the empirically-focused approach of SWB (reviewed and championed by Diener 1984), was noted at the time by Carol Ryff (1989b). For Ryff (1989b), the narrow focus on measures of affect and life satisfaction was little more than historical accident. In asking, rhetorically, whether 'happiness' was everything, Ryff noted how the focus on the balance of positive and negative affect as a measure of 'happiness' was based on a serendipitous finding by Bradburn (1969) that the two variables were independent (uncorrelated). Bradburn's main aim had been to understand how social change affected life outcomes and psychological wellbeing, rather than directly understanding the structure of wellbeing. Ryff similarly criticized reliance on scales that measured LS, arguing, again, that they were typically developed for reasons other than to understand the structure of psychological wellbeing (e.g., the Life Satisfaction Index, she noted, was used to identify persons who were aging 'successfully'). This led her to conclude that the work, to that point, on psychological wellbeing was not "strongly theory guided" and that, instead, instruments "developed for other purposes" had become "the standard bearers for defining positive functioning" (Ryff 1989b, p. 1070). As a result, what had been neglected was a plethora of work on positive functioning such as the efforts of humanistic and personality psychologists (e.g., Maslow's work on self-actualisation and Rogers' theory of persons and becoming, Allport's understanding of maturity), Jung's theory of individuation, and work on lifespan development (e.g., Erik Erikson's stage theory of psychosocial personality development).

Ryff's early challenge to research on SWB rested on an explicit front-footing of *eudaimonic* aspects of wellbeing. The Greek word 'eudaimonia', at least in its recent psychological co-option, emphasizes personal *aspiration* in a way that is only implicit in SWB research (it was also implicit in the 'manifesto' for Positive Psychology that would appear at the turn of the millennium). While Diener (1984, p. 542) simply noted that work on SWB "is concerned with how and why people experience their lives in positive ways", a eudaimonic approach explicitly elevates the pursuit of a 'positive experience' of life to a paramount, aspirational virtue. The strong hedonic bias in the science of SWB, as Ryff (1989b) points out, blurs the distinction between the "gratification of right desires and wrong desires" that the word 'eudaimonia' (translated loosely as 'happiness') was meant to establish and defend. These 'right desires'—also known as '*Daimon*'—represent "an ideal in the sense of an *excellence*, a *perfection* toward which one *strives*, and it gives *meaning* and *direction* to one's life" (Ryff 1989b, p. 1070, emphasis added).

It was at this point that the term Psychological Well-Being (PWB) became a rival for—or, more generously, a complement to—SWB, though both depend upon subjective reports. Ryff's (1989b) six dimensions of PWB were first detailed in her work on 'successful ageing' where—prefiguring her later comments on SWB—she contended that research on aging had neglected theory (Ryff 1989a). That work had also displayed a 'negativism' about aging and ignored the possibility of continued psychological growth (and wellbeing) in the later years of life. Even in these final years, according to Ryff (1989a), there was still 'potential growth' and improvement rather than steady decline. These claims were an early expression of the now common push back against notions of 'retirement' as a time of rest from the relentless activity characteristic of earlier stages of life (a push back that, perhaps not coincidentally, is happening at a time of concerns over the affordability of social security as the population ages and of actual and proposed increases in the age of entitlement to pensions and public superannuation schemes). As with all other periods of life from infancy onwards, old age is now seen as a site of aspiration, change, growth, and improvement despite the imminence of the end of life.

Ryff (1989b) operationalised the PWB dimensions of 'self-acceptance', 'positive relations with others', 'autonomy', 'environmental mastery', 'purpose in life', and 'personal growth' that she drew from previous theoretical work. For Ryff (1989b, p. 1071), these dimensions suggested aspects of wellbeing that were likely distinct from the "reigning indexes of positive functioning" (i.e., affect and life satisfaction measures) yet which captured "key components of well-being". What she found was that four of these dimensions—positive relations with others, autonomy, purpose in life, and personal growth—were not as closely correlated with the standard measures of affect balance and life satisfaction (used in SWB research) as were environmental mastery and self-acceptance. This provided evidence that there were additional components of wellbeing that needed integrating into wellbeing theory. Further evidence came a decade later when Keyes et al. (2002) found distinct demographic profiles for those who scored higher on SWB versus PWB. They confirmed that SWB and PWB were related but distinct constructs and that there were many adults who either had higher levels of PWB than SWB or lower levels of PWB than SWB. That is, people could often report being happy and satisfied with life but with "diminished thriving and self-realization in their life pursuits" or who say they are thriving in various aspects of life "but do not feel very satisfied or happy" (Keyes et al. 2002, p. 1018). Those with these disparate levels of SWB and PWB comprised almost half the sample (45.2%), with 18.6% scoring high on both (they had 'optimal well-being'), a full 19.3% low on both and the remaining 12.6% having moderate levels of each. Even more interestingly, the combinations of SWB and PWB showed distinct patterns when it came to the sociodemographic variables of age and education. Overall, those who scored low on both SWB and PWB tended to be young people with less education; adults who scored lower on SWB but higher on PWB were more likely to be young people with much higher education; those who scored high on SWB but lower on PWB tended to have less education and be mid-life and older adults; and, finally, adults who scored high on both SWB and PWB tended to be mid-life to older and more highly educated. These findings led to the conclusion that the relationship between SWB and PWB can be either complementary or compensatory. That is, because SWB and PWB have some overlap they can boost each other (or depress each other) and, because of their distinctness, they can compensate each other so that a low level of one can be partly off-set by a higher level on the other.

While tempting, it is too simplistic to see SWB as solely hedonic and PWB as solely eudaimonic. As Keyes, Shmotkin and Ryff (2002) pointed out, the cognitive evaluation of LS is not especially or neces-sarily hedonic despite being central to SWB accounts. Similarly, while dimensions of purpose in life and personal growth in PWB are strongly eudaimonic, other dimensions such as self-acceptance and positive relations with others are less so (and correlate more closely with SWB dimensions). Nevertheless, there is a potential trade-off between feeling good and being satisfied with life, on the one hand, and pursuing a fulfilling life, on the other: "higher SWB may help preserve positive feelings when PWB is not possible" or "the high demands of striving to make the most of one's talents may undermine SWB but boost PWB" (Keyes et al. 2002, p. 1018).

## The Happy or the Meaningful Life?

This potential opposition between a happy life and a meaningful life has been a perennial theme in understanding wellbeing. It is behind the dis-tinction between hedonistic and eudaimonistic approaches (e.g., Deci and Ryan 2008; Waterman 1993; Ryan and Deci 2001). Just what that distinction involves has been disputed. One view is that an hedonic focus concerns 'outcomes' (e.g., the affective and cognitive states meas-ured in SWB research) while a eudaimonic focus emphasises the 'con-tent' (meanings) of life and the 'processes' that are part of living well (Ryan et al. 2008). That is, the two accounts of wellbeing do not dif-fer because they claim that wellbeing involves different outcome states (perhaps a superficial outcome of immediate pleasure versus a 'deeper' outcome of an inner sense of meaningfulness). The difference comes, instead, from a focus either on (psychological) 'states' or on a 'pro-cess' or way of living. Like most oppositions, the state/process opposi-tion depends upon the use or practical concern we have in mind. If we want to track wellbeing in individuals or populations then, in one way or another, we need some kind of 'state' measure. But to understand how wellbeing gets generated, we need some kind of 'process' theory. It is no coincidence that hedonistic approaches have been criticized for their (over)emphasis on measurement (of states) rather than theory (of processes and content) (Ryff 1989b), while eudaimonistic approaches have been criticized for their *lack* of robust, agreed upon measurements ('operationalisations') of their theoretical terms (Kashdan et al. 2008). This is the familiar contrast between 'empiricist' and 'rationalist' tendencies in science that goes all the way back to Ancient Greek philosophy (Hergenhahn 2005). Once again, this is a point I will return to as it finds an echo in the distinction between the present, on the one hand, and the past and future, on the other (discussed below). Heraclitus' famous (empiricist) dictum that it is not possible to 'step into the same river twice' neatly captures both the need constantly to test (i.e., 'measure' or continuously sense) the world and the importance of the present moment (at which one 'measures' or 'senses/experiences' the world) in establishing what is true knowledge. The contrast with the (rationalist) Platonic world of eternal 'ideal forms' that persist through, or even beyond, past, present, and future and constitute the basis of true knowledge could not be starker. That temporal distinction— between the present moment, and all past and future moments—plays no small part in differences between 'selves' and 'persons', as we will see in Chapter 4.

Despite these debates, most approaches to wellbeing, whether hedonistic or eudaimonistic, acknowledge the close links between happiness and meaningfulness in life. The good life, as a rule, also entails the pleasant life. But despite that acknowledgment, there are still striking instances of their independence. Satisfying needs and wants, for example, increases happiness (SWB) but is largely irrelevant to having a meaningful life (Baumeister et al. 2013), which provides some pause for thought for any desire theorist. This finding chimes with another from a national comparison study which found that, at the population level, Gross Domestic Product (GDP) is highly and positively correlated with LS but is negatively correlated with meaning in life (Oishi and Diener 2014). In the same study, low levels of meaning in life were associated with higher suicide rates which meant that wealthier nations (those with a higher GDP) had significantly higher suicide rates than poorer nations. In this case religiosity was found partly to explain the link between GDP and meaning in life. That is, wealthier countries were also less religious and had lower meaning in life. Other possible explanatory factors at the nation level such as higher levels of education and individualism and lower fertility levels (children per female) in wealthier countries were tested but not found to be mediators of lower levels of meaning. When the analysis was done at the individual level, however, the effect of GDP on meaning in life was still significant after taking into account religiosity. That is, "If two individuals were equally religious, those living in wealthy nations were less likely to report having meaning and purpose in their lives than those living in poor nations" (Oishi and Diener 2014, p. 427).

There is another aspect of 'meaning in life' that is worth emphasizing. Meaning is a process of connecting events over time, including the events that we initiate (i.e., acting with agency) or have responsibility for. As I will argue in the following chapter, mainly because of the way it provides continuity over time, meaning is also the medium within which persons come to be and continue to exist. Persons are agents who act within a sociocultural web of meanings and moral obligations—they have both agency and responsibilities. They also have continuity over time, partly as a result of that culturally presumed agency and responsibility. While each of us can, in a sense, have 'personal' meanings, meaning is ultimately culturally derived (Baumeister et al. 2013). Despite potentially being idiosyncratic, any personal meanings we experience are part of the ongoing human 'conversation' (Harré 1983) that is fundamental to the very possibility of meaningfulness in our lives. It is those culturally grounded meanings that, when transformed into 'personal' goals (e.g., buying a house) and their associated cultural tasks (e.g., finding a decent paying job), connect our daily efforts, sometimes unpleasant, with the future. In this way, higher levels of meaning are associated with consideration of longer timeframes. If we think a lot about the past and the future we tend to report higher levels of meaningfulness—but we are also less happy (Baumeister et al. 2013). To make matters worse, this focus on the future (and the past) means that "[p]eople with very meaningful lives worry more and have more stress than people with less meaningful lives" (Baumeister et al. 2013, p. 512). Conversely, if we are oriented more towards the present and the short-term, we are likely to report being happier.

I will say much more about this later, but for now it is useful to see that the meanings of life that we set for ourselves (which, very often, are also culturally set or organised *for us*) can be linked to a life that is not particularly happy, or even to one that is miserable. There is a potential disconnect between the meanings we take life to have and the happiness we experience. A clear example of this concerns the 'parenthood paradox', the finding that parents experience lower levels of happiness ('marital satisfaction') but greater levels of meaningfulness in their lives (Twenge et al. 2003; Lyubomirsky and Boehm 2010). This disconnect has implications for the entire project of positive psychology since, as Baumeister et al. (2013, p. 511) pointed out, it suggests "that people will pursue meaningfulness even at the expense of happiness". To connect the dots: (1) if cultures provide the array of meanings (or the parameters for 'meaning-making') available for individuals; (2) if those meanings principally serve the imperatives of an 'aspirational culture'; (3) if people truly do tend to pursue meaningfulness "at the expense of happiness"; then, (4) there is no guarantee that aspirational cultures will generate happy people. And, if the 'meanings of life' gained "at the expense of happiness" turn out to be unattainable or hollow where does that leave the pursuit of wellbeing?

It is one thing to claim that meaningfulness and happiness can conflict. It is quite another to consider the question, "Who's 'meaningfulness' and 'happiness' can conflict?" Most animals would have little conflict of this kind. The, as yet unanswered, question that hangs in the air around all our understandings of wellbeing is: 'The wellbeing of what?' What kind of entity has to wrestle with the potential task of reconciling meaningfulness and happiness? What kind of entity is, at the same time, subject to experiences of pleasure and pain that have been refracted through an evanescent web of meanings? There is little chance of understanding human wellbeing without at least some careful reflection on questions such as these.

## Notes

1. My focus is on human wellbeing. Concern over the wellbeing of other species—or the planet as a whole—is another matter. Yet, even here, the discussion of ultrasociality in Chapter 2 is also an argument that it is the subordination of human autonomy, and hence wellbeing, to the

ultrasocial ecological-economic system that has been part of the creation of the diverse and massive environmental problems we currently face. Understanding human wellbeing, then, is probably central to solving the environmental issues that affect the wellbeing of so many other species.

2. In that address Seligman pushed for two changes. The second he mentioned was the focus on a 'Positive Psychology'. The first concerned the role that psychology and psychologists could play in what he perceived as the future increase in 'ethnopolitical conflict', and consequent refugee and migrant concerns. At the time, the Kosovo crisis was topical. Seligman thought that psychology could "train today's young psychologists who have the courage and the humanity for such work to better understand, predict, and even prevent such tragedies".

3. In subsequent chapters, I will be raising questions about the nature of the kinds of self-reports that inform standard SWB measures (and many other psychological measures). For now, it is probably enough just to say that self-reports can be understood either as 'reports' about psychological states and processes or as contributions to a conversation (with the researcher but also with oneself) that can be understood as a feature of the sociocultural activity of a person. I favour the second interpretation of self-reports (which are therefore misnamed) since I am skeptical both of the existence of such a subjective, inner realm of psychological experience and, even if one did exist, of the ability of an individual to report knowledgeably upon the nature of the internal psychological states and processes thought to populate such a realm. But I am getting ahead of this book's narrative.

4. Beginning from a very different set of assumptions about human psychology, discursive psychologists such as Edwards and Potter would simply argue that the claims people make in their accounts of themselves are typically constructed to achieve 'discursive work' rather than to report on some supposed inner world of psychological states.

5. For those interested, similar groupings of authors have been involved in another dispute, over the extent to which hedonic and eudaimonic experiences of wellbeing are related to differential gene expression (e.g., see Brown, MacDonald et al. 2014, 2016; Fredrickson et al. 2013, 2015, 2016).

# References

Allport, G. W. (1985). The historical background of social psychology. In G. Lindzey, & E. Aronson (Eds.), *Handbook of social psychology* (3rd ed., Volume 1: Theory and Method). New York: Random House.

Baumeister, R. F., Vohs, K. D., Aaker, J. L., & Garbinsky, E. N. (2013). Some key differences between a happy life and a meaningful life. *The Journal of Positive Psychology, 8*(6), 505–516. https://doi.org/10.1080/17439760.2013.830764.

Bradburn, N. M. (1969). *The structure of psychological well-being.* Chicago: Aldine.

Brown, N. J. L., MacDonald, D. A., Samanta, M. P., Friedman, H. L., & Coyne, J. C. (2014). A critical reanalysis of the relationship between genomics and well-being. *Proceedings of the National Academy of Sciences, 111*(35), 12705–12709. https://doi.org/10.1073/pnas.1407057111.

Brown, N. J. L., MacDonald, D. A., Samanta, M. P., Friedman, H. L., & Coyne, J. C. (2016). More questions than answers: Continued critical reanalysis of Fredrickson et al.'s studies of genomics and well-being. *PLoS ONE, 11*(6), e0156415. https://doi.org/10.1371/journal.pone.0156415.

Brown, N. J. L., Sokal, A. D., & Friedman, H. L. (2013). The complex dynamics of wishful thinking: The critical positivity ratio. *American Psychologist, 68*(9), 801–813. https://doi.org/10.1037/a0032850.

Brown, N. J. L., Sokal, A. D., & Friedman, H. L. (2014). The persistence of wishful thinking. *American Psychologist, 69*(6), 629–632. https://doi.org/10.1037/a0037050.

Bryan, W. L., & Harter, N. (1897). Studies in the psychology of the telegraphic language. *Psychological Review, 4,* 27–53.

Csikszentmihalyi, M. (1990). *Flow: The psychology of optimal experience.* New York: Harper and Row.

Deci, E. L., & Ryan, R. M. (2008). Hedonia, eudaimonia, and well-being: An introduction. *Journal of Happiness Studies, 9*(1), 1–11.

Diener, E. (1984). Subjective well-being. *Psychological Bulletin, 95*(3), 542–575.

Diener, E. (1994). Assessing subjective well-being: Progress and opportunities. *Social Indicators Research, 31*(2), 103–157.

Diener, E., & Emmons, R. A. (1985). The independence of positive and negative affect. *Journal of Personality and Social Psychology, 47,* 1105–1117.

Diener, E., Emmons, R. A., Larsen, R. J., & Griffin, S. (1985). The satisfaction with life scale. *Journal of Personality Assessment, 49*(1), 71–75.

Ewen, S. (1988). *All consuming images: The politics of style in contemporary cultures* (1st ed.). New York: Basic Books.

Fredrickson, B. L. (2013). Updated thinking on positivity ratios. *American Psychologist, 68*(9), 814–822. https://doi.org/10.1037/a0033584.

Fredrickson, B. L., Grewen, K. M., Algoe, S. B., Firestine, A. M., Arevalo, J. M. G., Ma, J., et al. (2015). Psychological well-being and the human conserved transcriptional response to adversity. *PLoS ONE, 10*(3), e0121839. https://doi.org/10.1371/journal.pone.0121839.

Fredrickson, B. L., Grewen, K. M., Algoe, S. B., Firestine, A. M., Arevalo, J. M. G., Ma, J., et al. (2016). Correction: Psychological well-being and the human conserved transcriptional response to adversity. *PLoS ONE, 11*(6), e0157116. https://doi.org/10.1371/journal.pone.0157116.

Fredrickson, B. L., Grewen, K. M., Coffey, K. A., Algoe, S. B., Firestine, A. M., Arevalo, J. M. G., et al. (2013). A functional genomic perspective on human well-being. *Proceedings of the National Academy of Sciences, 110*(33), 13684. https://doi.org/10.1073/pnas.1305419110.

Fredrickson, B. L., & Losada, M. F. (2005). Positive affect and the complex dynamics of human flourishing. *American Psychologist, 60*(7), 678–686.

Fredrickson, B. L., & Losada, M. F. (2013). "Positive affect and the complex dynamics of human flourishing": Correction to Fredrickson and Losada (2005). *American Psychologist, 68*(9), 822.

Friedman, H. L., & Brown, N. J. L. (2018). Implications of debunking the 'Critical Positivity Ratio' for humanistic psychology: Introduction to special issue. *Journal of Humanistic Psychology, 58*(3), 239–261.

Goodman, F. R., Disabato, D. J., Kashdan, T. B., & Kauffman, S. B. (2018). Measuring well-being: A comparison of subjective well-being and PERMA. *The Journal of Positive Psychology, 13*(4), 321–332. https://doi.org/10.1080/17439760.2017.1388434.

Gowdy, J., & Krall, L. (2016). The economic origins of ultrasociality. *Behavioral and Brain Sciences, 39,* E92. https://doi.org/10.1017/S0140525X1500059X.

Harré, R. (1983). *Personal being: A theory for individual psychology.* Oxford: Blackwell.

Haybron, D. M. (2008a). Philosophy and the science of subjective well-being. In M. Eid & R. J. Larsen (Eds.), *The science of subjective well-being* (pp. 17–43). New York: The Guildford Press.

Haybron, D. M. (2008b). *The pursuit of unhappiness: The elusive psychology of well-being*. Oxford: Oxford University Press.

Heathwood, C. (2005). The problem of defective desires. *Australasian Journal of Philosophy, 83*(4), 487–504. https://doi.org/10.1080/00048400500338690.

Heathwood, C. (2016). Desire-fulfillment theory. In G. Fletcher (Ed.), *The Routledge handbook of philosophy of well-being* (pp. 135–147). London: Routledge.

Hendriks, T., Warren, M. A., Schotanus-Dijkstra, M., Hassankhan, A., Graafsma, T., Bohlmeijer, E., et al. (2018). How WEIRD are positive psychology interventions? A bibliometric analysis of randomized controlled trials on the science of well-being. *The Journal of Positive Psychology*, 1–13. https://doi.org/10.1080/17439760.2018.1484941.

Hergenhahn, B. R. (2005). *An introduction to the history of psychology*. Belmont, CA: Thomson/Wadsworth.

Hsee, C. K., & Hastie, R. (2006). Decision and experience: Why don't we choose what makes us happy? *Trends in Cognitive Sciences, 10*(1), 31–37.

Huppert, F. A., & Baylis, N. (2004, September 29). Well-being: Towards an integration of psychology, neurobiology and social science. *Philosophical Transactions of the Royal Society of London B: Biological Sciences, 359*(1449), 1447–1451.

Huppert, F. A., Baylis, N., & Keverne, E. B. (2004). Introduction: Why do we need a science of well-being? [Introduction to a special issue]. *Philosophical Transactions of the Royal Society B-Biological Sciences, 359*, 1331–1332. https://doi.org/10.1098/rstb.2004.1519.

Kahneman, D. (2011). *Thinking, fast and slow*. Australia: Penguin Group.

Kashdan, T. B., Biswas-Diener, R., & King, L. A. (2008). Reconsidering happiness: The costs of distinguishing between hedonics and eudaimonia. *The Journal of Positive Psychology, 3*(4), 219–233. https://doi.org/10.1080/17439760802303044.

Keyes, C. L. M., Shmotkin, D., & Ryff, C. D. (2002). Optimizing well-being: The empirical encounter of two traditions. *Journal of Personality and Social Psychology, 82*(6), 1007–1022. https://doi.org/10.1037//0022-3514.82.6.1007.

King, P. E., Barrett, J. L., Greenway, T. S., Schnitker, S. A., & Furrow, J. L. (2018). Mind the gap: Evolutionary psychological perspectives on human thriving. *The Journal of Positive Psychology, 13*(4), 336–345. https://doi.org/10.1080/17439760.2017.1291855.

Lazarus, R. S. (2003). Does the positive psychology movement have legs? *Psychological Inquiry, 14*(2), 93–109.

Leahey, T. H. (2000). *A history of psychology: Main currents in psychological thought* (5th ed.). Upper Saddle River, NJ: Prentice Hall.

104   K. Moore

Linley, A. P., Joseph, S., Harrington, S., & Wood, A. M. (2006). Positive psychology: Past, present, and (possible) future. *The Journal of Positive Psychology, 1*(1), 3–16. https://doi.org/10.1080/17439760500372796.

Lyubomirsky, S. (2013). *The myths of happiness: What should make you happy, but doesn't, what shouldn't make you happy, but does.* New York: The Penguin Press.

Lyubomirsky, S., & Boehm, J. K. (2010). Human motives, happiness, and the puzzle of parenthood: Commentary on Kenrick et al. (2010) [Editorial material]. *Perspectives on Psychological Science, 5*(3), 327–334. https://doi.org/10.1177/1745691610369473.

Mercier, H., & Sperber, D. (2011). Why do humans reason? Arguments for an argumentative theory. *Behavioral and Brain Sciences, 34*(2), 57–74. https://doi.org/10.1017/S0140525X10000968.

Meyers, M. C., van Woerkom, M., & Bakker, A. B. (2013). The added value of the positive: A literature review of positive psychology interventions in organizations. *European Journal of Work and Organizational Psychology, 22*(5), 618–632. https://doi.org/10.1080/1359432X.2012.694689.

Oishi, S. (2010). The psychology of residential mobility: Implications for the self, social relationships, and well-being. *Perspectives on Psychological Science, 5*(1), 5–21. https://doi.org/10.1177/1745691609356781.

Oishi, S., & Diener, E. (2014). Residents of poor nations have a greater sense of meaning in life than residents of wealthy nations. *Psychological Science, 25*(2), 422–430. https://doi.org/10.1177/0956797613507286.

Parfit, D. (1984). *Reasons and persons.* New York: Oxford University Press.

Park, N., Peterson, C., & Seligman, M. E. P. (2006). Character strengths in fifty-four nations and the fifty US states. *The Journal of Positive Psychology, 1*(3), 118–129. https://doi.org/10.1080/17439760600619567.

Pavot, W. (2008). The assessment of subjective well-being: Successes and shortfalls. In M. Eid & R. J. Larsen (Eds.), *The science of subjective well-being* (pp. 97–123). New York: The Guildford Press.

Pavot, W., Diener, E., & Eunkook, S. (1998). The temporal satisfaction with life scale. *Journal of Personality Assessment, 70*(2), 340.

Peterson, C., Ruch, W., Beermann, U., Park, N., & Seligman, M. E. P. (2007). Strengths of character, orientations to happiness, and life satisfaction. *The Journal of Positive Psychology, 2*(3), 149–156. https://doi.org/10.1080/17439760701228938.

Peterson, C., & Seligman, M. E. P. (2004). *Character strengths and virtues: A handbook and classification.* New York: Oxford University Press.

Ryan, R. M., & Deci, E. L. (2001). On happiness and human potentials: A review of research on hedonic and eudaimonic well-being. *Annual Review of Psychology, 52,* 141–166.

Ryan, R. M., & Deci, E. L. (2017). *Self-determination theory: Basic psychological needs in motivation, development, and wellness.* New York: Guilford Press.

Ryan, R. M., Huta, V., & Deci, E. L. (2008). Living well: A self-determination theory perspective on eudaimonia. *Journal of Happiness Studies, 9,* 139–170. https://doi.org/10.1007/s10902-006-9023-4.

Ryff, C. D. (1989a). Beyond Ponce de Leon and life satisfaction: New directions in quest of successful aging. *International Journal of Behavioral Development, 12,* 35–55.

Ryff, C. D. (1989b). Happiness is everything, or is it? *Journal of Personality and Social Psychology, 57*(6), 1069–1081.

Seligman, M. E. P. (1998). *The President's address.* https://positivepsychologynews.com/ppnd_wp/wp-content/uploads/2018/04/APA-President-Address-1998.pdf. Accessed 9 Dec 2018.

Seligman, M. E. P. (2002). *Authentic happiness: Using the new positive psychology to realize your potential for lasting fulfillment.* New York: Free Press.

Seligman, M. E. P. (2011). *Flourish: A visionary new understanding of happiness and well-being.* New York: Free Press.

Seligman, M. E. P. (2018). PERMA and the building blocks of well-being. *The Journal of Positive Psychology, 13*(4), 333–335. https://doi.org/10.1080/17439760.2018.1437466.

Seligman, M. E. P., & Csikszentmihalyi, M. (2000). Positive psychology: An introduction. *American Psychologist, 55,* 51–82.

Sin, N. L., & Lyubomirsky, S. (2009). Enhancing well-being and alleviating depressive symptoms with positive psychology interventions: A practice-friendly meta-analysis. *Journal of Clinical Psychology, 65,* 467–487.

Turner, S. (2018). The belief-desire model of action explanation reconsidered: Thoughts on Bittner. *Philosophy of the Social Sciences, 48*(3), 290–308. https://doi.org/10.1177/0048393117750076.

Twenge, J. M., Campbell, W. K., & Foster, C. A. (2003). Parenthood and marital satisfaction: A meta-analytic review. *Journal of Marriage and Family, 65*(3), 574–583. https://doi.org/10.1111/j.1741-3737.2003.00574.x.

Waterman, A. S. (1993). Two conceptions of happiness: Contrasts of personal expressiveness (eudaimonia) and hedonic enjoyment. *Journal of Personality and Social Psychology, 64*(4), 678–691.

Watson, D., Clark, L. A., & Tellegen, A. (1988). Development and validation of brief measures of positive and negative affect: The PANAS scales. *Journal of Personality and Social Psychology, 54,* 1063–1070.

# 4

# Persons, Selves, and Wellbeing

## Introduction: 'The Wellbeing of What?'

No matter how we categorise the many psychological theories of wellbeing, they all aspire to fulfill the progressivist promise of the discipline. The practical application of research findings and theories to improve the wellbeing of individuals and society was, from the start, an unquestioned and explicit goal of 'Positive Psychology'; its focus would be on "building positive qualities" and not just on "repairing the worst things in life" (Seligman and Csikszentmihalyi 2000, p. 5). If effort and research focus is any indication, positive psychology has been increasingly successful at developing and testing wellbeing 'interventions', both at the individual (Bolier et al. 2013; Sin and Lyubomirsky 2009) and organisational levels (see Meyers et al. 2013 for a review). It has also, from the start, been adept at popularizing to the wider public research-based advice, hints, and interventions for a better life (Seligman 2011, 2002, 2018; Lyubomirsky 2013). There is a great hope that, individual-by-individual, organisation-by-organisation, and nation state-by-nation state (Diener and Seligman 2004) positive psychology will leverage human flourishing as more of these interventions are implemented.

© The Author(s) 2019
K. Moore, *Wellbeing and Aspirational Culture*,
https://doi.org/10.1007/978-3-030-15643-5_4

The recent book by leading SWB researcher Sonja Lyubomirsky—*The Myths of Happiness: What Should Make You Happy, But Doesn't, What Shouldn't Make You Happy, But Does*—is a paean to Positive Psychology and empirical work on SWB. Its main message is that, in our 'affective forecasts' we systematically over-estimate the gains in happiness from some events (e.g., getting married, finding a new job) and the loss of happiness from others (e.g., losing a job, getting divorced). After reading the book and, so, "knowing where happiness truly can be found—and where it can't" you should be able to "transform your crisis points into straightforward passages of life that are not only unexceptional but growth promoting" (Lyubomirsky 2013, p. 250). In this disarmingly innocent project, personal knowledge about wellbeing is presented as transformational power. It is worth observing the tenor of this advice more closely. All that individuals need do, it seems, is grasp the opportunity to make use of the knowledge provided by researchers to improve their emotional lives: "the healthiest responses … all involve *effortful happiness boosting strategies* that *spur you to invest* in your emotional life"; "it may help to *consider the bigger picture*", "*strive* to redirect your attention to something else [that is more positive]", "*look on the bright side* of negative situations" but "*be creative* about how you do it" and be sure to "*inject* variety and novelty into your life" while not forgetting to "*pursue* intrinsic, authentic, and flexible goals" and "*make them your own*" (Lyubomirsky 2013, p. 251, emphasis added). The conscious, rational self is both prominent and in control in this world of advice. Once your 'self' sees that it is "*your beliefs* about what will make you happy and unhappy" that have been "*driving your reactions* to life's challenges" you will be well-equipped to "*decide how to behave* in ways that promote happiness" by "relying on *reasoning* rather than instinct" (Lyubomirsky 2013, p. 251, emphasis added).

This kind of practical account is not some simple eschewing of the relevance of broader social structures and circumstances, which are acknowledged throughout. But the tone is unmistakable—with this knowledge *you* can make wellbeing an aspirational project. You can 'take back control' through consciously managing your*self*, your beliefs and your reactions to what life throws your way. This belief in, and promotion of, the efficacy of individual agency and action to accomplish personal change is completely unremarkable in the context of professional psychology. Belief in conscious agency as the route to 'becoming' all that you can (and should) be—"to be that self which one truly is" as Søren Kierkegaard put it—is fundamental, for example, to the humanistic psychology and therapeutic philosophy of psychologists such as Carl Rogers who pioneered 'client-centred therapy' and 'person-centred' psychology. Despite the term 'person-centred', Rogers (1959) conception of the 'person' was expressed as the idea of the 'Self Concept' which became the forerunner to renewed interest in the 'self' in psychology, an important development in our current discussion.

Efforts to apply wellbeing science have not been without their critics. The spread of wellbeing policies in private and public sector organisations and through government policy has been criticised as yet another worrying attempt to manage, measure and control the activity of individuals, and to delegate responsibility for wellbeing away from governments and corporations and towards the individual (Davies 2015; Cederström and Spicer 2015). The 'wellness ideology', for example, is seen as a not-so-subtle means of demonizing any supposed mistreatment of the body through smoking, over-eating or not exercising enough which then leads to an over-emphasis on individual responsibility to maintain wellness (Cederström and Spicer 2015).

But beyond criticisms of the social and political consequences of imperatives for personal wellbeing are those that claim that the culture behind those imperatives strikes at the heart of who we are. As mentioned in Chapter 2, the new and 'liquid' modernity that has erupted in recent decades not only affects social institutions but also "affects the most personal aspects of our experience" (Giddens 1991, p. 10). An increasing number of psychologists have picked up on those sociological insights and have come to see Positive Psychology and work on wellbeing as part of the overall disruptive process that is fashioning new 'subjectivities' and selves. Some argue, for example, that Positive Psychology is part of the broader capitalist and, especially neoliberal, project in that it has persuaded us to see ourselves as 'enterprises' (Binkley 2014) designed for optimising happiness. The "psychological individual, like the contemporary corporation, is urged to be opportunistic and enterprising, an entrepreneur of themselves in a manner that resonates with the economic and political discourse of neoliberalism" (Binkley 2018, p. 406). A special issue of the journal *Theory and Psychology* has recently been devoted to 'Psychology in the social imaginary of neoliberalism', and it is not only Positive Psychology but the entirety of psychology that comes within its sights. According to the editor of the special issue, one "could make the case that the ascendance of American psychology since World War II facilitated neoliberal thinking, but even more that it *prepared individuals to think and act neoliberally*" (Pickren 2018, p. 576, emphasis added). Another contributor detects the emergence of a 'neoliberal form of self' (NLFS) that has "given up on the idea of a transcendental ego" (i.e., on an aspect of one's being that is distinct from the self) and in which "the pinnacle self is achieved, when 'I' not only have an instrumental, entrepreneurial relationship to the 'self,' but 'myself' *is* an entrepreneurial entity" (Teo 2018, p. 585). As the artist Jay-Z (quoted in Teo 2018, p. 585) expressed it: "I am not a businessman, I am a business, man".

What does all of this mean for our wellbeing? Do we have a 'nature', as individuals, that can survive or even thrive in this world? What are the conditions that might help us survive and thrive? Are these conditions mostly 'inside' or 'outside' us (assuming that distinction itself even makes sense)? All of these questions depend upon a more fundamental one: *Just what kind of beings are we, in our totality*? And what on earth might we mean by the 'wellbeing' of that kind of being?

In this chapter I defend the claim that the wellbeing that we are interested in is the wellbeing of persons. I begin with the curious observation that the person, nevertheless, is almost entirely absent from our theories of wellbeing and, in fact, from most psychological theories.

## The Missing Person

To understand human wellbeing and its connections to our aspirational world it is necessary to go, theoretically, where many psychologists have feared to tread. The main argument of this chapter is that the person should be the focus of our wellbeing concerns and theories. Those who experience, report, investigate, and worry about wellbeing are persons.

They are not 'minds' or 'selves' or 'egos' or any number of other potential candidates that researchers could, and perhaps unfortunately have, focused upon in their investigations of wellbeing. Certainly, I might wish *my* mind or *my* 'self' or, for that matter, *my* body to be 'well' but that's largely because *I* want to be well—and 'I' am a person, not a mind or a self or a body (though what I might think about my mind, self, and body or how I might evaluate them, could affect my wellbeing as a person).

This idea that the person is central to our wellbeing concerns and so should have a prominent position in theories of wellbeing will not come as a surprise to most lay people. Yet the 'person' is notoriously difficult to locate in research on wellbeing; even, surprisingly, in that large body of work on *Subjective* Well-Being (SWB). At best, the person is something of a methodological cypher who 'reports' on their own wellbeing but, elsewhere, is absent from theory. It is the person, then, who is assumed to 'have' all the experiences that, together, comprise one's wellbeing—even including the experience of its own 'sense of self'—but, despite that, it largely goes unremarked and is effectively invisible in theories of wellbeing.

In fact, the person is remarkably absent from psychological theory in general. As Martin and Bickhard (2012, p. 86) observed, despite psychology's chosen subject matter supposedly being the "actions and experiences (albeit more typically rendered as the behaviors, cognitions and emotions) of persons" it is surprising just "how little attention most psychologists have given to conceptualizing and theorizing persons". There is an enormous amount of research on human psychology but mostly it involves the elucidation of all sorts of putative bits and pieces that presumably interact to generate the person and their experiences. Along with the quite literal 'bits and pieces' of neurology, physiology and genetic material there is now also a vast pantheon of psychological terms, each ruling over some psychological domain and generated, in turn, by some even lesser processes or sets of 'sub-routines'. In this approach, the person is like some unanalysed 'horizon concept' looming in the far-off scientific distance that, one day, we will come to understand once we know all of the bits and pieces and all the ways in which they interact. Forgotten entirely is the fact that we already have a robust account of persons which, once acknowledged, allows the psychological clutter to be sorted in a way that does more than justice to our actions and experiences as persons. And this is no more in evidence than in the case of human experiences of wellbeing.

As Martin and Bickhard (2012, p. 86) go on to note, it is also true that despite—or perhaps because of—this lack of theoretical interest in persons there has been no shortage of investigations by psychologists into the apparently complex nature of the human 'self' which in turn have led to a proliferation of "a variety of 'self' studies". These studies include the familiar work on self-concept, self-esteem, self-regulation, self-enhancement, etc. as well as everything from the self's evolution (e.g., Leary and Buttermore 2003; Sedikides and Skowronski 1997) to its unity (Baumeister 2011b) and supposed continuity over time (e.g., see the introduction to the Special Issue on 'self-continuity' in the journal *Self and Identity* by Sedikides et al. [2018] and the accompanying articles). Starved of the meatier notion of a person, it is as if psychologists have had to feed themselves on the less nourishing theoretical fare provided by the construct of the 'self'. Unfortunately, as I will argue, the self is not best conceived as some kind of *internal site* of psychological activity (complete with its own needs, processes, states, etc.). Instead, it is a dynamic production—a 'fiction' or 'theory'—that arises within the psychological activity of persons, out in the world. Selves—as anyone who is aware of their own self can testify—constantly shift, morph, twist and turn, largely as required by one or other of a person's 'projects' in the world. These projects, in turn, typically concern one or other of the demands or tasks placed upon persons by the relevant cultural milieu (e.g., being seen as a good parent, a responsible member of the community, a hard worker).

Why has the 'self' drawn so much attention from psychologists yet the 'person' so little? The answer is partly about the reluctance psychology, as established, has in incorporating the normative and conventional aspects of human life into a strictly causal (and, hence, supposedly scientific) account. It is as if there is a fear that any acknowledgment that psychological phenomena are fundamentally normative in character would jeopardise the scientific status of psychology. It is along those lines that Harré (1998, p. 133) speculates on a likely "metaphysical assumption" that "to be scientific an investigator must offer causal explanations rather than normative ones". This then leads psychologists to invoke "causally potent but unobservable properties"—that is, the full gamut of traits, attitudes, beliefs and so on that are claimed to generate (causally) the behaviour to be explained. This flight not just to unobserved but to, in principle, *unobservable* generative mechanisms is unnecessary. There is no reason to believe that the obviously normative dimension of actions and experiences is somehow beyond the purview of a science.

There is another related reason. Psychology has made an evidential mistake. It has taken the sociocultural and discursive invention known as a 'person' and seen in all its remarkable ascribed features direct evidence for an underlying, internal psychology. Persons are said to 'believe', and so psychologists see that as evidence of internal beliefs. Persons are said to be 'motivated', and so psychologists see that as evidence of internal motivational processes. Persons feel things—their bodies and their circumstances—and so psychologists see that as evidence for an internal world of feelings as the place where feeling *really* happens. Persons have a sense of being themselves and being authentic, and so psychologists conclude that there is a self, which persons essentially *are*. In other words, rather than seeing all of these psychological features as being just what they appear to be—the activities of persons—they are transformed into pieces of evidence for some deeper, yet still psychological, internal world of complexity.

This difficulty is no doubt responsible for many of the schisms and pendulum swings in the history of theory in psychology. Overall, it appears that psychological theory has most often taken the seemingly easy path of assuming that the deeply conventional features of psychological activity *must* ultimately be just a consequence of particularly complex internal causal processes. And, if nothing else, the brain (in its assumed role as the material site for the instantiation of our psychology) is clearly an immensely complex set of causal processes. Surely—so goes the thinking—somewhere deeply embedded in the unfathomably interconnected web of connections that is the brain the 'miracle' is finally achieved, and the conventional (or normative) at last yields to the causal. As I will argue, that hope is not the best prospect for resolving the dilemma between the normative and causal aspects of our experience. It is far better to deal with what we are given: persons (and their psychological attributes) exist as normative characterisations of material objects. As Harré (1998, p. 119) states, "In the human world people, as psychological beings, do not have parts, though they produce complex patterns of action that give the illusion of psychological parts". We have to go beyond that illusion.

A final point needs to be made before sketching the details of the notion of a person. Much of this chapter concerns the question of why the notion of the 'person' is conceptually and theoretically preferable to that of the 'self', especially in inquiries into human wellbeing. That means confronting some important theories that have been applied to the study of human wellbeing (and, in fact, to many other areas of psychology). Foremost amongst these theories is Richard Ryan and Edward Deci's widely invoked Self-Determination Theory (SDT) but it is also strongly in evidence in the work of other psychologists such as Roy Baumeister (e.g., Baumeister 2011a, b). SDT, specifically, is an extraordinarily well-considered and thought through theoretical structure. From its philosophical bases to the empirical hypotheses and findings it has generated, it stands as a remarkable achievement. But what I present in this chapter is a challenge, and an alternative, to that theoretical structure and to the way it helps us interpret discoveries about human wellbeing.

Let me be specific. A good deal of SDT involves categorisation of various different degrees of self-determined (or *not* self-determined) behaviour. The most completely self-determined behaviours, values, and so on have to be integrated into the 'self'—a psychological construct that, amongst other things, has the universal needs (i.e., needs that are part of our nature) of autonomy, competence, and relatedness. Acknowledging the fact that we can often perform behaviours that we would not necessarily have determined to do ourselves (e.g., working two jobs at a time) but that we, nevertheless, can *endorse* at a deep level (e.g., as part of a value of the importance of working hard to achieve one's goals). Once endorsed, the behaviour becomes closer to 'pure' self-determined behaviour. However, there is also the possibility that we act in ways that, similarly, we would not necessarily have determined to do ourselves but, in this case, when doing them we experience ambivalence or even conflict. Our behaviour is experienced—by our 'self'—as being externally controlled rather than under our own control. The relevant passage is worth quoting at length (Ryan and Deci 2017, p. 83, emphasis added):

> Importantly, the referent for the term internal, when used in the phrase "internal perceived locus of causality," is not the person but rather the self. This is a critical conceptual issue, because in the SDT framework there can be *intrapsychic* (or *intrapersonal*) pressures that, although *internal to the person*, can be experienced as *self-alien* and controlling (Ryan, 1982). Specifically, introjected attitudes or regulations are in some sense internal to the person but external to the self, and as such they would have a relatively external PLOC. They are an instance of non-self-determination. They can even diminish one's intrinsic motivation

This passage is exceptionally important, not only for understanding SDT but also for gaining a clear understanding of the kind of view of personhood (and self) that, while dominant, is unhelpful. In this view, what we are, *in essence*, is a self. Hence, what is truly 'internal' to us is what is present, or integrated into, this inner core of our being. The person, meanwhile, becomes a composite that includes a 'self' and various other psychological features that potentially include "introjected attitudes or regulations". This idea that the person includes 'alien' content that can lead to "intrapsychic … pressures" represents a theoretical fracturing of the unity of our personhood. Rather than seeing such everyday experiences of conflicting tendencies as simply part of the task of being a person, the conflicts are rehoused in an internal, psychological world. As with Freudian theory, we are encouraged to see ourselves as arenas of 'inner conflict' rather than as persons doing their best to make their way in the external world in which they came to be and continue to live. It internalises what is actually a difficulty in living in a particular context and cultural milieu. The 'fix' for these difficulties then becomes the re-engineering not of our life in the external world (or, even, the external world itself) but of our inner world in which, supposedly, our 'true selves' grapple with what to 'endorse' and what to reject. As with Freud's account, the enemy is within and the potential for psychic 'splitting' is ever-present as part of being human. The extreme forms of dissociation become explicable in terms of this abstract architecture in which the 'core' or 'true' self sits at the centre surrounded by potential 'introjected' threats that have been socially and culturally imposed on one's pre-existent, or at least independent, inner being.

The irony from the perspective advocated in this book, is that this understanding of one's true self as some inner citadel defending its territory is *itself* one of the most 'introjected', 'alien' notions imposed upon us by our aspirational culture. It is, in fact, a crucial mechanism in the perpetuation of aspirational culture. Over twenty years ago, social psychologist Kurt Danziger (1997, p. 139) wrote about the 'social formation of selves' and observed that "Before there could be anything for the discipline of psychology to study, people had to develop a psychological way of understanding themselves, their conduct, and their experiences". The modern sense of self had to emerge before psychology as a discipline was even possible as, without those kinds of self as "discursive objects", "the science of psychology would have had nothing to study" (Danziger 1997, p. 139). This new 'Lockean' self "was a private possession that each individual discovered in him or herself" and so "could become an object of concern as well as an object of knowledge" (Danziger 1997, p. 143). Historically, this 'self' came to be seen as a self-monitoring mechanism, a way that judged the person's own conduct against appropriate behaviour: "Persons no longer lived in their actions but adopted an observational, monitoring stance towards them" (p. 144).

To close the loop on this discussion, Danziger (1997, p. 145) quotes a passage from Adam Smith's *Theory of Moral Sentiments* that is explicit about the same 'splitting' of the person produced by this modern concept of the self as adopted, at least implicitly (and perhaps unintentionally), by (Ryan and Deci 2017): "When I endeavour to examine my own conduct, when I endeavour to pass sentence upon it, and either to approve or condemn it, it is evident that, in all such cases, I divide myself, as it were into two persons; and that I, the examiner and judge, represent a different character from that other I, the person whose conduct is examined into and judged of". It could not be clearer;

our 'selves' are a means of social control through becoming the constructed magnet of a "flow of approval and disapproval" that would now
"accompany individuals throughout their lives" which in effect means
that the "objectified self that persons now harbor within them is above
all an object of approval and disapproval, both by others and by the person herself" (Danziger 1997, p. 145).

Many psychologists slip unreflectively from speaking about selves
and then, without missing a beat, referring to persons or 'people' and
their experiences as if an account of selves and their structure just *is* an
account of personal experience. As I will try to show, that could not be
further from the truth.

## Why Persons?

As much of the literature reported in previous chapters testifies, in the
main the psychological study of wellbeing has followed the same conceptual and methodological paths trod repeatedly in other areas of
psychology over the past decades. Whether seen as an outcome or an
antecedent of some other conditions, processes or states, wellbeing has
been assumed to be a measurable component or attribute of psychological experience. It has also been assumed itself to have an internal complexity, a componential make-up (e.g., affective states and cognitive life
evaluations), and each of its components can be measured as aspects of
the psychological experiences of individuals. In other words, wellbeing—like most other psychological phenomena—has been taken to be
both a part of a broader set of psychological (and sometimes biological
or social) processes and as having *internal complexity*. This complexity is
thought to be internal in the sense that it arises out of the interaction of
psychological processes and states that are, themselves, internal to individuals (e.g., affective states, processes of evaluation, attribution, social
comparison).

In following these paths, research on wellbeing has also inherited
assumptions that hinder its understanding. In this chapter, the main
argument is that, in the study of wellbeing, the conceptual shortcomings of much work in psychology comes to a head around the fact that

the person is absent. To that extent, the psychological study of wellbeing provides a crucial testing ground for psychological theory itself.

These conceptual shortcomings produce an impoverished account of our psychological experiences—and the crucial sense in which these experiences are considered by most (but not all[1]) individuals to be '*mine*'. What—or who—is the 'I' that has these experiences? If they were not *my* experiences, then they could not possibly matter to me. Yet they do. That they do matter to me is also how the experiences I have concern *my* wellbeing.

Part of the difficulty, however, is that this crucial feature of our experiences—including experiences of wellbeing—can seem to produce a paradox: On the one hand, 'I' ordinarily see myself as the *subject* of all my experiences (that is, of everything I know, believe, am aware of, am conscious of, sense, etc.). In that sense, the sum of these experiences represents the *limit of my 'world'*. My experience is everything; 'The world is my world' as the philosopher Ludwig Wittgenstein put it in his early work (the *Tractatus Logico-Philosophicus*). On the other hand, 'I' see myself also (and obviously) as only *a part of the world*. I am only one of many other people and things. How is this possible? How can the world be 'all mine' yet also quite independent of me? It does not usually trouble us in our everyday life, but it is a major conceptual problem. How is it that sometimes we see ourselves as a 'subject' but, at others, as one 'object' amongst many others? There is a switch in perspective involved here, but is there some singular 'entity' doing the switching? (To anyone who is familiar with these kinds of reflections the danger of sliding inevitably into an infinite recursive loop will be obvious!)

This ambiguous and potentially paradoxical understanding of ourselves is at the heart of the many problems psychological theories encounter when they try to do justice to our experience of our psychological lives. In fact, these problems may explain, in part, Martin and Bickhard's (2012) observation that most psychologists choose to avoid engaging theoretically with this conceptually complicated sense we have of ourselves and our experiences as persons. For those of us interested in wellbeing, coming to grips with this reflexive, dual view of ourselves is unavoidable.

It has often been noted how cognitive scientists will often use the terms 'brain' and 'mind' interchangeably, slipping perhaps unwittingly between their respective uses. But less often remarked is how frequently psychologists will slide from discussions of putative internal psychological processes (including such theoretically complex processes as 'selves' and 'egos'), on the one hand, and the lived and reported experiences of people, on the other. One moment the talk might be of the mechanistic (i.e., causal) operation of an evolved 'hip-to-waist ratio' cognitive module and the next moment conclusions are drawn about the everyday experience—and reporting—of sexual desire by persons (the putative module supposedly being the partial cause of the experienced, usually male, desire). The move results in a failure to notice that a major grammatical shift has occurred, a shift that is vital to understanding the sense in which persons can be said to *have* experiences (e.g., of satisfaction, happiness, contentment, meaningfulness, etc.) and how, and when, they *report* them (both to others and to themselves).

Underpinning the problematic aspect of this unacknowledged grammatical shift is an inadequate conceptualization of the relationship between persons and the activity of their nervous systems (and, in fact, of their bodies in general). Neural architecture—no matter how dynamic or plastic it is thought to be—has come to be seen as the site where psychological states and processes exist. Certain neural pathways, and the parts of the brain they connect together, are simply taken as where such phenomena as remembering, deciding, evaluating, and so on, ultimately take place. There are well known problems with this simple identification of neural activity with psychological activity. Without an alternative plausible account of the relationship between psychological and neural activity that view of the relationship is likely to remain the default. But if it is the default then, once again, we—as the persons who have our psychological experiences—will remain forever out of the picture.

As Harré (1983) remarked, there could not be a greater contrast between two very different understandings of people. On the one hand is the 'high-grade automaton' view that, in various versions, dominates explanations in psychology of how our experiences arise—that is, as the outcomes of *causal processes*. On the other hand, there is the more familiar—but, because of that, the often overlooked or derogated—accounts used in everyday life that express (if not articulate) a much more fluid and transparent sense of the nature of our experiences as the outcome of *normative or conventional processes*. While this distinction oversimplifies—on both sides—it nevertheless serves as a pointer to the perennial difficulty psychology has had in putting the proverbial 'Humpty-Dumpty' together again. Put bluntly, how does a collection of causal mechanisms and processes, even in complex arrangements, do justice to our experiences, especially their sense of continuity and their meaningful and holistic aspects (they are *all my* experiences, feelings, memories, beliefs, etc. and *they matter to me*)?

This problem runs much deeper and wider than just how we think about wellbeing. It has played its part in the generation of several schools of thought within psychology. Humanistic psychologists, for example, were motivated by the sense of something being amiss—and missing—in both the behaviourist and psychoanalytic understandings of human experience (DeCarvalho 1991). By inserting the 'human being' or the 'organism' into the behaviourist stimulus-response scheme they hoped to inject humanity—in more ways than one—into psychological theories and practice. And, by highlighting the aspect of conscious *intentionality* in people's actions they also hoped to dispel the image of people being driven by—and being the passive victims of—unknown, unconscious causal processes or external contingencies.

No doubt the emergence of the cognitive approach was appealing to many psychologists for much the same reason that the humanistic approach was attractive. It too seemed to fore-front the *internal complexity* of the individual human being and so, once again, put the individual back into the supposedly barren landscape of behaviourism. The simple equation was perhaps that the more internal complexity we can get 'inside' individuals the greater the degree of *autonomy* and *agency* we can attribute to them. As possessors of massive and intricate cognitive machinery each individual could be seen as a powerful site for the initiation of behaviour and so no longer a 'mere' puppet of external (conditioning) forces. 'We' could be back in the driver's seat.

There is, however, an interesting irony to this appeal. A lot of work in the cognitive tradition explains human behaviour as a product of hybrid neuro-cognitive mechanisms that operate well outside the awareness of the individual who is meant to be the agent of her own actions. Not unlike Freud's hypothesized and baroque set of unconscious processes, once again the individual (the person) seems to be just coming along for the causal ride rather than doing the driving. The sort of familiar autonomy and agency claimed by most people, at least some of the time, once again disappears even in psychological accounts that purportedly put individual agency and autonomy back into the frame.

We are increasingly immersed in a culture unprecedented in its rhetorical emphasis on the sovereignty of the individual. It is commonly believed that each of us has the ability—and is in the best position—to create our own lives and our own experiences through the exercise of choice in line with our personal preferences and values. Wellbeing theories have not been immune from that influence despite problems with the claim that individuals have those abilities to the degree that they would generally choose well (Haybron 2008). This assumption that we have personal agency is implicit in the functioning of the aspirational culture I highlight in this book. One way or another, then, some kind of being that has agency has to be incorporated into our understanding of wellbeing in aspirational cultures.

The answer to the question 'The wellbeing of what?' is not obvious for two reasons. First, is the 'what' an entity (e.g., a 'human being', a 'self', a 'mind', etc.) or should we think more of the verb-sense of 'being'—the *process* of being (as in the process of 'living' or perhaps of 'being human')? In the first sense, research might focus on the wellbeing of an entity like a 'soul', 'mind' (as in a 'healthy mind'), an 'ego' (though Freud's concept of an 'ego' actually refers to a supposed psychic process, rather than an entity), or a 'self' (again not understood as a process). In the second sense, wellbeing might be understood more as a property of some processes such as the interactions of a complicated array of cognitive mechanisms or modules, needs (and their fulfillment or not) or, perhaps, of a 'life'.

The second reason that the answer to the question of 'The wellbeing of what?' is not obvious is that there is a large *diversity* of possible answers. Relevant entities include: the body (notions of 'wellness' tend to focus on this); the mind; the self; the ego (the Freudian tradition, for example, emphasizes the need for a strong ego); the human being (the biologically, evolutionarily and ethologically designated nature of a member of the species *Homo sapiens*); the individual; the child; the adult; the consumer; the worker; the parent; and so on. There is even recent concern for the health of the human 'microbiome', the bacterial colonies that make up so much of the human body (e.g., Clarke et al. 2012). This numerosity of possible targets of our wellbeing concerns no doubt goes some way to explaining the proliferation of interest in wellbeing from psychologists, social scientists, philosophers, economists and biologists whose concern is with some particular aspect of the human and broader natural world.

Further, for some, a wellbeing concern and focus may even 'dig deep' into our internal psychological workings. That means that the target of wellbeing research could be the specific wellbeing of individuated psychological phenomena including such psychological features as our decision-making skills, memory faculty, emotions, motivational processes, self-regulation systems, self-esteem, and creativity. Popular psychology books and blogs, for example, routinely dispense advice on keeping each of these skills and capacities 'well' and fit for purpose.

Of these numerous possible targets for our concerns about wellbeing, which one(s) should take priority? By 'priority' what I mean here is simply the identification of the 'target' for which, without its wellbeing, the wellbeing of other targets would be neither necessary nor sufficient to produce wellbeing in 'us'. After all, it is possible, at least logically, to have an excellent memory, a fit body, a strong 'ego' and yet still report that one does not have high wellbeing. Certainly, reports that people can perceive—or admit—that their lives can rationally be assessed as 'good' while, simultaneously, they are experiencing some degree of mental pain or a lack of vitality are not unheard of and may go some way to explaining the appeal, for lay people and experts alike, of biological explanations of their malady.

The simple answer to the question of what should take priority in concerns for wellbeing would be 'us' or 'ourselves', but the obviousness of this answer glosses a large theoretical hole in psychology. As a discipline, psychology has largely failed to clarify just what 'we' are. Or perhaps it has just assumed that the answer to that question—to the extent that it falls within the purview of psychology—will be arrived at through analysis of our component parts and their interactions (e.g., from some combination of mental and behavioural entities or processes, perhaps attached to a biological substrate). But there is an inherent problem with this analytic tactic. For all analytic approaches in psychology the 'hard problem' is how to synthesise the 'whole' out of the parts. We may truly be a 'bundle of bits'—whether those bits be bundles of conditioned responses or cognitive processes—but the question that matters most for *our* wellbeing is how those bits cohere—or do not.

This inherent problem can be lessened if a promising candidate for what the 'whole' is can be identified ahead of time (a priori). The rest of this chapter makes the case for that candidate being the notion of a 'person'. From the start, I claim that it is the concept of a 'person' that can best resolve the paradox previously highlighted. In our everyday use, the concept of a person is commonly understood as both a subject of *all* a person's experiences yet also as just *one* person in an array of many other persons. That is, it is commonly taken to be both a centre of 'holistic' experience of the world of persons, objects and events and yet also just one part of a much larger world of persons, objects and events that can affect it, sometimes in worrying ways.

There are further important reasons why persons are the most likely candidates to fill the conceptual gap over the kinds of beings we are and, therefore, to be the answer to the question 'The wellbeing of what?'. First, much of the literature on SWB is based on self-reports. For better or worse, self-reports have become the 'gold standard' for the presence of wellbeing in the individual (and they are correlated with other, so-called objective, measures of wellbeing—Diener 1994). Who—or what—provides such reports? While they are called 'self'-reports there is good reason to see the word 'self', in this instance, as standing in for the particular person who provides the report. It is, after all, the person who, in ordinary conversation, will be held accountable for the provision of such reports. When we ask someone, in a serious manner, 'how they are' we hold the person we are speaking to as both authoritative and responsible for the report that is given. In terms borrowed from Edwards and Potter's (1992) 'Discursive Action Model' (DAM), it is the person who utters these reports who is held *accountable* for their content (and function). In the social world, at least, it is the person (not some notional 'self') who is taken to be providing a 'self-report'.

Second, the notion of a person—as will soon be discussed—entails another, socially monitored and enforced, responsibility. A person is responsible for navigating its way to some normatively acceptable or defensible life—persons, that is, are creatures of, and operators within, what Harré (1983) has called the 'local moral order'. And, to the extent that wellbeing is seen as a facet of the normatively acceptable life, it is persons that have the responsibility to navigate towards an acceptable form and degree of wellbeing within that moral order. To be successful in this navigational goal, it is the person who must use its various nominal resources to achieve wellbeing. The person, for example, has the responsibility of using its mind, body, social status and affective experiences in an optimal manner, which—in the present context—is to say in a manner that will most effectively generate the kind of wellbeing associated with local moral orders and accounts of personhood.

Third, persons have an inherent temporal orientation in a way that other, related, concepts do not (e.g., the 'self'). By dint of their sociocultural origins and from the necessity of their social functions, persons are taken as unitary across time. Without that assumption of unity, being held socially accountable for one's past actions would be meaningless and, of course, unjust. However else we may change during our lives, the very fact that these are *our* lives and, hence, that the changes within them occur to just such particular lives is given by the related fact that we are particular persons (and, hence, the same person throughout a life). Short of identity fraud and the onset of delusional states (i.e., the belief that one is, or has become, some other person), this avowed and experienced temporal unity is a marker of personhood.

While it is possible to understand wellbeing as a momentary state (e.g., as is the tendency in more hedonically-oriented approaches to wellbeing), it is also commonly seen as a process or motivational project (e.g., a motive to flourish or, in the case of humans in particular, to 'self-actualise', etc.). That is, wellbeing is a continual—if not continuous—concern of organisms in general, especially when understood within an evolutionary frame. For related reasons, much of the interest in wellbeing research involves the way in which temporal trade-offs affect wellbeing (e.g., short-term versus long-term trade-offs). It is persons—rather than bodies, selves or the array of putative cognitive 'modules'—that are at the sharp end of just these sorts of temporal concerns. For example, consider the fascinating thought experiments discussed by Stokes (2017, p. 204, original emphasis) about the conflicting concerns of the "phenomenally figured *self*, understood as a present tense subject of experience, and the diachronically extended *person*". This distinction is related to the famous cold-pressor experiment and subsequent studies of 'duration neglect' when it comes to our choices based on past experiences (Fredrickson and Kahneman 1993; Kahneman et al. 1993). It was studies such as these that led Daniel Kahneman to the conclusion that there are two kinds of 'selves'—an experiencing self (Stokes' present tense 'self'), and a remembering self (Stokes' diachronic 'person') (see Kahneman 2011). Kahneman (2011, p. 390) makes this distinction clear when he claims that "I am my remembering self, and the experiencing self, who does my living, is like a stranger to me."

The concerns of the 'self' (the 'experiencing self') are immediate and so focus particularly on present and proximate future *states*—and discount past states—while the 'person' has a greater concern for life as a whole and, so, the total sum of a life's value. What has happened to a 'self' in the past is gone and, therefore, of little or no concern at least to the self. By contrast, what has happened to—or been *done by*—a 'person' in the past remains a feature of a person's experience that requires some degree of reconciliation to the life trajectory of the person (it may, for example, impact one's reputation, one's understanding of who one *really* is, etc.). The same asymmetry in valuation of experience between the 'self' and the 'person' is true of the distant future. While selves are concerned with the present and the more immediate future, persons tend inherently (that is, as a matter of the usual grammar of the concept of 'person') to have a concern for even the distant future. That is, they have concerns over what, ultimately, a life amounts to and how it might be evaluated by 'posterity', whether of the broader social posterity or a more localized notion within one's family or social circle. What remains to be considered, and will be discussed shortly, is just how the notion of a 'self' relates to the notion of a 'person'.

The argument presented here, then, is that the wellbeing that we should be most concerned about is the wellbeing of persons. That argument therefore requires detailed understanding of just what a person is or, more accurately, to see how personhood comes to be ascribed, both to ourselves and to others. In one sense, few would disagree that, 'of course', our concern should be with the wellbeing of persons. The difference in this account, however, is that the person becomes a central conceptual feature of our understanding of wellbeing rather than being seen simply as the unproblematic beneficiary of all the research and informed advice on how persons can *achieve*—or *aspire to*—wellbeing. Persons, that is, are treated here not just as 'end users' or consumers of research knowledge on wellbeing but as part of the theoretical account. By making the level of persons explicit in a theory of wellbeing the advantage is that the questions of just what persons are and how being a person connects with the concept of wellbeing are not begged through adoption of culturally pervasive, but unanalyzed, assumptions about personhood.

The remaining sections in this chapter present theories of personhood—the condition and quality of being an individual person. I first lay down some conceptual foundations so that what we mean when we talk about persons can be brought into focus. 'Person' is a word that is so ordinary that we probably are not that aware about how tricky the notion is. Taking for granted that we know what kind of 'thing' we are talking about when we speak of 'persons' can easily mislead us.

## The Concept of a 'Person'

I start by staking out my own commitments: I subscribe to an understanding of psychology that draws deeply from the philosophy of Ludwig Wittgenstein. I believe he is one of the few philosophers to have broken free from the tenacious hold that Cartesian dualism still has over our view of ourselves. That hold remains particularly strong in psychology but is also firmly part of the ideology of aspiration which, today, means it is part of most people's understanding of themselves and of their relationship to the world.

The philosopher Daniel Dennett, in his book '*Consciousness Explained*' wrote of how—despite all the flaws it is acknowledged to have—we remain under the thrall of this picture of our inner life; a picture he called the 'Cartesian Theatre' (Dennett 1993). We see our minds along the lines of an 'inner theatre' with a stage populated by psychological states and events. 'We' (whoever we are) sit like a spectator in the theatre, able to observe the action, report on what is going on, and even reflect upon and judge those states and events. This is an odd idea. Yet most people seem to subscribe to it, if the way they talk about themselves and their psychological experiences is any indication. Notice that once we accept that we are composed of an interior mind counter-posed to an exterior reality the world immediately splits in two. On the one side is the 'real' world of sticks, stones, animals, plants, planets, and other people; on the other side are our 'experiences'. Disturbingly, today even one's own body is now often seen as much a part of this 'exteriority' as is the planet Jupiter.

The harm that this 'split-view' can create at the extremes has long been recognised. In the social sciences, that split is sometimes called 'alienation'. That is, we feel like an 'alien' in relation to more and more of the world and what we may have to do in it (e.g., Karl Marx spoke of the alienation of the worker from their work). In psychology it goes under various terms: social psychologists might simply talk of 'loneliness'—the sense, perhaps even in the presence of other people, that one is entirely alone, psychologically and emotionally; in psychiatry and clinical psychology the corresponding term is often 'dissociation' which comes in various forms—all including some level of dissociation from reality—from the reasonably innocuous experience of daydreaming to more severe dissociation from one's memory of one's past (dissociative fugue), dissociation from one's feelings, depersonalisation (the feeling that the self is not real), and derealisation (a general sense of the unreality of the world). Why might we be susceptible to this kind of 'splitting' of our experience? Might it have something to do with the notion of a 'person'?

In his book *Individuality*, Peter Strawson (1959) provided what has become a seminal analysis of the concept of a person. He begins with some preliminary comments about Wittgenstein's (1961/1922) propositions in the *Tractatus* (5.631–5.641) to the effect that there is "no such thing" as the "thinking, presenting subject" and that it does not "belong to the world" (hence, there is no such thing in the world) but it "is a limit of the world" (just as the eye is not 'in' the visual field but represents its limit). Strawson (1959, p. 330) accepts that "when I talk of myself, I do after all talk of that which has all of my experiences" but points out that he—and all of us—also "talk of something that is part of the world in that it, but not the world, comes to an end when I die." This is the seemingly paradoxical aspect of being a person mentioned previously. We are at the same time only ever aware of our own experiences but also aware that we are in, and have to deal with, a world that is not of our making. Strawson summarises his position: it "may be difficult to explain the idea of something which is both a subject of experiences and a part of the world" but "it is an idea we have" so "it should be an idea we can explain". But how, exactly, can it be explained?

Strawson begins by noting that we tend to predicate (or ascribe) to the 'I' a very wide range of attributes. In particular, we ascribe both the kinds of attributes that we would of a material object (e.g., spatial location, size, weight, etc.) and the kinds of attributes that we "would not dream" of ascribing to material objects (e.g., feelings, beliefs, intents, etc.). We could respond in two ways here: either that each of these two types of ascriptions reference two quite distinct kinds of 'stuff' (the material body and the spirit/mind, for instance); or, that they, in one case, can be ascribed to a material body and, in the other case, are only mistakenly taken as ascriptions at all. Strawson, however, simply accepts the fact that we have a single concept (a 'person') to which we make *both* kinds of ascriptions. We just have to live with that fact rather than try to explain it away.

Strawson's argument is in opposition to two other types of account both of which are what he sees as kinds of 'dualism'. That is, they associate two types of 'thing' with the two types of predicates (material and mental). The first, as I have already suggested, is an account in which the use of the pronoun 'I' is sometimes thought to reference a material body (e.g., when we say 'I am sunburnt' or 'I am 75 kilograms') and, at other times, is thought to reference some kind of special 'stuff' or entity (the soul or spirit) which has attributes quite different from those which we typically ascribe to material entities (e.g., when we say 'I am confused' or 'I feel concerned' or any other self-ascriptions of what might be called states of consciousness or mental states). This is the familiar dualism of René Descartes in which the world is made of two kinds of stuff—matter and spirit.

The second account Strawson also argues against accepts that 'I' sometimes refers to a body but *denies* that in its other uses it refers to anything at all. It is, instead, a "linguistic illusion" that states of consciousness are ascribed at all because there is no such subject of the supposed ascriptions and so states of consciousness are not states of anything at all. When we say 'I am confused' we are, indeed, confused if we think there is 'some-thing' that is confused ('I' does not refer to an entity at all in these cases). So, in a sense there are still two sorts of 'things'—a body; and, a 'no-thing'. He calls these two accounts the Cartesian (for obvious reasons) and the 'no-ownership' views, respectively. With all the apparent complications that follow, Strawson instead argues that the 'I' should, in all its uses, be seen as referring to a *singular* entity about which both kinds of ascriptions can be made: a person.

The concept of a person can therefore be seen as 'logically primitive' which is to say that it is *not* composed of two (or more) distinct parts—a body and a 'soul'/mind (as in the Cartesian view); a body and a 'non-subject' (in the 'no-ownership' view). This is because in order to argue that—to take the Cartesian approach as an example—we know that there is a particular body *and* particular states of consciousness that go along with just this body (e.g., conscious states that are *mine*) we already need to have the unifying concept of a person, to whom both the body and the states of consciousness can be ascribed. The sense that there even *are* particular states of consciousness (that is, states of a *particular* subject of experience) and that these states go along with a *particular* body are derivative of or contingent upon the prior use of the concept of there being a 'person' whose states and body they are. This all means that there is the concept of a 'person' and that concept is not decomposable into components. The notion of a person is not analyzable either as "an animated body" or "an embodied anima". Further, Strawson (1959, p. 340, original emphasis) convincingly argues that "a necessary condition of states of consciousness being ascribed at all is that they should be ascribed to the *very same things* as certain corporeal characteristics, a certain physical situation, etc." In other words, a 'belief', 'feeling', etc. can only be ascribed to something that *can also have* such characteristics ascribed to it as we would normally ascribe to a material thing (e.g., spatial location, colour, physical attitude—'leaning', 'lying down', etc.). Believe it or not, Strawson is saying that a completely non-material thing—as is claimed in some understandings of a 'soul', 'ego', or 'self'—just cannot have states of consciousness. To say that something has a state of consciousness we must also be able to say that, at least in some respects, that 'thing' also can have ascribed to it the kinds of ascriptions we make of material objects (e.g., about their size, weight, colour, location, and so on).

The implications of this analysis are profound. There is not, to put it bluntly, a psychological referent (an 'ego', 'self', etc.) of the word 'I' which, when combined with a (biological) body, comprises the concept of a person. Persons do not have parts. There is also—to put it even more bluntly—not just a body in motion, on the one hand, and merely an *illusion* of agency, unity and continuity of experience on the other. In one very simple step, Strawson challenges the 'layering' that is so pervasive in our understandings of ourselves. In effect, he argues against a dualism in being a person: Not only against the dualism of two types of 'stuff'—Cartesian dualism—but also the dualism of two types of ascriptions—legitimate ones and illusory ones. We are exactly what we appear to be: persons who can not only be 175 cm tall but can also experience a sense of irritation at the latest tweet we have read. It might seem to be an odd sort of thing that can be both, but that kind of 'thing' is just what we are. Rather than question this strange fact we would do better to challenge—or discover—the assumptions that make it seem so odd.

There is not sufficient space to provide much more detail, but Strawson's analysis draws out several other important points. First, the very sense of experiences being *one's own* is dependent upon the concept of a person. Without that concept it would make no sense—even to me—to say 'I see/ hear/ think/ feel', etc. Awareness of one's own states of consciousness only comes along with mastery in employing the concept of a person to oneself: "The concept of a person is logically prior to that of an individual consciousness" (Strawson 1959, p. 341). That awareness is not, therefore, the result of some complicated and mysterious reflexive, inner psychological ability; the employment, for example, of some kind of 'inner spotlight' that shines at one moment on *this* memory, at another on *this* feeling and, at yet another moment, on *this* sense of determination, etc. There is no need for such a spotlight seen as some native ability that highlights the otherwise unconscious contents of one's mind (or 'psyche') in a serial manner—all upon the stage of the 'Cartesian Theatre'. Instead, it is the result of knowing how to talk about yourself, express yourself, and *take* yourself as a person.

Second, for Strawson there is no sense in ascribing such states to oneself unless there is already an ability to ascribe at least some states of consciousness *to others*. Put another way, for the concept of a person to make sense—to have a proper use—it must refer to a member of a broader category of persons; it must refer to one amongst similar instances of a 'person'. And while many people today may rebel at the claim, it is therefore not possible to argue from your own case of experiencing your own states of consciousness to the inference that others must (or may) have such states too. If you are not already proficient in knowing how to ascribe states of consciousness to others there is no way you can learn to ascribe them to yourself. Or, there is simply no use for an individual in seeing itself as a subject of experience unless, or until, there is a use in seeing others as subjects of their experiences (and this 'usefulness' is no doubt closely linked to the facility to use the kind of language that we do). This is probably one of the reasons that personhood seems to be very rare in the animal kingdom—there is not much call for it. It is also useful here to notice that our 'evidence' for ascribing states of consciousness to ourselves versus to other people can seem quite different. In our own case, the 'evidence' that we are feeling sad seems directly 'knowable' (but, as the scare quote marks are meant to indicate, this is not actually a case of knowledge—it is 'expressive'). In the case of someone else, the 'evidence' appears simply to be their behaviour, their facial expression, tone of voice, manner of moving, and other seemingly 'objective' or 'external' criteria. That is, we feel that we ascribe states of consciousness to ourself based on direct and immediate evidence; we ascribe states of consciousness to others using indirect and 'circumstantial' evidence. We do not ascribe sadness to ourselves solely because we notice how we are moving, speaking, etc.—that kind of evidence can come into our ascriptions but not definitively; it would not decide the matter, since we could be doing all of that and—as is of course also possible in the case of someone else—still not *feel* sad (we might be acting a part on stage or pretending as part of a joke).

Finally, Strawson provides some suggestions as to how we might make sense of how these two kinds of ascriptions (predicates) can be made of one and the same 'thing'. His main suggestion is the observation that there are certain kinds of 'intermediate' ascriptions which do not strike us as quite so odd when seen *either* as properties of a material body *or* as states of consciousness. These ascriptions, or predicates, are ones that involve us *doing* things. When a person is understood to have *done* something there is a clear sense in which an intention or some other state of consciousness is implied. (As discussed in the next chapter, Harré (1998, 2016) notes that in the use of the 'person ontology', things are *done*; in a 'molecular ontology' things *happen*). But there is also a clear sense in which such a 'doing' involves typical or characteristic patterns of behaviour—of bodily movement. These instances include things such as "playing ball", "writing a letter" and "going for a walk". We ascribe 'going for a walk' to others, for example, on the basis of observation (of the 'typical' pattern of behaviour, and perhaps also the typical site or situation in which it might occur such as a footpath or track). Yet, typically, when we, ourselves, go for a walk we do not ascribe the action of going for a walk on the basis of observing what we are doing (observing the typical pattern of behaviours, the site, etc.). Despite these two quite different ways by which we come to ascribe 'going for a walk' we do not feel particularly awkward in saying that we are ascribing *the same activity* to others as to ourselves. Both of us are *doing* the same thing—we are both 'going for a walk'. According to Strawson, the reason we do not feel awkward in doing this is because 'going for a walk' does not imply a particular or specific type of (subjective) experience so it is the *pattern* of movement that dominates. So, we can ascribe the fact that someone is 'going for a walk' without either observation (in our own case) or inference about private experiences (in the case of others).

More familiarly, the suggestion Strawson is making here is that we can treat these typical patterns of bodily movement as *meaningful actions*. That is, we do not simply perceive bodily movements but, instead, we perceive coordinated actions towards some end (we literally see someone going for a walk), with all the implications of intent and various other relevant conscious states, likely outcomes, likely causes or reasons, and so on. By treating these kinds of patterns as actions, we gain the advantages, amongst others, of knowing what is likely to happen (especially in the case of others), providing advice (e.g., of where a good local walk might be), and of regulating what we, ourselves, do (in our own case). Seeing other people as persons is, in large measure, recognising their patterns of action as meaningful 'doings'. This way of relating to others in the manner of persons comes first. We do not build it up from the 'evidence' we observe about how they behave; we presume it.

In emphasizing these instances of 'doing' things—as opposed to instances of states of consciousness themselves—Strawson is making use of a conceptual tool often used by Wittgenstein. In his later philosophy, Wittgenstein often explored *intermediate cases* to resolve apparent paradoxes. That is, he made use of instances where our problem does not seem to shine quite so bright or be so insoluble. The best example of this tactic in Wittgenstein's work is his discussion of two ways of determining meaning that appear to be in conflict. These two ways relate directly to just the kinds of issues that Strawson sought to resolve in the context of the wide range of ascriptions that can be made to persons.

When we use the concept of 'meaning', its grammar (i.e., the way it is used) provides us with two different ways to determine the meaning of something (of a word, a behaviour, an event). The first way is that sense we sometimes have of '*grasping the meaning in a flash*'. The meaning seems to present itself directly to us like a picture flashed before our mind (this is like the direct 'evidence' of our own sadness in the example above). The second sense involves some kind of use over time. The meaning that a set of written instructions has for someone (usually someone else) we determine by seeing what they do over time. If we give someone instructions for driving into the central city, we work out whether or not they have understood their meaning by noticing the turns they make at relevant intersections. We might even argue with the person if they keep insisting that—irrespective of how inappropriately they behave in trying to drive to the central city—they have actually grasped (or 'seen') the right meaning of the instructions.

Wittgenstein was interested in how we resolve these two ways of determining meaning since it seems, at first sight, that they clash with each other. How can something that is 'grasped in a flash' or an instant, *also* be something that is actually extended over time? This is the same question about the seeming ability of people (persons) to have minds (that can 'grasp' ideas and meanings instantaneously) while 'only' being bodies (material objects moving about in space over time). The resolution Wittgenstein suggested came from looking for an intermediate case: the concept of an 'application'. There is a sense in which the blueprint for a building that has not yet been built 'grasps' the meaning of the completed building. But, of course, its meaning depends upon a builder making use of the blueprint in a certain way (hopefully in a well-trained way that results in a building that will stay upright). While we might be able to get away with the idea that the meaning is 'in' the blueprint ('caught' or 'grasped' by the blueprint), the proof of the meaning it has or hasn't 'grasped' is in its application. The same is true of the meaning of all the words and concepts we use, as persons, to talk about ourselves, others, and the things that all we persons do.

Whatever might supposedly come before our minds when we grasp a meaning in a flash (a mental image, a word, etc.) still needs to be 'applied' or 'used' in order for its sense to be clear. If I do absolutely nothing with, for example, an image of my grandmother that comes to my mind as part of the experience I have when I 'grasp a meaning in a flash' (e.g., of the word 'grandmother') then, odd as it may sound, I will have no way of knowing what the image is of. I need to make use of it, perhaps by *drawing* it, *describing* it to someone else or *declaring* to myself 'silently' what the image means. Importantly, all of the italicised words in the previous sentence are instances of 'doing' or action—specifically, they are instances of applying the image (or whatever happens to come before my mind).

So far, the conceptual account of persons may seem to be far removed from the daily experience we have of being in a 'concrete' real world.

It is the world of hard substances, soft flesh and blood, and real, physical occurrences (I live in a city that experienced massive earthquakes not so long ago). What is surprising is that this conceptual account has its resonance, and even its advocates, amongst scientists immersed in that same real world. Nick Chater (2018), for example, in his book *The Mind is Flat: The Illusion of Mental Depth and the Improvised Mind* has come to the reluctant conclusion, based on decades of scientific research, that there is no hidden, inner world of unconscious psychological events, processes and experiences. Just as with fictional characters such as Anna Karenina, questions about inner motives, thought processes, and experiences of 'real' people are answered 'on the hoof', speculatively, often providing inconsistent answers (what he calls the 'improvised mind'). While it is fine, even advantageous, to think of the brain as an information processor of the most exquisite type, none of that processing activity amounts to evidence of 'inner depth' to our mind. We attend to—and are conscious of—only one thing at a time, in just the same linear manner that our conscious life is experienced. Our minds, beliefs, motives, and everything else we are used to thinking of as inhabitants of our inner, private world are jury-built, momentary productions in response to the moment. What continuity we feel we experience therefore must come from elsewhere—from the regularities maintained in the social and cultural world of meanings and meaningful activity. That means that our experiences of wellbeing—or of any other nominally psychological experience—have the meanings they have by virtue of how they form part of our activity out in the world (and not in our heads). As we will see in the next chapter, persons—and their wellbeing—are all about activity.

## Note

1. There are the interesting cases of so-called 'depersonalisation disorder' in which sufferers report that they often have no sense of 'ownership' of their experiences. They feel as if they are on the outside looking into the world of what is their experience.

# References

Baumeister, R. F. (2011a). Self and identity: A brief overview of what they are, what they do, and how they work. In D. Braaten (Ed.), *Perspectives on the self: Conversations on identity and consciousness* (Vol. 1234, pp. 48–55, Annals of the New York Academy of Sciences). Oxford: Blackwell Science.

Baumeister, R. F. (2011b). The unity of self at the interface of the animal body and the cultural system. *Psychological Studies, 56*(1), 5–11. https://doi.org/10.1007/s12646-011-0062-5.

Binkley, S. (2014). *Happiness as enterprise: An essay on neoliberal life.* Albany: SUNY Press.

Binkley, S. (2018). The work of happiness: A response to De La Fabián and Stecher (2017). *Theory & Psychology, 28*(3), 405–410.

Bolier, L., Haverman, M., Westerhof, G. J., Riper, H., Smit, F., & Bohlmeijer, E. (2013). Positive psychology interventions: A meta-analysis of randomized controlled studies. *BMC Public Health, 13*(1), 119. https://doi.org/10.1186/1471-2458-13-119.

Cederström, C., & Spicer, A. (2015). *The wellness syndrome.* Cambridge: Polity.

Chater, N. (2018). *The mind is flat: The illusion of mental depth and the improvised mind.* London, UK: Allen Lane.

Clarke, G., Grenham, S., Scully, P., Fitzgerald, P., Moloney, R. D., Shanahan, F., et al. (2012). The microbiome-gut-brain axis during early life regulates the hippocampal serotonergic system in a sex-dependent manner [original article]. *Molecular Psychiatry, 18*, 666. https://doi.org/10.1038/mp.2012.77, https://www.nature.com/articles/mp201277#supplementary-information.

Danziger, K. (1997). The historical formation of selves. In R. D. Ashmore & L. Jussim (Eds.), *Self and identity: Fundamental issues* (pp. 137–159). Oxford: Oxford University Press.

Davies, W. (2015). *The happiness industry: How the government and big business sold us well-being.* London: Verso.

DeCarvalho, R. J. (1991). *The founders of humanistic psychology.* New York: Praeger.

Dennett, D. C. (1993). *Consciousness explained.* London: Penguin Books.

Diener, E. (1994). Assessing subjective well-being: Progress and opportunities. *Social Indicators Research, 31*(2), 103–157.

Diener, E., & Seligman, M. E. P. (2004). Beyond money: Toward an economy of well-being. *Psychological Science in the Public Interest, 5*(1), 1–31. https://doi.org/10.1111/j.0963-7214.2004.00501001.x.

Edwards, D., & Potter, J. (1992). *Discursive psychology*. London: Sage.

Fredrickson, B. L., & Kahneman, D. (1993). Duration neglect in retrospective evaluations of affective episodes. *Journal of Personality and Social Psychology, 65*(1), 45–55.

Giddens, A. (1991). *Modernity and self-identity: Self and society in the late modern age*. Stanford: Stanford University Press.

Harré, R. (1983). *Personal being: A theory for individual psychology*. Oxford: Blackwell.

Harré, R. (1998). *The singular self: An introduction to the psychology of personhood*. London: Sage.

Harré, R. (2016). Hybrid psychology as a human science. *Theory and Psychology, 26*(5), 632–646.

Haybron, D. M. (2008). *The pursuit of unhappiness: The elusive psychology of well-being*. Oxford: Oxford University Press.

Kahneman, D. (2011). *Thinking, fast and slow*. Australia: Penguin Group.

Kahneman, D., Fredrickson, B. L., Schreiber, C. A., & Redelmeier, D. A. (1993). When more pain is preferred to less: Adding a better end. *Psychological Science (0956–7976), 4*(6), 401–405.

Leary, M. R., & Buttermore, N. R. (2003). The evolution of the human self: Tracing the natural history of self-awareness. *Journal for the Theory of Social Behaviour, 33*(4), 365–404. https://doi.org/10.1046/j.1468-5914.2003.00223.x.

Lyubomirsky, S. (2013). *The myths of happiness: What should make you happy, but doesn't, what shouldn't make you happy, but does*. New York: The Penguin Press.

Martin, J., & Bickhard, M. H. (2012). An introduction to the special issue on "The new psychology of personhood". *New Ideas in Psychology, 30*(1), 86–88.

Meyers, M. C., van Woerkom, M., & Bakker, A. B. (2013). The added value of the positive: A literature review of positive psychology interventions in organizations. *European Journal of Work and Organizational Psychology, 22*(5), 618–632. https://doi.org/10.1080/1359432X.2012.694689.

Pickren, W. E. (2018). Psychology in the social imaginary of neoliberalism: Critique and beyond. *Theory & Psychology, 28*(5), 575–580. https://doi.org/10.1177/0959354318799210.

Rogers, C. R. (1959). A theory of therapy, personality, and interpersonal relationships, as developed in the client-centered framework. In S. Koch (Ed.), *Psychology: A study of a science: Study 1* (Vol. 3, pp. 184–256). New York: McGraw-Hill.

Ryan, R. M., & Deci, E. L. (2017). *Self-determination theory: Basic psychological needs in motivation, development, and wellness.* New York: Guilford Press.

Sedikides, C., & Skowronski, J. A. (1997). The symbolic self in evolutionary context. *Personality and Social Psychology Review, 1,* 80–102.

Sedikides, C., Wildschut, T., & Grouzet, F. (2018). On the temporal navigation of selfhood: The role of self-continuity. *Self and Identity, 17*(3), 255–258. https://doi.org/10.1080/15298868.2017.1391115.

Seligman, M. E. P. (2002). *Authentic happiness: Using the new positive psychology to realize your potential for lasting fulfillment.* New York: Free Press.

Seligman, M. E. P. (2011). *Flourish: A visionary new understanding of happiness and well-being.* New York: Free Press.

Seligman, M. E. P. (2018). PERMA and the building blocks of well-being. *The Journal of Positive Psychology, 13*(4), 333–335. https://doi.org/10.1080/17439760.2018.1437466.

Seligman, M. E. P., & Csikszentmihalyi, M. (2000). Positive psychology: An introduction. *American Psychologist, 55,* 51–82.

Sin, N. L., & Lyubomirsky, S. (2009). Enhancing well-being and alleviating depressive symptoms with positive psychology interventions: A practice-friendly meta-analysis. *Journal of Clinical Psychology, 65,* 467–487.

Stokes, P. (2017). Temporal asymmetry and the self/person split. *Journal of Value Inquiry, 51,* 203–219. https://doi.org/10.1007/s10790-016-9563-8.

Strawson, P. F. (1959). *Individuals: An essay in descriptive metaphysics.* London: Methuen.

Teo, T. (2018). *Homo neoliberalus*: From personality to forms of subjectivity. *Theory & Psychology, 28*(5), 581–599.

Wittgenstein, L. (1961/1922). *Tractatus logico-philosophicus* (D. F. Pears, & B. F. McGuinness, Trans.). London: Routledge and Kegan Paul.

# 5

# Persons and Their Wellbeing

## Two Accounts of Personhood

What are persons? To answer this question, I am going to rely on two prominent accounts of persons, or 'personhood', though these will be supplemented by other contributions at times. The first account is from the work of Rom Harré and colleagues (Harré 1983, 1998, 2016; Harré and Gillett 1994; Harré and Madden 1975; van Langenhove and Harré 1991). The second account is the theoretical framework developed by Jack Martin and his colleagues (Martin 2003, 2005, 2006a, 2010; Martin et al. 2010).

While the differences between each of these accounts are important and interesting, the broad outlines of each have considerable similarities. In both, persons are understood as embodied sites of agency, unity, continuity and uniqueness ('singularity') as well as locations from which skills, powers and capacities are exercised. That makes these theories capable of just the kinds of accounts of human action and experience (and, as I intend to show, wellbeing) that incorporate the sense we have of ourselves to which Strawson's analysis stays true but with which other approaches in psychology struggle. More interestingly, they incorporate

© The Author(s) 2019
K. Moore, *Wellbeing and Aspirational Culture*,
https://doi.org/10.1007/978-3-030-15643-5_5

these aspects within a naturalistic and objective account both of how these aspects arise and how they develop. The natural properties of our bodies are not neglected or seen as peripheral to who we are. A person, of necessity, is embodied so that she can engage in the kinds of activities characteristic of being a person. The 'hard problem' of holistic unity of our experience also becomes much clearer and more intelligible largely through being understood as a presumptive activity involved in being seen as, and seeing oneself as, a person. What I did yesterday is experienced by me as being one of *my* experiences just because that continuity over time is guaranteed and enforced by the world of persons, since that is why other persons take me as a person—in order to generate the reliable regularities required for the kind of human cooperativity and sociality within which they, themselves, exist. Similarly, the feature of continuity of our experiences (that they are all 'ours') no longer has to be seen as some neat trick achieved by our memory faculty (following the philosopher John Locke) or as being based on some kind of other evidential basis such as a psychic tag attached to our own experiences that we perceive through inner reflection and are able to show to ourselves to confirm our ownership of our experiences. Instead, it follows from the continued—largely discursive—use, and reporting, of materially and socially situated actions. Simply, we do not 'know' an experience is ours: we, and other persons, *take* it as ours—and that is more than enough to achieve the sense of continuity we experience.

The same is true for 'agency'. So often, agency is understood as some mysterious psychological capacity that, if it exists, would seem to defy notions of causal determinacy. Understandably, psychologists have a wariness about acknowledging this kind of agency (though belief in 'free will' can be accommodated—see Feldman et al. 2018). In everyday use, agency can too easily be seen as a magical power that bootstraps our actions and, in the ethical and political realms, that guarantees our individual human dignity. Without the assertion of agency, we might feel that our claims to be treated with dignity are under challenge. More relevantly to the focus of this book, the idea that we do not have such a mysterious agentic power may also threaten the logic of the entire ideology of aspiration. Yet, people talk about their experiences of being and acting in a free manner in ways that show that "freedom is not

something that one has; human freedom is something that one does …
[one] negotiates, constructs, and practices human freedom differently at
different times and under different circumstances, with varying degrees
of success" (Westcott 1992, p. 27).

By contrast, in these accounts of personhood, the apparent
'under-determination' of human action—which amounts to the conviction of agency—comes to be understood as either a grammatical
feature of the use of first-person pronouns or, relatedly, as the normative assessment (including one's own assessments) that actions are not
fully accounted for by either internal or external factors. Finally, the
uniqueness or 'singularity' of our point of view (or 'perspective') is able
to be rendered in theory in a way that avoids the conceptual trap of
solipsism and the paradoxes so often encountered when attempts are
made to explain the putative relationship between our (internal) experience and (external) reality. Accounts of this sense of a unique point
of view emphasise our training in the discursive uses of the pronoun 'I'
(in English) and its typical attachment both to a particular body and as
a substitute for natural expressions of feelings of that body, that occur
within arrays of material things and other persons. Such accounts of
personhood go a long way to demystifying—and resolving—the puzzles
that seem to flow from the uniqueness of our subjective experiences.

Rom Harré's account of personhood has developed over decades
(Harré 1983, 1998; e.g., see Harré 2016; Harré and Gillett 1994). At
its base, it concerns the way that the social and discursive activities we
carry out (i.e., speaking, listening, dialoguing, doing, and, now, writing)
produce a 'conversation' which is the "fundamental human experience"
and into which we make our individual contributions (Harré 1983, p.
20). It is an activity-based understanding of mind and the kind of activity that is its main focus is discursive (which includes our actions that,
of necessity, incorporate features of the material world). Out of that
'conversation' we come to have a 'theory' of ourselves as persons, based
on the particular cultural accounts of persons dominant at the time.
The "personal unity of unities" is how Harré (1983, p. 14) describes the
way we become a person by discursively connecting the three basic unities of (1) *consciousness* (i.e., our cognitive and affective unity); (2) *action
and agency* (i.e., a unity that entails our accountability, responsibility,

and social continuity as a person in a world of persons—and which, in this way, folds us into the 'local moral order'); and (3) of *biography* (i.e., the continuity of our life expressed in a meaningful life narrative). Being a person, in this view, means being able to accomplish each of these unities more or less successfully in a particular cultural milieu (this focus on the importance of 'unity' has been highlighted by Roy Baumeister, though he applies it to the notion of the 'self'—see Baumeister 2011).

Persons also are conceptually and practically related to their 'selves'. Early in his thinking, Harré (1983, p. 26) described the self as a "central constructing concept of individual human psychology" but its acquisition involves its appropriation from the "source analogue" of the "socially defined and sustained concept of 'person' that is favoured in the society under study". That is, we gain our 'theory' of our 'self' by idiosyncratically modelling it on our society's notion of a person. This happens through a process first described by Lev Vygotsky. Vygotsky (1978) famously argued that our higher psychological processes arise in two stages: first in the social world and, second, internalised in our personal psychology. Similarly, the 'self' begins as the cultural notion of a person but is then acquired by a person as her theory of herself. A person, therefore, is simply "a being who *orders his or her activities according to a theory* of his or her own nature" and "[t]o realize that one is a person is to learn a way of thinking about and *managing oneself*" (Harré 1983, p. 22, emphasis added). The kind of self we have affects how we manage, or navigate, our lives.

Harré (1998) argues that it is useful to distinguish three ways in which we talk about such a 'self'. All three ways can ultimately be seen as 'theoretical' or as 'fictions' and relate to our behaviour in much the way that any theory might. Self 1 is the origin point of action, which includes one's point of view or perspective. This self is typically—almost always, in fact—associated with a particular body which can be easily located and 'indexed' by other persons. It is this self that gives us our sense of 'singularity'—our uniqueness as a single person. Self 2 is our reflection on the value, meaning, and implications of that action (originating from the singularity of Self 1) and it does so in the form of our (actual) personal history, attributes and—importantly—our reflexive beliefs about our 'self'. Self 3, in keeping with George Herbert Mead's notion of the 'me', comprises others' interpretations of the components of Self 2. That is, it is what others make of us, irrespective of what we might believe about ourselves. It is also worth emphasising that, as Harré (1998, p. 70, emphasis added) phrases it, "[i]t is not generally true that each person has but one Self 2 and one Self 3"—since circumstances and situations can conjure variant forms of each—but that the "maintenance of the singularity of Self 1 *takes us to the borders of pathology*".

Self 1 is inherently singular but also dynamic; we change our point of view and perspective (spatially, psychologically, and socially) as part of our activity. That dynamism means that Self 2 (our actual attributes and our beliefs about those attributes) cannot fully determine our action— Self 2 gets applied from quite different perspectives and positions from moment to moment. This is why our life can appear, to ourselves and to others, as quite unpredictable and under-determined by either internal factors (e.g., our supposed 'personality') or external factors (the apparent 'situation'). This under-determination is also how Jack Martin (Martin 2006b; e.g., Martin 2012; Martin and Bickhard 2012) explains the sense we have of our agency and the agency of others. Further, "the pronoun 'I' is used not to refer to oneself but to *express* oneself as a singular, responsible being" (Harré 1998, p. 43, emphasis added) and "'I' is part of the grammatical machinery by which I *express* my point of view, not a device for referring to a subject to which properties and states are being ascribed" (Harré 1998, p. 61, emphasis added). This insight about the expressive aspect of most of our first-person utterances is borrowed from Wittgenstein's analysis. They are expressive *in our action*, in our world of 'doing' things as a person. In this way, our activity creates what we usually call our 'psychology' and psychological experiences through a steady stream of expressive acts. Also, these acts gain their sense of being expressive by virtue of being taken as the acts of a person (by ourselves or by other persons).

For Harré, persons exist within a personal ontology of things being *done* (Harré 2016). But persons—following Strawson's key insight—are also embedded in a material world which is taken as part of a 'molecular ontology' (of objects, causes, and processes). His call for a 'hybrid psychology', then, depends upon seeing how these two ontologies can be integrated, or at least sensibly shown to intersect. It is here that Harré (2016) echoes both Strawson's examples of less problematic (i.e., less seemingly dualistic) ascriptions we make (such as 'going for a walk') and Wittgenstein's intermediate case of an 'application' that makes sense of how meaning can be said to be both 'grasped in a flash' and 'extended over time'. His suggestion as to how a hybrid psychology could be understood is through what he calls the 'tool-task metaphor'. A person is a being that makes use of 'tools' (some of which come from the 'molecular ontology', such as brains) in order to carry out culturally constituted 'tasks' (such as being a—'good'—parent, demonstrating care of others and oneself, working hard eight hours a day, and the like). (I will make use of this metaphor when considering the wellbeing of persons.)

Martin et al. (2010, p. 27) provided a definition of a person that aligns well with Harré's account: "an identifiable, embodied individual human with being, self-understanding (self), and agentive capability". The 'identifiable' aspect of a person is that they are present in a physical array of objects (via their bodies) and in a social array of persons. Being 'embodied' is necessary for personhood but not sufficient. The self-understanding referred to is an understanding "that discloses [to others and oneself] and extends a person's being and activity in the world" in much the way that Harré's theoretical 'selves' operate (Martin et al. 2010, p. 28). The aspect of agency has already been discussed so I will not repeat myself here. What Martin highlights in much of his work is the importance in the development of persons of the ability to adopt 'perspectives'. He and his colleagues (Martin 2006a, b, 2012; Martin and Gillespie 2010) see this as central to the successful acquisition of personhood. The process is 'neo-Meadian' as it takes as its base the way George Herbert Mead emphasized the importance, in creating the self, of taking the perspective of the 'other'. (In fact, Mead apparently gained that insight from Adam Smith's focus on trade and market exchange—to happen, it requires each person in the trade to take the perspective of the other.) The importance of this point is that personhood is embedded, developmentally, in interactions with other persons. The form of those interactions will determine the extent to which this perspectivalism will successfully develop. It is not hard to imagine that modern forms of interaction (e.g., social media) will have their impact on that development.

These accounts of personhood, with their focus on discursive interactions, may seem to under-emphasise one aspect of our experience that can seem so dominant: feelings. But, as it turns out, the same analysis, based in the *activity* of persons, can be applied to our feelings. John Cromby and Willis (2016, p. 484) have argued that, based on Susanne Langer's and Alfred North Whitehead's philosophical accounts of feeling, we 'feel' in the verbal sense and to "say that what is felt is a 'feeling' is a deception of language". (More technically, the notion of a 'feeling' is a verbal noun.) On this account, our 'feelings' are also 'processes' or *actions* which—as with thoughts and speech and writing—are meaningful (and intentional) via their conventional incorporation into, and expression through, the grammar of their relevant concepts. To feel anger, upset, joy or disgust is to make a move in the grammar of those concepts. In making those moves, we frequently use our bodies and our physiology, including their 'natural expressions'. Flying into a violent rage—a classic example of the seemingly 'biologically driven', spontaneous and, in effect, uncontrollable nature of our 'emotional reactions'—is only taken (by us or by others) *as* a violent rage to the extent that it *is* a move in the grammar of 'anger'. Otherwise, it might be seen as a 'violent fit', a violent reaction to a psychoactive drug or some other expression of uncontrollable behaviour.

This understanding of feelings also means that what we normally call our thoughts or 'cognitions' can also be understood as imbued with feelings and supported by processes of feeling. To restate it in the terms of the way the 'I' expresses itself, feelings are encounters with the expressiveness of the world (e.g., the expressiveness of our bodies, social situations, the predicaments of others and ourselves). Our intuitions about what is going on, we could say, are felt by us as part of this expressively oriented activity.

If persons are these kinds of beings, and have the kind of being described above—including their feelings and affective life—what does this mean for our consideration of the wellbeing of persons? How should we think about what contributes to their—which is to say 'our'—wellbeing?

# The Wellbeing of Persons

Watching the continuous generation of nylon is one of my enduring memories of chemistry classes at school. The fibre was originally
released to the public in 1938 after over a decade of research at DuPont,
headed by Harvard chemist Wallace H. Carothers (who committed suicide in the same year nylon was brought to market). In house, it had
been known by a variety of names—Rayon 66 and Fiber 66 (named
after polyamide 6,6), and 'Duparon'. But I prefer the urban myth that
its name is composed of the abbreviations of the two major world cities
at the time: New York (NY-) and London (-LON). It would be nice
to think that its name reflects a process similar to its chemical creation
through the coming together of two chemical monomers: adipoyl chlo-
ride and hexamethylene diamine, each with six carbon atoms. The two,
acting as repeated six-carbon links in combination, provide an endlessly
repeating polyamide—'nylon'. The process is magical. In a beaker, one
chemical is poured on top of the other and, with the use of something
as simple as a fork, a chemistry teacher with steady hands can slowly
wind off a thread or even sheet-like creation of nylon. As it is wound
off, more of the chemicals interact and continue to create nylon until
one or other of the chemicals is fully used.

The way our personhood is continuously formed is much like the
production of nylon. Personhood is created and sustained by the constant coming together of our biological endowment and human culture.
Each one of us is 'wound off' from this interaction but, just as with
nylon, if the winding is too swift or jerky stresses can occur. The fabric
of our personhood can have holes, discontinuities, and 'impurities'. The
metaphor should not be pushed too far, but I find the image helpful to
understand the experience of personhood, and its vulnerabilities.

How should we understand the wellbeing of persons given the
account of persons and personhood just presented? To answer this question, I first reprise some of the central features of personhood. That
leads into a discussion of what it might mean to speak of persons being
'well' (as opposed to 'selves', 'human beings', 'bodies', 'minds', 'con-
sciousnesses', etc. being well). In brief, and at the most abstract level,
I argue that the wellbeing of persons depends upon (a) a particular

culture's requirements for personhood, including the demands and specific tasks given as requisites for the attainment of full-personhood; (b) access to the range of 'tools'—and the resources to develop them—necessary for a person to perform and master these requisite tasks; (c) the coherence or 'fit' between these kinds of 'tools' and the requisite tasks; and (d) the condition in which these tools are typically available to persons, relative to the requisite tasks.

To speak more plainly and to put some 'flesh' onto these abstract bones, it is important to remember that many of the 'tools' we use to be persons are parts and processes of our bodies such as our nervous systems, physiological functions and bodily capabilities (e.g., to enable the kinds of 'natural reactions', gestures, actions, activities and the like that may go along with a culture's conventional criteria for personhood). That implies that the process of development (ontogeny) not only determines the *extent* to which we are able to meet the requirements of personhood but also determines the 'condition' of the tools each of us develops individually with which personhood is established and then maintained. Just as digging and maintaining a vegetable garden depends on the condition of the tools we have for gardening, becoming a person similarly depends on the condition of the tools we have for establishing and maintaining the continual performance that is personhood. If all we have managed to acquire by way of appropriate tools is a flexible, rubber trowel we just will not do as well at gardening as someone who has acquired, through luck or social inheritance, a set of full-sized, hardened steel spades and other gardening tools. That is especially the case if the ground we have to dig is dry, compact and hard. As every worker knows, poor quality tools also have a predictable habit of breaking under the pressure of the everyday tasks for which they are supposedly made.

It is now well understood that both our neurodevelopment and general physical development is highly sensitive and responsive to environmental, especially social, contexts (e.g., see Keverne 2004; Lamblin et al. 2017). At least in today's world, for the first 20 years or so of life we are in a 'social womb'—or, to use a less biological metaphor, a neurological 'tool-making factory'—that fashions the neurological apparatus we get to use to generate personhood in line with the requirements of our culture. How the social environment (e.g., peer interactions during adolescence) interacts with brain development, especially those social-regulatory 'tools' or 'gadgets' (Heyes 2018) in the Pre-Frontal Cortex (PFC) that ramify out to deeper brain structures, will help determine susceptibility or resilience to mental health issues (Lamblin et al. 2017).

There is increasing appreciation of the embodiment that underpins our psychological experiences and capacities (e.g., see Anderson 2003). The nervous system evolved to coordinate motor activity and that original use is reflected in our cognitive and affective lives. It is this embodiment that is the first vital aspect of personhood.

Beyond the personhood 'tools' that are directly dependent upon the development of our bodies and organs, the presence and condition of the social and cultural prostheses implicitly or explicitly required for full personhood in a particular culture (e.g., health, literacy, a middle-class standard of education, etc.) also affect our performance on the tasks constitutive of personhood. In some instances, access to these tools may compensate for the lack of, or deterioration in, the necessary biological tools (e.g., hearing aids). In other cases, they may enhance the necessary personhood skills (e.g., public libraries). But it is the acquisition, mastery and employment of the basic discursive tools to achieve the culturally determined 'tasks' of personhood that has most bearing on our efforts to achieve and maintain personhood projects.

As I will discuss in more detail in Chapter 6, what I have called 'aspirational culture' has created a 'perfect storm' when it comes to establishing and maintaining personhood and its associated senses of self: as a starting point, aspirational culture involves a *particularly difficult* version of personhood to establish; at the same time it provides highly complex sets of tasks that, in the aggregate, are often mutually incoherent, contradictory (requiring quite different sets of 'tools' or skills to perform) and even incompatible in practical terms; its inherent mode of operation also systematically presents serious *obstacles to gaining access* to the 'tools' necessary for personhood and its sustainability; it then acts, in the majority of cases, to *degrade* the process by which the 'tools' required for the tasks of personhood are constructed (both in the development of bodily and neurological 'tools' and in the acquisition of discursive, social and economic 'tools').

Why does an aspirational culture create such a perfect storm for the prospects of personhood? As an economist might put it: Making something efficient at producing one thing does not necessarily make it efficient at producing other things. An aspirational culture—from its economic settings, social and political institutions, and legal and judicial systems through to the ordinary tasks and typical events of life— organizes its elements around the generation of quantifiably greater production and progress. Persons are one of the elements deployed to that end and they are therefore created to suit—or at least pursue—that purpose. The focus for persons then becomes what they can do or achieve, not how they can be reproduced, sustained or regenerated. Reproduction and regeneration are 'steady state' or 'maintenance' activities and are seen solely as a means to the end of more aspirational striving and outcomes. In short, persons cease to be ends. The guiding aphorism is 'to be *in order to* do' and not 'to do *in order to* be'. 'Merely' living is a waste of a life. And the legacy of a life is not measured in terms of how 'good' a person was but what that person achieved.

A major advantage of this account over current ones is that it provides a straightforward way to make sense, theoretically, of the otherwise perplexing paradoxes that surround the experience of wellbeing in today's world. By organizing personhood around the processes that have produced the sorts of objective improvements and progress that some argue characterize the modern world (e.g., economic prosperity, reductions in violence) we have, in effect, increasingly produced, as a more or less direct outcome, an experience of personhood that is weighted towards psychological suffering. As economists are fond of pointing out, there is no such thing as a free lunch. The difficulties we have with personhood—that is, difficulties in being a person—is the price we have collectively paid, and continue to pay, for the opportunity to dine on this progress.

As noted, I will return in Chapter 6 to the question of how our wellbeing as persons is faring in aspirational culture. But, for now, I want to consider how the wellbeing of persons could be understood in general terms, irrespective of the cultural context. Persons are 'doings' rather than things. They exist in action, not in brains. To say that a person 'has' a mind is really to say that they act with 'mindedness'—the complex patterns in their activity conform, more or less, to the 'grammar' of psychological concepts such as being cautious, thoughtful, angry, gullible, or any other number of psychological ascriptions we make about each other or ourselves.

This focus on activity means that persons are sociocultural artefacts that have no *internal* psychological complexity. All psychological complexity is in the activity of a person, made meaningful by its deeply conventional nature. The purpose of persons is therefore to perform tasks in the social world, and they can be judged on, and be held responsible for, the performance of those tasks. Nevertheless, by virtue of being taken as persons, either by themselves or by each other, they are deemed to have certain powers and capacities that they then use to accomplish the cultural tasks associated with being a person in a particular culture. That is, they have—or are ascribed—agency. In the world of persons, things are *done*, not caused.

Their lack of internal psychological complexity is a *grammatical* aspect of personhood, rather than an empirical feature, and follows from mastery of both first-person pronouns and the gamut of psychological concepts available in a particular culture. Persons create their psychology in the meaningful activities—discursively mediated—that they carry out in their lives primarily in interaction with other persons. That psychology (with its experiences, feelings and meanings) is therefore occurrent, situated and plastic. But, in keeping with the primary purpose of the sociocultural evolution of personhood, it is also directed towards the degree of continuity, stability and unity requisite for persons, and personhood, in the relevant cultural setting.

This siting of psychological phenomena in the activity of persons (often with other persons), rather than *within* persons, follows from two arguments. The first is Strawson's account of the concept of a person as 'logically primitive'. That concept is the starting point, rather than the consequence, of our understanding of other (psychologically relevant) concepts such as 'self', 'belief', 'memory', even 'body' (as in 'one's body'), etc.. That is, persons are not the products of pre-existing psychological processes. In the same way that a skein of nylon can be drawn out from the continuing interactions at the interface between two chemicals, persons are continuous enactments arising from the interplay of biology and culture (similar to the production of the 'self' as envisaged by Baumeister 2011).

The second argument from which the siting of psychological phenomena in the activity of persons follows is the pragmatic sociocultural concern with tracking and identifying the *actions* of members of a culture. Personhood, that is, was a necessary sociocultural invention to allow for the coordination of human beings (in the state to which they had evolved to that point) in such a way that generated the distinctive form of human sociality. It may well be that this basic requirement of personhood (to act as a social tracking mechanism) is closely associated with the parallel evolution of reciprocal altruism that Barresi (2012) has argued was central to the evolution of human personhood and the moral orders that are essential for our being as persons. This distinctive and cooperative (as opposed to competitive) aspect of human sociality no doubt required the development of ever more subtle means of tracking reciprocated encounters, especially as the forms of behaviour that needed to be tracked themselves became subtler. These enduring, repeated encounters would, in the evolutionary past, have occurred amongst dozens or scores of closely interacting persons and so could easily have driven a turbo-charged acceleration of the refinement of the discursive skills required to navigate these relationships.

If persons are, and should be, the target of our wellbeing concerns, then how can the wellbeing of persons be understood? What dimensions might characterize it? What activities and experiences might be said to manifest it? The starting point to answer questions of this type is to consider the general concept of wellbeing. As Huppert et al. (2004) defined it, wellbeing involves "a positive and sustainable state that allows individuals, groups or nations to thrive and flourish". If this definition is pared down to its essentials and made more general than its focus on individuals, groups and nations, 'wellbeing' becomes the general feature of *any* entity that allows that entity to thrive and flourish in a sustainable manner. This is a particularly useful definition, despite its generality, since it combines both 'state' and 'process' conceptualizations of wellbeing. An entity (any entity) has wellbeing when it is in some positive *state*—presumably dependent on the kind of entity it is and the kind of environment within which it exists—which allows it to thrive and flourish (i.e., the *process* of developing or growing to its fullest).

The wellbeing of persons then can be understood as the 'positive states' of persons which allow them to thrive and flourish in a sustainable manner. Those states are dependent upon the nature of the environment within which persons arise and the kind of 'entity' a person is. The discussion of theories of persons and personhood provides a first approximation of a characterization of both of these; the kind of entity that persons are, and the environment in which persons arise.

The 'positive states' of persons amount to the coherence of the performance of being a person based upon sufficient mastery of the broadly discursive skills in navigating the (locally appropriate) grammar of personhood. That is—and in Harré's terms—persons, as 'powerful particulars', are in 'positive states' to the extent that their powers, skills and capacities are sufficient to the demands of the tasks required of them as persons. These tasks are largely established culturally and may often require a combination of physical skills (behaviours) and linguistic skills (e.g., pointing, handshakes, bowing, a Māori hongi, the Añjali Mudrā (namaste) gesture).

This moral order is the normative and conventionally recognised system of standards of appropriateness or correctness in the performance of discursive acts. To participate fully in such a system is to be acting as a person; to be deemed—either by oneself or by others, or by both—as having acted in accord with these standards is to be deemed to be a person in good standing. Every local moral order will have its particular (normative) ways in which such standing is indicated or expressed, both by oneself or by others. For example, an act that is deemed to accord with the local moral order will likely be followed by the normative forms of support and acknowledgment by others (e.g., expressions of congratulations, back-slapping, applause) and by normatively appropriate expressions of pride, humility or the like by the person whose act it was seen to be.

Out of these considerations it is possible to isolate one centrally important aspect of being a person: The ability to 'go on' in one's culture. It is also possible to isolate one important obstacle to this ability to 'go on'—*disruption*. A person is the site at which disruptions to this ability to 'go on' are encountered and need to be navigated.

Continuity of action is a ubiquitous feature of animal life. A unicellular *Paramecium* under the microscope is fascinating to watch as a simple example of this need to go on. Their cells are surrounded by thousands of small hair-like extensions called 'cilia'. Like an array of oars on the sides of a Viking ship, the cilia propel the microbe through water until it encounters some obstacle. Almost instantaneously, the cilia will redirect their propulsion—even leading to the *Paramecium* reversing. Through trial and error it moves off somewhere else in its pursuit of food.

Examples of this principle of the continuity of action can be found elsewhere. At the other extreme, Ludwig Wittgenstein famously said that his aim in philosophy was to 'show the fly the way out of the fly-bottle'. This expressed his view that philosophy had become caught within its own 'fly-bottle' and could not escape—it did not know how to 'go on'. In fact, that was another way that he described his type of investigations—finding out how to go on or, even, escape from philosophising entirely. But continuity is also valued in very practical and everyday ways. Our 'quality' social relationships involve a degree of familiarity and comfort that means that our interactions can proceed with continuity and relative effortlessness. Long-lasting relationships provide this most clearly.

Most relevantly, we have already come across a significant role for continuity of action in accounting for experiences of deep happiness and wellbeing. The notion of 'flow' (see Chapters 3 and 6) and related concepts of 'engagement' are all about this ability to 'go on'. The effortlessness and enjoyment experienced in moments of flow experience, for example, are characteristic of the coming together of ability and setting in an uninterrupted and experientially seamless manner.

The opposite experience is of disruption and that, too, is familiar and recurrent in life. In evolutionary theory there is the idea—as part of 'strategic interference theory'—that humans are especially attuned to any threats to the completion of strategic goals (e.g., finding a mate, gaining access to valued resources such as food). 'Negative' emotions such as anger and envy are, in effect, signalling systems to let us know that the achievement of some goal has either been frustrated or is under threat (Hill and Buss 2008). More personally, the experience of consciousness is itself a response to disruption (Baumeister et al. 2011).

This is not surprising as the complicated feedback and 'over-ride' features of human neurology—especially from the PFC—appear to have been evolved for just this kind of 'interruptive' function. Certainly, self-consciousness is disruptive of the experience of flow and of performance in general (Baumeister 1984). Beyond the individual, social hierarchies are complex social organisations that serve a similar role to the interruptive function of cortical brain areas. As anyone who has had a close encounter with a bureaucracy will know, the regulation, interruption and even disruption of ongoing activity is par for the course.

Life, as we all know, is far more complicated than conforming, as required, to transparent standards of appropriateness. It is often just a series of attempts to maintain some sense of personal continuity amidst frequent disruption—by others, by social institutions, by ourselves (as we 'self-monitor' our activity). Sometimes we may feel no such wish to conform or, indeed, we may actively feel like rebelling against conventional standards. At other times, the discursive accounts people provide of our actions may conflict with either our own accounts or those of others. Each of these incidents—encountered many times every day—make the experience of continuity fleeting at best. Our skills at navigating these discursively fraught situations, along with the skills deployed by others in the same situations, will no doubt impact our standing in, and as a result of, these encounters. But, to add more complication, in order for this positive standing to be sustained over time (ultimately, over a lifetime) it will not be enough to successfully navigate particular situations. Given that we are persons whose actions are continually 'tagged' to us, there is also a need to provide a continuous and coherent narrative of our life, what Harré (1983) terms an 'autobiography'. The more disruptions we experience as part of our daily life, the more difficult it will be to construct such a coherent narrative, and the greater the narrative skills we will require.

If what I have briefly discussed here amounts to the beginnings of an account of the wellbeing of persons (i.e., of personhood) what is left to consider is the extent to which an aspirational culture can support this kind of wellbeing. The next chapter addresses this question but, as should by now be clear, the prospects for the wellbeing of persons in aspirational cultures does not look promising.

# References

Anderson, M. L. (2003). Embodied cognition: A field guide. *Artificial Intelligence, 149*(1), 91–130. https://doi.org/10.1016/S0004-3702(03)00054-7.

Barresi, J. (2012). On seeing our selves and others as persons. *New Ideas in Psychology, 30*(1), 120–130.

Baumeister, R. F. (1984). Choking under pressure: Self-consciousness and paradoxical effects of incentives on skillful performance. *Journal of Personality and Social Psychology, 46,* 610–620.

Baumeister, R. F. (2011). The unity of self at the interface of the animal body and the cultural system. *Psychological Studies, 56*(1), 5–11. https://doi.org/10.1007/s12646-011-0062-5.

Baumeister, R. F., Masicampo, E. J., & Vohs, K. D. (2011). Do conscious thoughts cause behavior. *Annual Review of Psychology, 62,* 331–361.

Cromby, J., & Willis, M. E. H. (2016). Affect—Or feeling (after Leys). *Theory & Psychology, 26*(4), 476–495. https://doi.org/10.1177/0959354316651344.

Feldman, G., Farh, J.-L., & Wong, K. F. E. (2018). Agency beliefs over time and across cultures: Free will beliefs predict higher job satisfaction. *Personality and Social Psychology Bulletin, 44*(3), 304–317. https://doi.org/10.1177/0146167217739261.

Harré, R. (1983). *Personal being: A theory for individual psychology.* Oxford: Blackwell.

Harré, R. (1998). *The singular self: An introduction to the psychology of personhood.* London: Sage.

Harré, R. (2016). Hybrid psychology as a human science. *Theory and Psychology, 26*(5), 632–646.

Harré, R., & Gillett, G. (1994). *The discursive mind.* London: Sage.

Harré, R., & Madden, E. H. (1975). *Causal powers.* Oxford, UK: Blackwell.

Heyes, C. (2018). *Cultural gadgets: The cultural evolution of thinking.* Cambridge, MA: Harvard University Press.

Hill, S. E., & Buss, D. M. (2008). Evolution and subjective well-being. In M. Eid & R. J. Larsen (Eds.), *The science of subjective well-being* (pp. 80–96). New York: Guildford Press.

Huppert, F. A., Baylis, N., & Keverne, E. B. (2004). Introduction: Why do we need a science of well-being? [Introduction to a special issue]. *Philosophical Transactions of the Royal Society B-Biological Sciences, 359,* 1331–1332. https://doi.org/10.1098/rstb.2004.1519.

Keverne, E. B. (2004, September 29). Understanding well-being in the evolutionary context of brain development. *Philosophical Transactions of the Royal Society of London B. Biological Sciences, 359*(1449), 1349–1358.

Lamblin, M., Murawski, C., Whittle, S., & Fornito, A. (2017). Social connectedness, mental health and the adolescent brain. *Neuroscience and Biobehavioral Review, 80,* 57–68.

Martin, J. (2003). Emergent persons. *New Ideas in Psychology, 21*(2), 85–99.

Martin, J. (2005). Real perspectival selves. *Theory & Psychology, 15*(2), 207–224. https://doi.org/10.1177/0959354305051364.

Martin, J. (2006a). Positions, perspectives, and persons. *Human Development, 49*(2), 93–95.

Martin, J. (2006b). Reinterpreting internalization and agency through G.H. Mead's perspectival realism. *Human Development, 49*(2), 65–86.

Martin, J. (2010). The psychology of personhood: Conditions for a viable, neo-meadian pluralism. *New Ideas in Psychology, 28*(2), 219–226.

Martin, J. (2012). Coordinating with others: Outlining a pragmatic, perspectival psychology of personhood. *New Ideas in Psychology, 30,* 131–143. https://doi.org/10.1016/j.newideapsych.2009.11.007.

Martin, J., & Bickhard, M. H. (2012). An introduction to the special issue on "The new psychology of personhood". *New Ideas in Psychology, 30*(1), 86–88.

Martin, J., & Gillespie, A. (2010). A neo-meadian approach to human agency: Relating the social and the psychological in the ontogenesis of perspective-coordinating persons. *Integrative Psychological and Behavioral Science, 44*(3), 252–272. https://doi.org/10.1007/s12124-010-9126-7.

Martin, J., Sugarman, J., & Hickinbottom, S. (2010). *Persons: Understanding psychological selfhood and agency.* New York: Springer.

van Langenhove, L., & Harré, R. (1991). Varieties of positioning. *Journal for the Theory of Social Behaviour, 21,* 393–407.

Vygotsky, L. S. (1978). *Mind in society.* Cambridge, MA: Harvard University Press.

Westcott, M. A. (1992). *The psychology of personal freedom.* New York: Springer-Verlag.

# 6

# Aspirational Culture in the Balance

Persons are continuous creations that emerge at the boundaries of our biology and our culture. In a rough sense, a person's wellbeing depends upon the fit between that biology and culture and, so, on the smoothness of that emergence. With the caveat that the concept of an 'aspirational culture' is as much theoretical as descriptive, the question that needs to be answered is how good aspirational culture is at establishing and maintaining personhood? Aspirational culture, I have argued, is not just expressed by individuals. Each of us can be more or less aspirational in our own lives. We can aspire to 'intrinsic' or 'extrinsic' goals (Kasser and colleagues' work). But irrespective of our individual predispositions or propensities, we all have to live in a world that is deeply structured for aspiration. It is not only individuals that aspire but entire economies and societies. Schools, universities, private homes, services, goods, social 'networks', cities, transportation, technology, and the prodigious offerings around self- and other-care have all arisen imbued with, and in support of, aspirational ends. Yet, all of this growth, progress, change, improvement—and the widespread 'creative destruction' it brings in its wake—mean that all adjustments and adaptive responses individuals may be able to enact provide increasingly brief periods of relief and

© The Author(s) 2019
K. Moore, *Wellbeing and Aspirational Culture*,
https://doi.org/10.1007/978-3-030-15643-5_6

refuge. This brevity of respite applies not only to individuals but also to organisations, firms, social institutions, governments, nation states and, most worryingly of all, the planet.

From the fateful shift to the agricultural way of life that started to drive human ultrasociality some 10,000–12,000 years ago; through the emergence of an array of experiments and variants of hierarchical societies, economic systems, civilisations and empires; to today's globalised 'risk society' or 'liquid modernity' with its unleashed dynamism, uncertainty, discontinuities and near-chaotic restlessness, the 'race' has become increasingly breathless. From life's accidental discovery of the remarkable trick of replication (using DNA or its precursors), the hallmark of the living world has been to find more and more creative ways to maintain stability via evolved systems that successfully self-regulate themselves long enough to reproduce, often with a degree of variation. Today, for our species at least, an experiment is underway. One of life's most complex creations—the sociocultural artefact known as a person—is being put to the test. Can it survive, or perhaps even thrive, in a world in which—to borrow a cliché—the only constant is change? Can this creation find in such a world a sufficiently robust regularity (perhaps at some advanced level of abstraction) that can support its sense of its own stability and, so, existence?

These questions remain unanswered, though the answers are working themselves out in real time. In this chapter, my aim is more modest. From what is known from theories of personhood and from the state of empirical work on individual wellbeing, I will provide an initial assessment of the extent to which aspirational culture supports or undermines our wellbeing. An initial caution is that my interpretation of the state of play of empirical findings on wellbeing will inevitably be partial and others may disagree with the work I highlight and the conclusions I draw from it. There is not the space in this book to defend my assessment of the intersection between aspirational culture and wellbeing as robustly as I could. Hopefully, however, the following is enough at least to provide stimulus for others to think in greater depth and detail about what it means to understand individual wellbeing through a focus on the prospects for personhood in an aspirational culture.

At first blush, there is much about an aspirational culture that appears conducive to personal wellbeing. Most obviously, if aspirational culture has achieved anything it has provided better material circumstances for many people (see Chapter 1). With more absolute wealth available there should be more opportunity to provide personal and social capabilities (see Dalziel et al. 2018 for a recent discussion of Amartya Sen's capabilities approach to wellbeing economics). Increases in (distributed) wealth should also be able to satisfy more desires, although it has no doubt generated many more targets for those desires. But these seemingly logical consequences of increased wealth are based on the assumption that human wellbeing depends fundamentally on the sovereignty of the individual to define, and be able to act upon, their own desires (see Haybron 2008 for a thorough conceptual consideration and critique of this assumption). The person-based account of wellbeing I have been arguing for suggests that individuals are struggling to exert that presumed authority. To live a life of wellbeing is not simply a matter of pursuing desires. It involves navigating a culture. That ceaseless project depends upon the tasks the culture presents and the 'tools', skills and capacities the culture has provided through each person's trajectory of psychological development and experience. Given the research on wellbeing, the question is how well, or to what extent, aspirational culture supports the generation and maintenance of our wellbeing.

When seen from the perspective of the daily lives of people, aspirational culture seems to support many features that are thought to be vital and central to wellbeing. Some of these features include the role of goals associated with achievement and accomplishment, the importance of personal autonomy and competence, the associated apparent freedom for the expression of curiosity, play, creativity, relatedness and other forms of immersed engagement, and the pursuit of one's true or authentic self. I will discuss each of these features in turn. They are some of the most likely candidates that might support the claim that today's aspirational culture is, overall, good for our wellbeing. I will ultimately conclude, however, that even these 'wellbeing-friendly' features are themselves undermined by that culture.

# Goals

The mere act of consciously having an important, valued goal, even if no progress is made towards it, provides an increment in SWB—though actually making some progress towards it adds further increments (King 2008). Goals are also advantageous in the way they provide structure for our daily lives, providing a sense of meaning, purpose and direction to them. We can establish daily routines—or even rituals—for fitness or to practice a skill. Being valued, personal goals also direct our emotional lives. We respond emotionally to the vicissitudes and events of life through the prism of our goals—does what has just happened help or hinder us in our goal pursuit? As part of that emotional mediation, goals can also make sense of aversive emotional events. The boring job needed to save money for the trip of a lifetime or the arduous effort of self-discipline to study for years to gain a qualification can be made sense of by a deeply held and valued goal. We suffer now to achieve our future goals, which helps us be reconciled to the suffering. Goals also allow us to counter what wellbeing researchers have called the 'hedonic treadmill', the finding that people adapt to any event or circumstance—such as, in a classic study, winning a lottery or having an accident—and return, more or less, to some previous hedonic 'baseline' (Brickman and Campbell 1971; Brickman et al. 1978). The pursuit of goals can counter this process by allowing a goal to be replaced by a new or modified goal if the initial goal is either achieved or been frustrated. That is, the 'hedonic treadmill' comes to be off-set by a 'goal-treadmill' which can continue to generate the kinds of affect and meaningfulness characteristic of wellbeing.

However, in my terms, the hedonic and goal treadmills together form the opposing forces that make up the 'aspirational treadmill'. As Bauman's notion of liquid modernity (Bauman 2000, 2007) suggests, aspirations themselves are subject to alteration and reconfiguration at a moment's notice as social forms continue in their constant process of shape-shifting and so "cannot serve as frames of reference for human actions and long-term life strategies because of their short life expectation" (Bauman 2007, p. 1). In a thorough-going aspirational world, goal-redundancy accelerates which requires, as a response, either the effortful ramping up of goal-setting activity and an increase in the speed of goal pursuit or, less positively, become reconciled to the need to surrender the option of structuring one's life around goals.

In his Ph.D. dissertation (and later publications), Robert Emmons called these personal goals 'personal strivings' (Emmons 1986a, b). 'Striving' emphasizes the requirement of effort; and effort does not always pay off. Emmons (1986a) was principally interested in formulating a motivational account of personality that would also help explain our emotions (affect). In a study of the 'personal strivings' of forty undergraduates, he found that positive affect was associated with how valued the 'striving' (as a noun) was to the person and, importantly, their past success at fulfilling goals through striving. Negative affect, by contrast, was associated with a low probability of striving success, ambivalence about the goal being pursued, and conflict between different valued goals ('between striving conflict'). In a related study, Diener and Fujita (1995) compared the kinds of resources people had with their reported SWB and how 'personal strivings' intersected with this relationship. There was a moderate positive relationship between total resources and SWB but reported life satisfaction (LS) was more closely associated with available resources than were measures of affect. It was also social and personal resources, rather than material resources (such as money), that best predicted SWB. The most interesting finding, however, was that the kinds of resources a person had correlated most closely with SWB when they were relevant to the kinds of 'personal strivings' (goals) the person had. Showing that people try their best to make the most of whatever resources they happen to have, participants in the study tended to choose goals that aligned with their available resources. Which is just as well, since SWB depended upon the congruence between the kinds of resources available to individuals and the types of 'strivings' they valued. Striving for a goal, no matter how valued, is a recipe for low SWB when you do not have the resources to achieve it.

It would be easy to assume that personal goals (or 'strivings') mesh neatly into an aspirational culture. As a sub-genre of popular books and articles on motivation and success, promotion of goal-setting occupies the heartland of aspirational advice. But there are good reasons to argue that, counterintuitively, today's aspirational culture is not fertile ground for goal pursuit to flourish. Our culture certainly implores and even harangues us to set our 'own' goals but how supportive is it of such efforts?

As already noted, aspirational culture is a culture of unrelenting change and, therefore, can only be navigated by constant adjustment of one's life. That includes goals. Goals themselves become fungible, subject to constant revision and even abandonment as the environment morphs (jobs are lost, bureaucratic processes are revised and reformed, people move away, relationships begin and end—all seemingly at an accelerating rate). It is no coincidence that encouragement for goal-setting as a way to wellbeing has been in lock-step with research on the wellbeing advantages of 'GRIT', self-regulation and perseverance. The Robert-the-Bruce injunction to 'try, try, try again!' is now extended into a near infinite series of self-exhortations if we hope to achieve our goals. The striving required in our 'personal strivings' is becoming harder and harder and their success is becoming less and less certain so what is called for is more GRIT, more self-control, and more perseverance.

The famous longitudinal Dunedin Study which followed a cohort of 1037 people from birth to (currently) their late 30s found that, in our world, self-control is as good a predictor of life-success as IQ or social class—though it is highly correlated with class and IQ to begin with (Moffitt et al. 2011). Health and wealth outcomes are significantly better for those with self-control than without and the former are also far less likely to end up with a criminal conviction by age 32. Not only that, but the better outcomes associated with self-control are on a steady gradient: The more self-control the better the outcomes. Simply, those persons who failed to acquire the 'powers' of self-control in an aspirational society—a society that is increasingly difficult to navigate—are at a marked disadvantage, often falling into so-called 'snares' during adolescence (e.g., dropping out of school, having children, taking up smoking). In the face of this escalation in effort, it is no wonder that fewer people seem able to summon the energy required to aspire to their goals or to maintain the conviction that they have what it takes to achieve them.

Goals are also set *for* us. While we may set ourselves personal goals, our world has goals of its own that we are required to achieve—and usually prioritise—not for our individual benefit but in order to meet the imperatives of the ultrasocial system upon which society depends and which aspirational culture enacts. While the most obvious example of this 'external' goal-setting is work (which, for most, is simply employment), it is also prominent in our leisure and social lives. An increasingly important aspect of those spheres of our lives is the need for 'emotional intelligence' and the corresponding amount of 'emotional labour' (Rojek 2010). The modern world requires us to become aware of a "pedagogy of the emotions" as a "pre-condition for smooth social relations and a robust personal image" (Rojek 2010, p. 243). The spread of demands for care of self ('self-care') and care for others (Rojek 2005) call forth a need to demonstrate what Rojek (2010) calls 'competent agency' and, crucially, "[s]elf-coaching is the axis around which care for the self and care for others is organized" (Rojek 2010, p. 251). Care for the self is, in effect, the province of the new applied science of wellbeing (with some 'care for others' attached, as advice to work on altruism and gratitude, as a further supplement to personal wellbeing). It includes "various coaching tips and styles of monitoring and reconnaissance that contribute to the physical, psychological, and emotional wellbeing of the individual" such as knowledge about "stress management, healthy diet, grooming, exercise, environmental risks to well-regulated embodiment, multi-cultural and multi-ethnic tolerance, and so on" (Rojek 2010, p. 245).

Tellingly, this ethic of self- and other-care arose as a "hallmark of modern personality" (Rojek 2010, p. 245) simultaneous with the algal-like blooming of the service sector in modern economies. When the economy depends upon ubiquitously available 'soft skills' in its workforce it is hardly surprising that the 'ethic' to demonstrate competency in these skills has also blossomed in leisure, social and interpersonal spheres. This 'competence' with emotional intelligence comes at a personal price. It requires *reconnaissance*—"the process of evaluating the classification systems, codes of communication, and representations of performance that indicate competence"—and *monitoring*—"the system of checks that individuals use to assess competence in themselves and other agents" (Rojek 2010, pp. 243–244). That is, we need to devote energy to finding out how we need to act to be taken credibly *and* to continuously 'test' our performance, and that of others, against those standards.

All of this laborious emotional work ('emotional labour') is part of acquiring the necessary emotional intelligence to operate credibly in the current, aspirational world. We must aspire to gain and demonstrate—at the right time and place and in the right circumstances—the skills needed to show our good standing relative to this culturally normative set of mores. Rojek (2010, p. 243) sees these efforts as arising from what Bourdieu famously referred to as *'habitus'*—the "frames of knowledge, mores of communication and systems of classification, and modes of interpersonal behaviour learned through socialization". Transmitted through family and community—now including and often dominated by digital and social media—the *habitus* amounts to "the *normative institutions of coercion* in society" (Rojek 2010, p. 243, emphasis added). Less ominously, they are simply the available cultural, practical and discursive resources a culture deploys to generate the persons—and the required tasks and projects they should adopt—that constitute and that, through their activity, will reconstitute the culture. To be a fully-fledged and acknowledged person in our culture—and therefore to see ourselves as fully competent persons in that culture—we have to achieve not just the 'extrinsic' aspirational goals of 'success' but also show that our 'self' manifests the achievement, or at least is in pursuit of, the appropriate 'intrinsic' aspirational goals (Kasser and colleagues' work).

Looked at in this way, even the 'deep' and 'authentic' intrinsic goals we have chosen and fully endorsed (Ryan and Deci 2017) can have their own 'agenda', one which cares little for us as persons. In fact, it has already been noticed that our goals may be 'selfish' in exactly the same sense that Richard Dawkins (Dawkins 1976) characterised the selfishness of our genes in his book *The Selfish Gene*. Though referencing the operation of 'unconscious' goals—in my view, mistakenly—Huang and Bargh (2014) have argued that 'goals' can be activated without any conscious intention by the person. Once activated, later cognitive processing of the environment (e.g., social situations) is constrained as the goal embarks on a path determined by its inherent tendency to achieve its own end. Meanwhile, that trajectory of behaviour may not be in the best interests of the individual person who enacts the goal pursuit—who, to echo Dawkins (1976), is a 'vehicle' for goal attainment. Huang and Bargh (2014) suggest that our capacity to pursue conscious goals evolved out of these 'unconscious' forms of 'triggered' goal pursuit. The advantage of this understanding of goals as having their own 'interests' is that it helps explains the ubiquitous inconsistency in the goals that we, as individual persons, pursue and the, often alarming, rate of chopping and changing of the goals we pursue as the environment 'triggers' these 'selfish goals', unchosen by us. That is, it helps explain the difficulty we have in maintaining personal consistency and 'integrity' across the highly differentiated and changing roles and settings we encounter on a daily basis in today's world—a difficulty that undermines establishment of a robust personhood.

It takes only a little theoretical tweaking to fit this 'Selfish Goal Theory' into the framework I have developed in this book. As Chater (2018) has convincingly argued (see Chapter 4), there is no need to think that our minds have 'depth', especially in the sense of some mythical inner realm of psychological processes. 'Yes', we can understand the brain as an information processor but, 'no', that does not commit us to the idea that 'unconscious'—yet still psychological—events and states exist somewhere buried in the brain's complexity. That picture may be necessary to sustain the modern notion of an inner self, but that is an ideological rather than scientific convenience. Once the theoretical focus on a supposed 'unconscious' inner world is foresworn it is then a short step to suggest that these 'goals' are embedded in individuals via a history of social and discursive interaction provided through the interlocked nature of cultural institutions and practices (as discussed in Chapter 2). That culture then developmentally inserts into us the particular neurocognitive 'gadgets' we need so that we can understand these goals and have the cognitive capacities to pursue them. These gadgets (e.g., ones to support 'metacognition'—'thinking about thinking') are the 'tools' that allow us to perceive life in terms of goals (in an aspirational culture). Through that developmental experience they are also preset to be activated (in the 'unconscious' way described by Huang and Bargh 2014) by the sociocultural situations and settings that prevailing institutions and practices ensure are the everyday circumstances of our lives. The most obvious examples of this predicament are the 'triggering' of goals such as for social acceptance, attractiveness, mating, and status through marketing and advertising. This pervasive experience of 'unconscious' activation of goals can lead to inconsistent goal pursuit (e.g., spending money on a product or service to achieve the goal of appearing attractive while pursuing a consciously determined budget, all resulting in the experience of what Greek philosophers called 'akrasia'—failure of the will). But there are less obvious examples. On one occasion we might laugh along with a racist joke to achieve the goal of social acceptance. At another time, we might re-tweet an anti-racism meme to achieve the goal of consciously supporting a cause we deeply believe in (or, less virtuously, to achieve the goal of self-enhancement or, again, social acceptance).

Aspirational culture certainly supports the experience of life as a goal-saturated phenomenon. At the same time, though, it can undermine the kind of goal pursuit that, by providing continuity of action, biography (personal narrative) and agency, could enhance one's well-being as a person. The speed of change, the heightened experience of uncertainty, and the ephemeral nature of 'social forms' (that is, of "structures that limit individual choices, institutions that guard repetitions of routines, patterns of acceptable behaviour"—Bauman [2007, p. 1]) all work together to make the goals a person sets for herself hard to achieve. Even worse, the cultural environment—with aspirational imperatives for progress, change and improvement infusing all its aspects and institutions—presents a hostile context for all but the most skilled and lucky persons to pursue their goals.

Finally, goal content has long been found to be related to wellbeing, especially the distinction between 'intrinsic' and 'extrinsic' goals (see discussion of the Aspiration Index in Chapter 2) (Kasser 2002; Kasser and Ryan 1993, 1996). Those who pursue the intrinsic goals such as personal growth, community involvement, and relationships have significantly higher vitality, physical health, social functioning and levels of self-actualisation than those who pursue extrinsic goals such as financial success, fame and image. The relationship holds not only for the *pursuit* of these two types of goals but also their *attainment*—attaining intrinsic goals is significantly related to wellbeing but attaining extrinsic goals is not (see review by Deci and Ryan 2000). How, then, does an aspirational culture enhance or impede pursuit and attainment of these two types of goals?

In a practical sense, the likelihood of attaining goals such as quality relationships and community involvement is reduced in modern aspirational cultures. High residential mobility, a feature of aspirational cultures, encourages a friendship strategy that involves many friendships but weak ties (Oishi 2010). By contrast, people in residentially stable societies have fewer friendships but far stronger ones, characterised by substantial (i.e., 'costly'), mutual obligations and commitments. Further, people who are frequently on the move also tend to have a very open and positive view of making friends. Conversely, people who are residentially stable are more cautious, or even negative, about adding potentially costly friends to their friendship network. Both are adaptive friendship strategies—in a 'cost-benefit' sense—relative to the prevailing degree of residential mobility. Having a large friendship network in a residentially stable society, for example, would be an extremely 'costly' strategy (since you could almost constantly be called upon by one or other friend for major obligations to support them through major crises). Instrumentally, both work. But it is the presence of high quality, established and enduring social relationships that are more supportive of wellbeing. If there is one finding that is 'gold-plated' in research on wellbeing (and, indeed, on human development) it is the crucial requirement of supportive, quality social connections. And the flipside is that loneliness is a stark indicator of human illbeing.

## Autonomy and Competence

Closely connected to goals and their pursuit are experiences of autonomy and competence. These are two of the three so-called 'universal needs' identified by Ryan and Deci (2017) as fundamental to self-determined behaviour and, by extension, human wellbeing. Self-determined activity also typically comes along with a serving of positive affect such as joy and optimism (see Chapters 3 and 4). Fulfilling these needs has repeatedly been found to improve wellbeing (Deci and Ryan 2000).

The sense of being in control of one's own life is also a consistent indicator of wellbeing.

It might be thought that an aspirational culture would positively encourage autonomy (literally, 'self-government') and competence since both of these attributes would seem necessary for the innovation and skills needed to support future economic growth, daily adjustment to rapidly changing technologies, increasingly mobile, multicultural and diverse societies and the fleet-footed adaptability that characterises the ideal individual in such a culture.

From the perspective advanced in this book, autonomy is less a human 'need' than it is a constitutive element that comes from the enactment of personhood. That is an important distinction. In effect, only by being taken as a person (again, by ourselves as well as by others) can we move out of the realm of a 'molecular ontology' of neurophysiological and bodily events and into the 'person ontology' of intention, agency and responsibility (Harré 1998, 2016). The assumption of autonomy is crucial to that movement. Without that assumption—made by both oneself and others—persons who can be seen as agents with moral obligations and responsibilities would be impossible. It is part of the practice of seeing people as morally responsible agents that they must be considered competent and autonomous enough in relation to the act for which they are held responsible. A person, for example, is not usually considered responsible for what they do when under the influence of a powerful psychoactive drug; but, of course, they can be held responsible for taking the drug in the first place (but, again, they are *not* held responsible if the drug was imbibed through a drink spiked by someone else without their knowledge). In other words, there would be no persons—taken to be acting as morally effective agents—if autonomy was not a given. The experience of autonomy is not, then, something that makes us (perhaps understood as 'selves') *feel good* through fulfillment of a 'need'; it is central to the experience of seeing oneself as a person and being taken as a person.

Autonomy, as we have already seen, is a casualty of the ultrasocial form of life our species adopted some 10,000 years ago (Gowdy and Krall 2016). Because of the extensive specialization and division of labour characteristic of ultrasociality, members of these societies evolve in the direction of relinquishing autonomy. (Put another way, autonomy remains but the circle within which it operates becomes increasingly constricted.) For our species, however, this is especially problematic since the evolution of ultrasociality has not occurred deep within our biological natures but, instead, through a powerfully selected process of cultural evolution. Ultrasocial human societies out-compete less ultrasocial human societies through the more or less ruthless way that they sacrifice individual human autonomy and wellbeing to the interests of a social and economic form that, partly through its inherent instability, can dominate ecosystems, which includes other human societies.

But, is there any evidence that humans, today, are experiencing reduced levels of personal autonomy? Yes, there is. There has been a remarkable shift in young people's sense of personal control over a forty-year period. The finding comes from a meta-analysis of 138 studies with a total sample size of 25,000 college students and children aged 9–14 years in the United States conducted from 1960 to 2002 that used Rotter's Internal-External Locus of Control scale and, for the younger children, the Children's Nowicki-Strickland Internal-External Control Scale (Twenge et al. 2004). Locus of Control (or 'Perceived Locus of Control') refers to our perceptions of where the control over our lives sits: Either with *external* events, people and forces (e.g., luck, fate, parents, society, etc.) or *internal* capacities, attributes and skills (e.g., intelligence, effort, choice, physical strength, personality, etc.). You might think that the modern world with its focus on individualism and personal freedom would generate young people who increasingly have the sense of being in control—what Twenge et al. (2004, p. 309) refer to as the 'Independence Model' which would suggest that, "Modern people are, in theory, strong, independent individuals in control of their own destinies and free of the confines of social forces". In fact, what was found is that the marked shift in Locus of Control was a full 0.8 standard deviations towards a perceived *external* locus of control. Young people increasingly feel less in control of their lives. In 2002, the average college student had a more external locus of control than 80% of college students at the start of the 1960s. This fits with the prediction of an 'Alienation Model' that is linked to an increase in negative social indicators over the same period (e.g., increased divorce rates, crime, political disengagement and cynicism) along with an increased tendency to what is known as the 'self-serving bias'—to take the credit for the good things that happen in our lives and to blame external factors for bad events. In an environment with more negative events, the self-serving bias is likely to increase given its role as a self-protective mechanism. Paradoxically, an individualistic society is likely to promote the self-serving bias (to avoid the judgment from others and from oneself that one has in some way failed as an independent individual). The self-serving bias is also known to be positively correlated with an external locus of control (Campbell and Sedikides 1998). The self-serving bias and the tendency to 'blame others' is often seen as a moral failing that demands a constant upbraiding of people who succumb to its temptation. But it might make more sense to see it as an adaptive response to a world that has 'upped the ante' on personal responsibility while, simultaneously, has produced an uncertain and unpredictable social and economic environment which has made it much harder to take responsibility. That is, in our attempts to maintain our personhood and good standing as a person in an increasingly hostile social environment, it is no surprise that we will try to categorise more and more of the outcomes we experience in life as products of 'causal' forces rather than moral capacities. We will tend to draw upon a 'molecular ontology' rather than a personal ontology. (Interestingly, these 'causal' forces that we deem 'external' to us are more and more likely to include a host of biological factors—such as genes and neurological conditions—that are actually internal to our bodies but seen as external to our 'self' as agent.)

The paradoxical result of this interplay between our culture and ourselves is that, in an aspirational culture, the more explicitly we subscribe to—and endorse ourselves as—autonomous agents the more of our behaviour we will tend to ascribe to forces beyond our control. The more the focus on being autonomous, the less autonomous we will experience ourselves as being. As the daily and enduring life projects that we co-opt, idiosyncratically, from the surrounding culture become riskier and more uncertain, the overarching project of sustaining personhood within the 'local moral order' requires greater moment-by-moment self-management and management of the impressions we project.

Development of ever-more refined and subtle discursive practices is required to perform that management. One consequence of this need for greater self-management, impression-management and skilled use of discourse is a greater focus on competence; the second universal need in Self-Determination Theory (Ryan and Deci 2017).

Does our need for competence fare any better than the need for autonomy in an aspirational culture? Being competent, judging oneself as competent and being judged by others as competent would be a clear wellbeing advantage in an aspirational culture. Those who have demonstrated 'competence' enough to succeed in an aspirational society—such as the very wealthy—certainly seem to demonstrate increases in SWB (Diener et al. 1985). And those who experience a sense of competence at other types of task also gain wellbeing—but there is an important caveat (Deci and Ryan 2000). Competence interacts with a sense of autonomy. Being competent can produce a sense of happiness or wellbeing irrespective of motivation (controlled/extrinsic or autonomous/intrinsic). But there is evidence that being competent while also feeling that the behaviour was performed autonomously provides not only more happiness but also a sense of subjective vitality or energy (Nix et al. 1999; Ryan and Frederick 1997). Aspirational societies may provide many opportunities to express competence but, as just discussed, fewer opportunities to feel that we are also acting with autonomy. At best, this likely reduces the 'quantum' of wellbeing available from acting competently.

It gets worse. The imperative to be and to demonstrate competence is heightened in aspirational cultures. The constant monitoring, measurement, assessment, surveillance, and judgment of competence (e.g., at work, at school and either by others of us, by us of others, and by us of ourselves) leads to an intense focus on the need to be, and to appear, competent. At the same time, this loudly and *externally* expressed imperative to be competent is in many circumstances likely to be experienced as a socially coercive expectation rather than an intrinsically and autonomously chosen value. It is also likely that this focus on competence is being reflected in the extraordinary increases in perfectionism that have been found over recent decades. A meta-analysis of 164 studies with a combined sample of over 41,641 American, Canadian, and British university students that sought to identify any birth cohort changes in perfectionism between 1989 and 2016 found linear increases in three distinct forms of perfectionism (Curran and Hill 2017). *Self-oriented perfectionists* are irrational or unrealistic in their desire to be perfect to the point of holding "unrealistic expectations of themselves" and being "punitive in their self-evaluations"; *social perfectionists* believe that their "social context is excessively demanding", "others judge them harshly", and "they must display perfection to secure approval"; other-oriented perfectionists "impose unrealistic standards on those around them and evaluate others critically" (Curran and Hill 2017, p. 1). The take home message from the analyses was that all forms of perfectionism rose over this period, but to different extents. Self-perfectionism actually showed the smallest increase, though still an increase of 10%. Other-oriented perfectionism rose by 16% over the period and social perfectionism by a huge 32%. Curran and Hill (2017) suggested that the relatively lower increase in self-perfectionism may be because it has a greater degree of heritability (i.e., its variation within a population is considerably affected by genetic inheritance). While they explained all increases as a likely result of the way that modern, neoliberal values and notions of 'self' have permeated these three societies, the cultural influences of 'neoliberal meritocracy' and the associated emphasis on competitive performance they saw as especially powerful causes of other-oriented perfectionism and social perfectionism. In sum, aspirational societies transform whatever wellbeing rewards we may get from a sense of personal competence into a nagging, and largely coercive, feeling of the need to be perfect. As with the 'need' for autonomy, our need for competence is used against us by an aspirational culture to the point of undermining any wellbeing benefits the expression of competency may have for us.

There is a further twist in the tale of perfectionism. Other-oriented perfectionism, remember, is about expecting others to be perfect. Anyone who has ever experienced even the incipient inklings of 'road rage' probably understands why other-perfectionism might be especially likely to be on the increase in aspirational societies. The greater the (coercive) experience of the need to aspire the more we are likely to be intolerant of any behaviour on the part of others that may 'strategically interfere' with our attempts to succeed in achieving the goal to which we aspire—even if that goal is simply getting to work on time. Intolerance to and frustration with any perceived lack of competency in others is likely to rise precipitously in an aspirational culture that emphasises the competent, even perfect, performance of individuals. This tendency is compounded by the radical interdependency that comes along with ultrasociality which means that one person's (judged) competency is highly dependent on others' performance. An individualistic but supremely interdependent society is thus a recipe for interpersonal conflict, resentment and bitterness. Who, today, has not frequently felt a sense of injustice at being judged as incompetent when, it seems to us, that any deemed failure on our part was actually due to the incompetence of others? And this sense of injustice can then easily spill into overt criticism of the person we see as being the cause of our unjust treatment. That, in turn, reinforces the sense, for the criticised person, that today's world is one that unrelentingly demands perfection. The experience of social perfectionism is in this way part of a self-reinforcing vicious circle formed between itself and other-perfectionism—each reinforcing the other.

Finally, this vicious circle is no doubt also toxic to the third 'need' identified in Self-Determination Theory—relatedness. The effects of the modern aspirational world on the prospects for positive experiences of relatedness have already been made clear (see Chapter 2). But an additional obstacle to fulfilling this need is the way that social relationships are tipped towards conflict by the imperative to demonstrate competency. This is in sharpest relief when it comes to the already mentioned spread of demands for care of self and care for others (Rojek 2005). The requirement to show 'competent agency' in regard to this ethic requires a lot of 'emotional intelligence' and corresponding amounts of 'emotional labour'. This 'competency' (i.e., in our care for self and others) is especially difficult to navigate since it potentially puts each of us into a psychological and social vice when the two commitments come into conflict. We must show ourselves to be competent in our efforts to care for ourselves (e.g., eat healthily, exercise, be knowledgeable about general health) and to care for others (e.g., show tolerance towards others who may be different in some notable way—race, gender, ability, sexuality). But the stress of daily life in the uncertain and shifting context of an aspirational culture can disrupt and even shatter any efforts we make to succeed at these delicate forms of competency. And, again, any sense that these efforts are not being carried out autonomously (i.e., that they are perceived to be imposed or coerced from us) can undermine the wellbeing benefits typically associated with relatedness.

## Engagement

The sense of deep immersion in our activities is sometimes known as 'flow' (Csikszentmihalyi 1990; Csikszentmihalyi and LeFevre 1989) or 'engagement' (Seligman 2011). Such engagement is often the dividend of the intrinsically motivated activities that form such a crucial role in Self-Determination Theory (Deci and Ryan 2000; Ryan and Deci 2017). In practical guise, engagement also emerges in one of the most often recommended personal ways to wellbeing. 'Mindfulness', at least in one form, describes a type of focused awareness of, engagement in, and openness to, situations and contexts. Typically, mindfulness involves being attentive to the present moment while being sensitive to the wider context and the perspective taken. Counterintuitively, it produces engagement by "*disengaging* individuals from thoughts, habits and unhealthy behavior patterns" and by providing "clarity and vividness of current experience and functioning" (Brown and Ryan 2003, p. 283, emphasis added).

Engagement or flow is not so much a mental state as a quality of action. Csikszentmihalyi (1997, p. 29) noted that 'flow' was the term that people use "to describe the sense of effortless action they feel in moments that stand out as the best in their lives." It is similar to the experiences described by expressions such as 'being in the zone', 'rapture', or 'ecstasy' and concerns some of the most intense feelings of being alive. During flow, awareness is utterly focused on the activity so that there is what Csikszentmihalyi (1990) describes as a merging of action and awareness to the point where consciousness of oneself disperses (there are no cognitive resources left over from the action to consider oneself as a subject of awareness). As we will see in the Chapter 7, because it is often dependent on settings that have clear goals and 'rules of the game' people actually report it more often when at work than when at leisure or socialising with others (Csikszentmihalyi and LeFevre 1989). People typically report experiencing it when the skills they have are optimally suited to the challenges involved. Any mismatch is experienced either as boredom (when skills are greater than challenges) or anxiety (when challenges are greater than available skills). Feedback on performance in the activity has to be rapid and accurate, allowing skilled adjustments to be made that seem to happen without any conscious deliberation or effort.

The possibility of engagement also implies at least the perception of freedom of action, which provides a link to SDT through the need of autonomy. Whether in play or creative pursuits, the feeling of freedom is integral to the experience of full engagement. If aspirational culture is thought to provide an arena of personal freedom within which each of us can pursue our own preferences and interests—as desire satisfaction theories of wellbeing might recommend—then it might also be thought to support wellbeing. Free play, for example, should be ideal for allowing engagement with the world in a way that makes the pursuit and possible satisfaction of momentary desires and interests relatively easy (see Chapter 7).

The possibility to experience engagement, however, is seriously under threat in an aspirational culture. If disruption, as argued in Chapter 5, is becoming a ubiquitous experience in daily life then it represents a serious challenge for the prospects of engagement. These disruptions are at a variety of scales. The most obvious are the interruptions to our activities that are simply a function of the size, form and complexity of our modern arrangements that themselves stem from general economic and social aspirations. The multiple channels of communication made possible through new communication technologies are an everyday—or every-moment—threat to engaged activity. Advice to 'turn off' devices both during public events (e.g., performances) and while pursuing private projects (e.g., such as trying to write a book) are now commonplace and deemed as 'common sense' for the modern person. But the difficulty of following this advice, paradoxically, arises as much from the need to stay 'engaged' or informed about changes in our social environments and matters of life administration (e.g., being available for people who want to inform you of changes in social plans at the last minute, or for notifications from a delivery company about the timing of the delivery of some important product needed for other business you are involved in). Just in pure practical terms, being too engaged in an absorbing activity—and for too long—can be a handicap in one's attempts to keep a complicated life afloat.

Beyond practicalities, engagement is also threatened 'internally' by the imperative constantly to monitor our own activities and performance, to see how well our 'self' is doing (the 'self-monitoring' self that arose as a historical novelty in the seventeenth and eighteenth centuries in Europe—see Danziger [1997] and related discussion in Chapter 4 and Baumeister [1984] for an early study of the effects of self-consciousness on performance). Aspirational cultures are inherently linked to a focus on self—its performance (how well are we doing at the tasks of life, are we failing, stumbling or succeeding), its attributes (are we extroverted enough, happy enough, industrious enough?), its presentation (are we seen as competent, reliable, talented, beautiful?). In fact, it is hard to imagine the possibility of a thoroughly aspirational culture without the elevation of the 'separate self' (Eckersley 2004)—in explicit or implicit competition with other separate selves—to be the central concern of our modern personhood. The 'emotional labour' required to monitor and judge the condition and performance of this self in the presence of the 'institutions of normative coercion' (Rojek 2010) creates a degree of self-consciousness that is inimical to focused engagement, flow, or mindfulness. The need to maintain this level of 'self' vigilance is also a source of pervasive anxiety which further undermines the prospects of complete engagement in the activities of life. That so many people are attracted to the possibility of engagement is perhaps the best evidence for the difficulty of achieving it: Often what we most frequently talk about is what we most lack. (I discuss 'engagement' in our work and leisure lives further in Chapter 7.)

At the level of a person's entire life—or her consideration of her life—'engagement' is similar to a sense of personal coherence and being at home in the world. That, in turn, leads to the feeling of living in a way that is 'authentic' and true to oneself.

# The True and Authentic Self

One of the most modern expressions of aspiration is the pursuit of one's own true self. It can seem paradoxical that something so close and so intimate (i.e., one's true self) could require such devoted and ceaseless searching. Yet the experience, no matter how fleeting, of 'being authentic' or 'who you really are' is clearly valued and of value. People who feel authentic also feel powerful in the world (Gan et al. 2018). Self-reflection—rather than self-rumination—can, interestingly enough, generate a sense of authenticity (Boyraz and Kuhl 2015). A study of the experience of authenticity in young people found that it enhances well-being, is apparently caused by satisfying the need for autonomy and is related to the other two needs in SDT (competence and relatedness), and is a link between satisfying these three needs and experiencing well-being (Thomaes et al. 2017). How easy might it be, then, to experience authenticity in an aspirational world?

The first observation I would make, is that the whole reason that authenticity is one of the well-known 'modern values' is that there is often a disjunction between how we need to present ourselves in the world and how we are actually disposed to be and to act in it. Simply, the modern experience is one of outwardly conforming to what is appropriate irrespective of one's inclinations. Once again, at the heart of this desire to be an authentic self is the reality that the 'Lockean self' (see Chapter 4) was established, in part, to enable social regulation through a steady "flow of approval or disapproval" (Danziger 1997, p. 145). In this context, the mere possession of such a self is a disadvantage to the experience of authenticity—and aspirational culture emphasises the importance of, and need for, just this kind of self. How such a self-which is likely to inform each person's own 'theory' of their self-could ever be the site of authenticity is hard to imagine.

Much of the anxiety (and reward) that comes from participation in social media is no doubt linked to this need to present well, irrespective of how one is feeling or how one's life is actually going. This is a heightened form of what social psychologists call 'self-enhancement', the "tendency to maintain unrealistically positive self-views" (Dufner et al. 2018,

p. 1). From a meta-analysis of 299 cases with an aggregate sample of 126,916 people, it was found that self-enhancement is positively related to what the authors called 'personal adjustment' (essentially SWB—LS, positive affect, negative affect, and depression) but mixed in relation to 'interpersonal adjustment' (general social valuation, agency, and communion). Agency self-enhancement concerns competence, dominance, and drive while communion self-enhancement concerns features such as warmth, morality, and prosociality. Specifically, self-enhancement that is aimed at agency-, rather than communion-, self-enhancement was found to be positively related to judgments of agency by others, negatively related to judgments by others of communion while communion enhancement was positively related to judgments by others, of communion. In the context of an increased emphasis on the ethics of self- and other-care (Rojek 2010) these findings are entirely predictable but they also indicate that an unrealistic sense of self (i.e., self-enhancement) is likely to make people feel better. Since it also seems to be the case that interactions with peers during adolescence 'sculpt' the developing brain in ways that augment either risk or resilience in relation to mental health issues (Lamblin et al. 2017) it may well be that, in an aspirational society, inauthentic self-presentation and self-enhancement may almost be an adaptive developmental strategy.

From the perspective of persons and personhood, what might this desired feeling of authenticity involve? Given that a person is an activity rather than an entity then the most obvious answer is that a feeling of authenticity arises when there is no disruption or interruption to the activity in which a person is fully engaged. This would explain the relationship between a sense of autonomy and a sense of authenticity. To be authentic is to feel oneself engaged in unfettered and unhesitant activity. The need to consciously regulate oneself (e.g., censor what one is about to say) is absent. But, once again, in a world where the focus is on aspiration, self-regulation is an increasingly acknowledged requirement for life success (Moffitt et al. 2011). And it is probably not a persuasive argument to tell yourself that you were actually being authentically you when you stopped yourself from contradicting your boss during a meeting. That is, not everything a person does is authentic, no matter that one has, in fact, done it.

It is time to weigh in the scales what we have found about wellbeing in an aspirational culture. How we have learnt to live in the uncertainty and unpredictable dynamism that is the distinctive feature of today's world demonstrates the human ability to adapt. It is perhaps our species' greatest strength—but also its greatest weakness—that it can 'adapt' to whatever kind of environment it finds itself in. We are remarkably inventive, even to the point of re-inventing ourselves on demand. But there is a price to pay for all of this adaptability. We must adopt 'separate selves', be satisfied with only 'tribal ties' (Eckersley 2004)—and, in wellbeing terms, suffer the consequences. The coherence, continuity, and surety of action that is fundamental to the notion of a person—and fundamental to our positive experience of being a person—is increasingly under threat. Where, then, can we turn to find some wellbeing? Perhaps to our work? Or our lives in leisure?

# References

Bauman, Z. (2000). *Liquid modernity*. Cambridge, UK: Polity Press.

Bauman, Z. (2007). *Liquid times: Living in an age of uncertainty*. Cambridge, UK: Polity Press.

Baumeister, R. F. (1984). Choking under pressure: Self-consciousness and paradoxical effects of incentives on skillful performance. *Journal of Personality and Social Psychology, 46,* 610–620.

Boyraz, G., & Kuhl, M. L. (2015). Self-focused attention, authenticity, and well-being. *Personality and Individual Differences, 87,* 70–75.

Brickman, P., & Campbell, D. T. (1971). Hedonic relativism and planning the good society. In M. H. Appley (Ed.), *Adaptation-level theory: A symposium* (pp. 287–302). New York: Academic Press.

Brickman, P., Coates, D., & Janoff-Bulman, R. (1978). Lottey winners and accident victims: Is happiness relative? *Journal of Personality and Social Psychology, 36,* 917–927.

Brown, K. W., & Ryan, R. M. (2003). The benefits of being present: Mindfulness and its role in psychological well-being. *Journal of Personality and Social Psychology, 84*(4), 822–848. https://doi.org/10.1037/0022-3514.84.4.822.

Campbell, W. K., & Sedikides, C. (1998). Self-threat magnifies the self-serving bias: A meta-analytic integration. *Review of General Psychology, 3,* 23–43.

Chater, N. (2018). *The mind is flat: The illusion of mental depth and the improvised mind*. London, UK: Allen Lane.

Csikszentmihalyi, M. (1990). *Flow: The psychology of optimal experience*. New York: Harper and Row.

Csikszentmihalyi, M. (1997). *Finding flow: The psychology of engagement with everyday life*. New York: Harper Collins.

Csikszentmihalyi, M., & LeFevre, J. (1989). Optimal experience in work and leisure. *Journal of Personality and Social Psychology, 56*(5), 815–822.

Curran, T., & Hill, A. P. (2017). Perfectionism is increasing over time: A meta-analysis of birth cohort differences from 1989 to 2016. *Psychological Bulletin*. https://doi.org/10.1037/bul0000138.

Dalziel, P., Saunders, C., & Saunders, J. (2018). *Wellbeing economics: The capabilities approach to prosperity*. Wellbeing in politics and policy (1st ed., pp. XVII, 196). London: Palgrave Macmillan.

Danziger, K. (1997). The historical formation of selves. In R. D. Ashmore & L. Jussim (Eds.), *Self and identity: Fundamental issues* (pp. 137–159). Oxford: Oxford University Press.

Dawkins, R. (1976). *The selfish gene*. Oxford, UK: Oxford University Press.

Deci, E. L., & Ryan, R. M. (2000). The "what" and "why" of goal pursuits: Human needs and the self-determination of behavior [Review]. *Psychological Inquiry, 11*(4), 227–268. https://doi.org/10.1207/s15327965pli1104_01.

Diener, E., & Fujita, F. (1995). Resources, personal strivings, and subjective well-being: A nomothetic and idiographic approach. *Journal of Personality and Social Psychology, 68*, 926–935.

Diener, E., Horwitz, J., & Emmons, R. A. (1985). Happiness of the very wealthy. *Social Indicators Research, 16*, 263–274.

Dufner, M., Gebauer, J. E., Sedikides, C., & Denissen, J. J. A. (2018). Self-enhancement and psychological adjustment: A meta-analytic review. *Personality and Social Psychology Review*. https://doi.org/10.1177/1088868318756467.

Eckersley, R. (2004). Separate selves, tribal ties, and other stories: Making sense of different accounts of youth. *Family Matters, 68*(Winter), 36–42.

Emmons, R. A. (1986a). Personal strivings: An approach to personality and subjective well-being. *Journal of Personality and Social Psychology, 51*, 1058–1068.

Emmons, R. A. (1986b). *Personal strivings: Toward a theory of personality and subjective well-being (motives, goals, affect)*. Urbana and Champaign: University of Illinois.

Gan, M., Heller, D., & Chen, S. (2018). The power in being yourself: Feeling authentic enhances the sense of power. *Personality and Social Psychology Bulletin, 44*(10), 1460–1472.

Gowdy, J., & Krall, L. (2016). The economic origins of ultrasociality. *Behavioral and Brain Sciences, 39,* E92. https://doi.org/10.1017/S0140525X1500059X.

Harré, R. (1998). *The singular self: An introduction to the psychology of personhood.* London: Sage.

Harré, R. (2016). Hybrid psychology as a human science. *Theory and Psychology, 26*(5), 632–646.

Haybron, D. M. (2008). *The pursuit of unhappiness: The elusive psychology of well-being.* Oxford: Oxford University Press.

Huang, J. Y., & Bargh, J. A. (2014). The selfish goal: Autonomously operating motivational structures as the proximate cause of human judgment and behavior. *Behavioral and Brain Sciences, 37,* 121–175. https://doi.org/10.1017/S0140525X13000290.

Kasser, T. (2002). *The high price of materialism.* Cambridge: MIT Press.

Kasser, T., & Ryan, R. M. (1993). A dark side of the American Dream: Correlates of financial success as a central life aspiration. *Journal of Personality and Social Psychology, 65*(2), 410–422.

Kasser, T., & Ryan, R. M. (1996). Further examining the American Dream: Differential correlates of intrinsic and extrinsic goals. *Personality and Social Psychology Bulletin, 22,* 280–287.

King, L. A. (2008). Interventions for enhancing subjective well-being: Can we make people happier, and should we? In M. Eid & R. J. Larsen (Eds.), *The science of subjective well-being* (pp. 431–448). New York: The Guildford Press.

Lamblin, M., Murawski, C., Whittle, S., & Fornito, A. (2017). Social connectedness, mental health and the adolescent brain. *Neuroscience and Biobehavioral Review, 80,* 57–68.

Moffitt, T. E., Arsenault, L., Belsky, D., Dickson, N., Hancox, R. J., Harrington, H., et al. (2011). A gradient of childhood self-control predicts health, wealth, and public safety. *Proceedings of the National Academy of Sciences, 108*(7), 2693–2698.

Nix, G. A., Ryan, R. M., Manly, J. B., & Deci, E. L. (1999). Revitalization through self-regulation: The effects of autonomous and controlled motivation on happiness and vitality. *Journal of Experimental Social Psychology, 35,* 266–284.

Oishi, S. (2010). The psychology of residential mobility: Implications for the self, social relationships, and well-being. *Perspectives on Psychological Science, 5*(1), 5–21. https://doi.org/10.1177/1745691609356781.

Rojek, C. (2005). *Leisure theory: Principles and practice.* Basingstoke: Palgrave Macmillan.

Rojek, C. (2010). Leisure and emotional intelligence. *World Leisure Journal,* *52*(4), 240–252.

Ryan, R. M., & Deci, E. L. (2017). *Self-determination theory: Basic psychological needs in motivation, development, and wellness.* New York: Guilford Press.

Ryan, R. M., & Frederick, C. (1997). On energy, personality, and health: Subjective vitality as a dynamic reflection of well-being. *Journal of Personality, 65*(3), 529–565.

Seligman, M. E. P. (2011). *Flourish: A visionary new understanding of happiness and well-being.* New York: Free Press.

Thomaes, S., Sedikides, C., van den Bos, N., Hutteman, R., & Reijntjes, A. (2017). Happy to be "me?" authenticity, psychological need satisfaction, and subjective well-being in adolescence. *Child Development, 88*(4), 1045–1056. https://doi.org/10.1111/cdev.12867.

Twenge, J. M., Zhang, L., & Im, C. (2004). It's beyond my control: A cross-temporal meta-analysis of increasing externality in Locus of Control, 1960–2002. *Personality and Social Psychology Review, 8*(3), 308–319.

# 7

# Wellbeing at Work and at Play

It might be thought old-fashioned to distinguish between work and play. A neatly tripartite daily routine of eight hours of work, eight hours of sleep and the remaining eight hours divided between maintenance activities and leisure can seem too mechanically modernist for our postmodern times. Surely today's world has sufficiently blurred those artificially constructed boundaries that we can dispense with them? No doubt for some people it is true that work, leisure, rest, recreation and maintenance are thoroughly interpenetrated in time and function. Organising domestic duties during the work day, checking work emails during a child's school concert, dealing with life administration problems while on holiday are examples of the kinds of 'blurring' that are increasingly commonplace—a blurring aided by new communication technologies. Also, if my analysis is correct, then all life domains are becoming similar in the sense that they are sites that aspirational culture has penetrated and, therefore, has homogenized in important experiential ways if not in their concrete particulars. For many others, however, these boundaries between 'work', 'play', and 'maintenance and recovery' remain clear. Walking away from a workplace at the end of the day can

© The Author(s) 2019
K. Moore, *Wellbeing and Aspirational Culture*,
https://doi.org/10.1007/978-3-030-15643-5_7

still mean not having to give work another moment's thought until the next work day.

Whatever particular experiences individuals may have, for the purposes of analysis there is good reason to persist in distinguishing between these domains. By thinking separately about the characteristics of each it is easier not only to see the wellbeing consequences for persons that might arise in each sphere on its own but also the wellbeing effects that might come from blurring and melding them together. A starting question, for example, might be whether such blurring has made the experience of daily life a more integrated, seamless experience of 'flow'? Or, as a result of this merging, has life become a highly disjointed and disrupted experience that diminishes whatever increments of wellbeing each domain, on its own, could potentially provide? And does this wellbeing effect depend on the kind of work and leisure a person might pursue? Taking the centrality of personhood for wellbeing as a starting point (see Chapters 4 and 5), in this chapter I focus on the question of how 'work' and 'play' intersect with wellbeing concerns in an aspirational culture.

## Persons at Work

As Twenge and King (2005) noted, for Sigmund Freud, the recipe for a healthy life was twofold: 'Lieben und arbeiten' ('To love and to work'). It is an unfortunate combination for those of us living in aspirational cultures. The conflict between having relationships with others ('to love') and having gainful work that, hopefully, is both satisfying and materially sufficient to live, is legendary. These two cultural and personal tasks, in part, are reflected in the two types of 'aspirational goals' identified by Kasser et al. (and discussed in previous chapters): the 'intrinsic' goals of affiliation, community feeling, and self-acceptance (often associated with social relationships, or 'love'); the 'extrinsic' goals of financial success and possessions (wealth), fame, and image (often associated with work). Perhaps encouragingly, Twenge and King (2005) found that people generally think that relationship fulfillment is an essential ingredient to the good life. Work fulfillment, by contrast, was seen as a useful bonus but not central to the good life. Similarly, there seem to be two kinds of 'prosperity' when it comes to SWB: Material or economic prosperity, which is most closely correlated to life evaluations (e.g., 'life satisfaction'–LS–measures); psychosocial prosperity, which is correlated with positive feelings associated with activities such as learning, autonomy, skill use, and respect (Diener et al. 2010).

The split between 'love' and 'work' is, in one sense, accentuated in aspirational societies, generating the familiar conflict. As Sennett (2006, p. 2) highlights, the "fragmenting of big institutions has left our lives in a "fragmented state" with, today, "the places [we] work more resembling train stations than villages, as family life is disoriented by the demands of work". In another sense, as just mentioned, the two are not so much 'split' as 'blurred'. Either way that relationship is probably why we have such an ambivalent relationship to our work. One of the areas of our life that generates the greatest frequency of experiences of 'flow', for example, is the work we do (Csikszentmihalyi 1997; Csikszentmihalyi and LeFevre 1989). This is not surprising since work is typically more structured than other parts of life and its tasks have clearer 'rules' and goals than we experience at home or at leisure. At least sometimes, our work can provide us with meaning, a sense of efficacy ('competence'), and a measure of social worth and connection.

Yet work is also the setting in which we report the least amount of positive affect (e.g., Csikszentmihalyi and Graef 1980; Killingsworth and Gilbert 2010). The amount of flow experienced while working also depends on the type of work. Using a 'liberal' definition of flow (whenever someone scored above their mean level for challenges and skills), Csikszentmihalyi and LeFevre (1989) found that blue collar workers spent 63.2% of the time that they were not in flow doing their primary work task (assembly work) while clerical workers (at 46.8%) and managers (at 57.8%) spent most of their non-flow time at work doing the miscellaneous 'Other' category of work-time activities (i.e., tasks not central to the job). It is perhaps not surprising, then, that work is also the time when our minds wander most from the task at hand (Killingsworth and Gilbert 2010) which suggests low levels of what, in terms of the concept of flow and wellbeing more generally, we would call 'engagement'. In fact, when directly asked how engaged they are with their work, modern people typically report low rates of engagement. A 2015 Gallup poll tracking employee engagement in the United States found that only 32% of employees could be described as 'engaged', with 50.8% 'not engaged' and 17.2% 'actively disengaged'. The typical response to this apparent general disaffection with, or apathy for, work from psychologists of happiness and wellbeing is to recommend that individuals bootstrap their levels of engagement. People are advised, for example, to identify and deploy their 'character strengths' in their work (Peterson et al. 2007) or make work personally meaningful so that flow is generated. As Csikszentmihalyi opined in a 2007 *Psychology Today* online article, "[w]hen approached without too many cultural prejudices and with a determination to make it personally meaningful, even the most mundane job can produce flow." But this response is too simplistic. When it comes to wellbeing at work, the evidence for low levels of affect, mind-wandering and employee disengagement is a strong argument to consider not just the worker but the nature of modern work itself. What is work now like, and how did it get to be this way?

Since the Industrial Revolution the world of work has been repeatedly transformed. No longer is work typically done in and around the home or neighbourhood (the traditional site for 'love' to be generated) and the expression '*going* to work' has come to seem unremarkable and entirely normal. This major shift began in Britain around 1760 and eventually led to the replacement of a largely agrarian and cottage handicraft society with a machine-based, coal-fueled, manufacturing society. Productive capital rather than land became the basis and the marker of wealth. Work became organised according to the factory system which drove increased division of labour and specialisation and a corresponding reduction in worker autonomy. (Which, as discussed in a moment, is quite a neat, amplified 'echo' of the markers of the ultrasocial arrangements that began 10,000–12,000 years ago.) Absence from other family members became obligatory while absence from work became punishable.

Hard on the heels of the industrial revolution—and in keeping with John Dewey's focus on education as the means to transform the modern population (see Chapter 3)—came mass compulsory schooling, as much an exercise in social regulation as education. In the United Kingdom the debate over compulsory schooling for children was partly over children's welfare (Gray 2013). From a very young age children would be put to work in the new factories, often performing dangerous tasks in unhealthy and cramped conditions for poor recompense. Education was resisted by some industrialists because it would remove a section of the workforce and potentially drive wages up. It was also resisted because of the belief that "too much education would give the people of the working class ideas above their station and they would no longer be content to work as servants or labourers" and, in the wake of the French Revolution, that "through education the masses would obtain tools for discontent and fanaticism" (Lemire 2013, p. 257). Before compulsory education in the nineteenth century, literacy in Britain had already been on the increase, driven by a number of factors including charity schools, religion and simple population growth. But, as economic requirements for greater regimentation and self-discipline increased, the case for compulsory mass education was finally accepted. School became good preparation for working according to the clock, following directions and assuming that others (adult teachers) were in charge of setting schedules and priorities.

It is easy to see how the logic of ultrasociality has played itself out in these changes to work and the establishment of widespread education since the Industrial Revolution. The ultrasocial form of life that began with the adoption of agriculture found its modern expression in the regulation and management of industrial work for the interests of the 'locked-in' but quickly transforming economic system. The hallmarks of ultrasocial organization—division of labour and specialisation—were metastasising rapidly and the interests and wellbeing of individuals was secondary to their reorganisation and reskilling for industrial production at the national level. Gowdy and Krall's (2013) ultrasocial 'superorganism' was undergoing a massive increase in scale—and wellbeing at work was a casualty.

The depredations, powerlessness and coercive social, political, economic and legal measures that kept working people in check in the nineteenth century were, however, matched by the formation of the labour movement and trade unions across Europe, the United Kingdom and United States. A growing impetus for popular revolt came to fruition in the aftermath of World War I. In America, an economic crisis (the 'Panic' of 1893) led to the Democratic Party selecting as its candidate a populist—William Jennings Bryan from Nebraska—who was eventually defeated in the 1896 election by Republican candidate William McKinley (Leahey 2000). Bryan was the Democratic candidate but, at the time, it was in an alliance with the Populist Party (which also selected Bryan as its candidate) and the Silver Party (formed by silver producing states such as Nevada and Colorado). He was, in effect, the representative of the values and favoured policies of the 'island communities' in the American rural heartland that were rapidly being depopulated by rural migration to the industrial cities on the east coast (see Chapter 3). The refashioning of an entire way of life and a new kind of person to live that life was well underway. As the industrial workplace and associated professions (such as the early industrial-organisational psychologists) began to dominate people's daily experience of work, concerns over wellbeing were slow to catch up.

Much has changed since that time but the need to manage and regulate the workforce has not. From the 'Scientific Management' of tasks for 'Factory Hands' to the more subtle concerns with the motivation and job satisfaction of the 'Sentimental Worker' espoused by the contemporary Human Resources orientation in industrial-organisational psychology (see the critical account by Hollway 1991), the principal problem in the workplace has been how to corall the efforts of a workforce in the most efficient manner possible and in the service of the economy understood as an entity (Gowdy and Krall's 'superorganism') in its own right. The 'win-win' rhetoric of both increased productivity and increased wellbeing became a mantra that remains with us to this day, expressed in the claim that a 'happy worker is a productive worker' (for a review see Cropanzano and Wright 2001). Criticism of the way that wellbeing has been promoted and implemented by organisations, corporations and governments has largely come from this critical and historical perspective on the economic management of the population (Cederström and Spicer 2015; Davies 2015). These criticisms make sense in the light of the historical circumstances that transformed the workplace.

Once we adopt a person-focused understanding of wellbeing the reasons for the difficulty in maintaining wellbeing in a workplace becomes clearer. As products of a culture, persons are constituted by these historical, economic and social changes and the requirements and tasks they generate for people. They also inevitably embody and express the tensions, contradictions and moral dilemmas that the cultural context expresses. If it was only biologically evolved 'selves' that went to work, rather than persons, it would be possible to tweak their inputs and internal structure to fit them to whatever work they carried out. Csikszentimihalyi's advice might then be an enduring intervention: once the checkout operator at the supermarket has been shown how her job can be made more meaningful by paying attention to the individual characteristics and needs of each customer, her 'self' would come to act in that way, habitually and automatically, and so gain (causally) the positive feelings and sense of purpose and meaning it presumably delivers.

But, if a 'self' is not some inner 'entity' or set of dynamic processes waiting to be engineered but, instead, is simply a protean 'theory' or 'fiction' (Harré 1998, 2016) generated by the person who is *actually* the checkout operator then the long-term outcome of the advice is less certain. For one thing, persons, as opposed to selves, are inherently oriented towards the 'whole-of-life' or 'diachronic' perspective (Stokes 2017) and so what has happened, what is now happening, and what might be thought to happen later all matter. It is the overall quality of one's life—and our worries about how we might judge that quality—that is of central concern to a person. For a 'self', by contrast, the main focus is on the quality of moment-by-moment experience that follows 'Time's Arrow' into the future. From the perspective of the self, what is gone is gone. From the perspective of the person, what is gone still matters, sometimes mightily—regrets, nostalgia, guilt, pride, shame, grudges, and fond memories are still present and so can affect a person's happiness and wellbeing. Persons are therefore most similar to Kahneman's 'remembering self' rather than the first-person, subjective 'experiencing self' present in the immediate moment (Kahneman 2011). They narrate, edit and reconstruct their 'selves' in response to the normative circumstances in which they find themselves. They can even come to see themselves as their 'self' (i.e., identify with their theory of themselves) through this dynamic narration. But they remain a person, with a person's responsibilities—and have their being in the complicated circumstances that are created in the world of persons. (And, as Rogers (1959) argued, if the feedback that you (as a person being taken as an agent in the world of persons) receive from reality (i.e., from other persons, social institutions, etc.) is a poor match with your 'self-concept' then that creates a psychological problem, or at least difficulty, that you (the person) must deal with.) These complicated circumstances are constructed by the world of other persons—each of whom, as an adult, is authoring her own long-term narrative about her life as a person (McAdams 2013). In that sociocultural world of persons *doing* things there is far more than the advice of psychologists of wellbeing to respond to. As Harré (2016) explains (see Chapter 5), the world of persons necessarily requires operation of the 'Person-grammar' associated with the ontology of persons (in comparison to the grammar associated with 'molecules', 'organisms', or 'souls'). As part of that grammar, persons act as agents who *do things* and who, recursively, monitor, judge, and are accountable for the things they do.

What must be navigated by the checkout operator, as a person, is therefore a fraught context of judgments, responsibilities, accountabilities, and narrative complexities. She may, for example, be reprimanded by work colleagues or a supervisor for talking too much to a customer, being too familiar, failing to notice or attend sufficiently to some other task while she is paying deep attention to the customer, and so on. Incidents such as this, over the long-term, fold into ongoing and overarching concerns she may have such as how she is being treated by her employer, how well she is getting on with workmates, the feeling that she is always getting into these kinds of difficulties, and whether or not this job is fulfilling her 'self' and taking her anywhere good. The half-life of the effectiveness of the advice of wellbeing psychologists in this kind of complicated—yet everyday—context that persons inhabit is probably quite short. The example of the checkout operator is everyday enough—I assume that we can all provide examples of this personally experienced complexity and difficulty from our own lives. In that sense it might seem that this complexity is simply the lot of being a person. But, in an aspirational culture, these everyday contexts are especially difficult to navigate. The imperatives of change, improvement, adjustment, uncertainty, and multi-layered fluidity—e.g., tomorrow our checkout operator may find she has lost her job, been rostered to work in the storeroom, or needs to learn new software on the till—are inherent features of aspirational cultures that would tax any person's 'will-power' and perseverance to implement the advice in the world in which, today, they are swimming (or drowning).

But there is more than just the complexity of the workplace that the checkout operator must, as a person, navigate. There is the entire economy and society within which she works. Her experience, especially with the threat of new 'self-service' technologies replacing checkout operators, is that "the shelf life of many skills is short" (Sennett 2006, p. 4). Even if she were to follow the recommended route and retrain to one day enjoy the benefits of professional life she would still be subject to Sennett's (2006, p. 4) 'spectre of uselessness' which means that even "in technology and the sciences, as in advanced forms of manufacturing, workers now need to retrain on average every eight to twelve years." (And that 'now' was over a decade ago.) If Sennett's (2006) account of modern work is accurate, then what sense of craft and achievement she may gain in however long she has at her job will soon dissipate or likely be incomplete as the 'flexibility' of modern work inevitably interrupts that project. Her loyalty to the company—as with the loyalty of the company that employs her towards her—will also find no sure-footing and soon stumble. Overall, if "[o]nly a certain kind of human being can prosper in unstable, fragmentary social conditions" (Sennett 2006, p. 3) then the low levels of engagement and affect and high levels of mind-wandering exhibited in the modern workplace suggest that there are precious few of this 'certain kind of human being' at work today.

Yet despite the shifting and unreliable context of this 'new capitalism' that has emerged as the latest form of aspirational culture, the hope remains that with enough focused research it should be possible to extract maximum wellbeing from the hours so many people spend at work. One of the most thoroughly researched dimensions of wellbeing in the workplace has been the notion of 'job satisfaction' (JS). In fact, it "may be the most extensively researched topic in the history of industrial/organizational psychology" (Judge and Klinger 2008, p. 393). JS is usually a self-report either of one's overall job satisfaction (like common measures of 'global' life satisfaction) or of the various facets involved in working at a job, the latter measures covering both 'extrinsic' features (e.g., pay and promotions) and 'intrinsic' features (supervision, the job itself, recognition, management, work conditions). Types of theories of job satisfaction can focus on the job itself ("situational theories"), the personality (or "personological makeup") of the worker ("dispositional approaches"), or the interaction between the two ("interactive theories") (Judge and Klinger 2008, pp. 398–399). The Job Characteristics Model, as the name suggests, is mainly concerned with features of the job and its component tasks. The characteristics in the model not only echo work in wellbeing on the importance of intrinsically motivated activity (as in Self-Determination Theory–SDT) and 'flow' but also express the qualities needed for the exercise of agentic personhood. '*Task identity*' concerns the unity of one's work. Does the work allow someone to see the task through from start to finish? '*Task significance*' is about the importance of the work, to others but also to the person doing the work. '*Skill variety*' focuses on the extent to which one gets to use a wide range of one's abilities and skills, both to avoid boredom (as in the theory of 'flow') and to fulfill as much of oneself as possible ('self-actualise'). '*Autonomy*' in the task concerns the degree of discretion and control available in the work and has clear connections to the need for autonomy in SDT. Finally, '*feedback*' describes the extent to which the job itself provides feedback on performance, similar to one of the conditions for a 'flow' experience.

Satisfaction with the work itself—which is the focus of the Job Characteristics Model—is one of the work features that is most strongly correlated with overall job satisfaction. But, interestingly, to make the fit between these two even closer, a 'moderator' of the relationship called 'Growth Need Strength' (GNS) has been suggested. In effect, GNS differs between individuals (some have a higher GNS, others a lower GNS) and so is a dispositional factor that has been added to a situational model to produce an interactive model. Most interesting of all, GNS is a construct that, in effect, formalises the importance of aspiration (and the importance of embracing aspiration) in the modern workplace. Workers who score a 'high-GNS' have a stronger relationship between the characteristics of their work and their job satisfaction than do those who have a 'low-GNS' score: "intrinsic characteristics are especially satisfying for individuals who score high on GNS" (Judge and Klinger 2008, p. 400). The modern world of work—if replete with intrinsic characteristics—rewards the most aspirational amongst us; if not in material rewards, then in job satisfaction. To put it in SDT terms, people who have managed to 'endorse' personal growth as a deep value—and therefore integrate it into their 'selves'—will be 'high-GNS' and so will be able to make the most of any jobs with these intrinsic characteristics. Which is not to say that those with 'low-GNS' do not also benefit from jobs with intrinsic characteristics, at least in terms of job satisfaction.

A further conceptual innovation to understand job satisfaction is the idea that each of us has a 'core self-evaluation' (CSE) (Judge et al. 1997), roughly a set of deep beliefs or understandings of ourselves. As a dispositional theory of job satisfaction, the aim of the CSE model is to determine the person-attributes associated with job satisfaction ratings. Aligned along four trait dimensions—self-efficacy, self-esteem, locus of control, and emotional stability—a person's CSE correlates with job satisfaction and, at least in one study, adds explanatory power to other dispositional theories that use either the well-known 'Big Five' personality traits from the 'Five Factor Model' (FFM) or a Positive Affect/Negative Affect typology (PA/NA) (Judge et al. 2008).

So much is interesting and informative. But in what way? Adopting the person as the theoretical focus leads to a different interpretation of these findings on job satisfaction from the interpretation normally offered. Aspirational cultures encourage persons to adopt the imperatives of aspiration into their theories of self. In Chapter 4, I noted Harré's (1983, p. 26) argument that while the concept of the self is the "central constructing concept of individual human psychology" it is a theoretical concept through-and-through. It is a theory not just for the psychologist but for the person too. Moreover, it is a theory that each of us generates from the "source analogue" that "is the socially defined and sustained concept of a person" favoured in a particular society. In an aspirational culture, the 'source analogue' of the person is imbued with aspirational motifs and imperatives. To be a person in good standing, therefore, just *is* to have a theory of one's 'self' as aspirational and in pursuit of its potential. The GNS score for a person, for example, then amounts to an expression, by the person, of their standing as a person in an aspirational culture. Through their responses, they characterize themselves as in conformity—or not—with conventional and normative understandings such as of the value of aspiring in life. What validity might exist between the self-report 'measure' and a person's observed behaviour (by others) is an indication of how congruent their claims about themselves are with how they act. This congruence is a matter of correctness, not evidence of a causal process. As Harré (1998, p. 133) explains, self-report (or, for that matter, other-report) questionnaires "are not instruments in the sense that thermometers are" since they "do not measure a property" but are "invitations to a conversation". This 'conversation'—as formalised through the institution of scientific research—takes a direction (i.e., 'provides data') that is not a result or indication of "underlying causal processes" but of "discursive conventions" that a person idiosyncratically applies in their own case. Whether completing questionnaires and scales on SWB, GNS or the CSE it is a *person* who is doing the completing, and persons always operate in the normative world of moral concerns, accountability, and responsibility. Each person's position in that world will differ and vary both from that of others and from the same person's position at other times—but it will always be a position in that world. Core self-evaluations just are expressions of persons operating in this arena of normative concerns. There is a clue to this when Judge et al. (1997) refer to core evaluations as fundamental, or even '*metaphysical*', value judgments. Our 'core evaluations', that is, are our metaphysical *commitments*; our firmly held theories of ourselves, the world, and of other people. To put it in Sennett's (2006, p. 3) terms, the worker who scores highest on the four traits comprising CSE is probably the closest we have today to the "certain kind of human being"—mentioned previously—who is able to "prosper in unstable, fragmentary social conditions". In that light, the finding that it is the 'emotional stability' core trait that provides much of the explanatory power of CSE on job satisfaction is not surprising. If you are a worker high in emotional stability you are like Kipling's ideal 'Man' and can 'keep your head when all about you/Are losing theirs and blaming it on you'.

## Persons at Play

If work is not always, or even often, a site of wellbeing in today's world it is often assumed that, once we are free of the constraints of work, our wellbeing is there for the taking. Whether we refer to it as 'free time', 'leisure' or 'recreation' the reasonable expectation would be that the times when we are free and at our ease should also be the times that our wellbeing would be at its peak.

We have already seen that flow experiences are reported more often at work than during leisure (Csikszentmihalyi and LeFevre 1989). Part of the reason for that is the typical activities people engage in during so-called 'free time'. The most common activities are passive and even demotivating such as television watching. In that same study, watching TV was the free time activity that generated the greatest difference between its contribution to flow and non-flow time for all three groups of managers, clerical workers, and blue collar workers ($-14.0$, $-9.3$, and $-17.5$, respectively—see Table 3 in Csikszentmihalyi and LeFevre 1989). Talking with friends 'broke even', providing similar proportions of the time spent in flow and non-flow.

If being engaged and in flow is so rewarding, why do people tend to spend so much of their available 'free time' in activities that do not provide engagement? The reason seems to be the degree of effort required and how daunting starting flow activities is perceived to be (Schiffer and Roberts 2018). Passive, non-flow activities are perceived not only to be easier and less daunting to access but also to be more enjoyable, especially in the immediate sense. Here, once again, we come across the effect of time on our wellbeing. Even when we are relatively free and able to decide what to do, we generally prefer activities that require little effort and that we suspect will provide the greatest increment of 'here and now' enjoyment. And we do this even though we are perfectly aware that the more effortful activities will, in the long-run, provide us with more happiness (Schiffer and Roberts 2018). Our rational selves, that is, will not save us from making a 'sub-optimal' decision for life-time happiness or wellbeing. If for no other reason, this should be caution enough for those positive psychologists who believe that providing information about the latest research findings on wellbeing will help people make better decisions and so improve their overall wellbeing (Lyubomirsky 2013). The dominant everyday experience for many people is that they need to 'expend psychological energy' (to use a metaphor) for a large part of their lives, either for their work or for maintenance—and often also in socializing—that they will frequently look for the least-effort option when they can.

To simply get by in our world we need to master the ability to 'pay attention'. But we are not particularly good at it (Jackson 2018). One of the reasons for our poor performance is that we have to do it too often (Kaplan and Kaplan 1983). According to the 'attention restoration hypothesis', we have two kinds of attentional capacities. The first is called 'directed' or 'voluntary' attention. This is when we consciously or deliberately focus on some event or task to which we feel we must pay attention. Despite being called 'voluntary' it can often feel effortful and at least partly coerced (in SDT, it might be said to be a relatively external 'perceived locus of control/causality'—Ryan and Deci 2017). The other type of attention is 'involuntary' but, more accurately, is largely spontaneous attention. This happens when something in the world draws our attention, seemingly effortlessly, and we experience a sense of fascination, interest, or curiosity towards the target of our attention. According to the theory, the effort we experience with directed attention is not actually from having to focus or concentrate. It comes from having to stop attending to other things. That is, directed attention is mainly the effort not to be distracted by stimuli that draw our attention 'involuntarily'. Electronic distractions are the obvious examples but even before their advent we could find plenty to distract us from arduous or boring tasks.

Today, we need to direct our attention not just for work tasks but also when socialising or at leisure. Partly this is because directed attention involves the self-regulation abilities and other executive functions carried out in that late-developing area of the brain, the pre-frontal cortex (Kaplan 2010). That means that it is also just the kind of effort and vigilance needed—with the help of our accumulated 'emotional intelligence'—to navigate the responsibilities associated with the ethics of self- and other-care; responsibilities that our now so demanded by our culture that they form the bulk of our 'emotional labour' (Rojek 2010, 2005). If you have ever wondered why you feel mentally drained after a social event or a leisure occasion it is likely due to the expenditure of effort involved in the directed attention necessary to be on your best behaviour.

Fortunately, the natural environment is just the kind of place where we can allow our directed attention to rest and recuperate. By operating at a pace conducive to the relaxed use of 'involuntary' attention, natural environments provide few circumstances that require directed attention. Nature also provides just the kinds of characteristics to support this recovery process and stimulate 'involuntary' attention: It is typically away from the (urban) environments that are so demanding of our directed attention; it provides a perceptual 'extent' (e.g., both in a physical sense and the intricate complexity of its features); it evokes 'soft fascination' in both aesthetics and processes; and it is often experienced as a 'fit'—or as compatible—with the person and with the activities we carry out there. Unfortunately, our experiences of natural environments appear to have been in decline. We are now officially an urban species—and increasingly so. In May 2018 the *United Nations Department of Economic and Social Affairs* announced that 68% of the world's population was predicted to be living in urban areas by 2050. In 2018, 55% of us lived in urban areas (about 4.2 billion people). One in eight people live in so-called 'mega cities', with Tokyo currently leading the pack with an astonishing 37 million inhabitants, New Delhi following quite far behind at a modest 29 million, and Shanghai at 26 million.

None of which would matter if we were an infinitely malleable species, but it seems we have our limits. The claim that an increasing lack of contact with nature is harmful to us has been widely popularized (e.g., Louv 2008) but there is plenty of evidence to support it. Simple interventions such as nature walks (compared to urban walks) that increase contact with nature for those suffering from major depressive disorder result in improved cognition and affect (Berman et al. 2012). It also seems that urban green spaces may not have quite the same level of benefit as 'actual' natural environments, especially rural and coastal—at least in terms of perceived restoration benefits and the sense of connectedness with nature (Wyles et al. 2019). Despite the benefits of natural environments, our propensity to avoid the amount of effort and resources (e.g., of time, equipment, transport, and income) increasingly needed to access them is worrying enough. But it is not just a matter of reduced access—of most concern has been what has replaced that access.

At the extreme, most concern has been over the replacement of time in nature with time on screen. In a massive meta-analysis of over half a million U.S. adolescents that covered the years 2010–2015, it was found that depressive symptoms had sharply increased over that period, especially for females, with a full 33% increase; 12% more also reported at least one suicide related outcome; and there was a 31% increase in suicides for the age group (Twenge et al. 2018). This was further evidence of increasing mental health issues for young people on top of recorded increases in the case loads of university clinicians. While, from the meta-analysis, it did not seem that economic circumstances were the cause, the one factor that correlated strongly with these increases was more time spent on social media and electronic devices. The results showed "a clear pattern linking screen activities with higher levels of depressive symp-toms/suicide-related outcomes and nonscreen activities with lower levels" (Twenge et al. 2018, p. 9). Those with the least in-person interaction combined with high levels of onscreen interactions fared the worst. Limited in-person interactions may also have an effect on the development of neural centres involved in the kind of social and self-regulation necessary in our world. In an ideal world, adolescent brain development is a carefully calibrated interplay between individual (genetic) differences, neural development and the social environment (Lamblin et al. 2017). Adolescence is well known as a time of risk for mental illness and also as a time when the brain is being equipped to help with social information processing and behaviour. The social environment is deeply implicated in the outcomes of this development. As Lamblin et al. (2017) argue, there is a process of mutual 'sculpting' occurring between the developing brain (which, is a 'tool' for the person to use) and the social environment; each affecting the other. Harsh and punishing social media experiences intruding into that developmental process are a potential risk for achieving anything like the development of a successful and robust set of social skills.

Social media is one of the most pronounced expressions of an aspirational culture. There are stark and disturbing descriptions of the experiences that young people, and girls in particular, have with it and how it mediates their social lives in extraordinarily stressful ways (Sales 2016). There are also methodologically refined studies demonstrating its perverse effects. As well as the 'Friendship Paradox' which results in most people having friends on social media who are more popular than them, there is also the 'Happiness Paradox'—most people have friends on social media who are happier than they are (Bollen et al. 2017). The implications of these 'by design' features of social media networks of friends are clear enough. That feeling you have that everyone seems happier than you are and more upbeat on social media may at least partially be true. Given that the direction of our social comparisons (either 'upwards' or 'downwards') are known to affect SWB, and that social comparisons are an inherent feature of aspirational societies, and that social media inevitably invites comparison, it is no wonder that time on social media, especially for young people, is so harmful (Twenge 2013; Twenge et al. 2018).

*How* we interact with natural environments—and any environment—also has wellbeing consequences. The birthright of most mammals has been, of practical necessity, the opportunity to play in the world. For humans, particularly those of us in aspirational societies, the opportunities and time for 'free play' during childhood has declined over recent decades (Gray 2011). Whether that decline is part of the causal chain that leads to the increase in psychopathology in youth, which (Gray 2011) argues, is arguable but it is hard to see how it might support wellbeing either during childhood or into the future. Play has long been seen as essential to human beings (Bock 2004; Byers 1998; Fredrickson 2004; Pellegrini 2006, 2009). Famously, it has even been claimed by anthropologist Johan Huizinga in his book '*Homo Ludens*', that play is so inherent to humans that we, in effect, 'play' our lives and this playing is the basis of civilisation. Play enables skill development for use later in life, which is probably why the larger an animal's brain (cortex in particular) the more the animal tends to play while young. It has evolved to be enjoyable and is the original site for intrinsically motivated behaviour. In play, "behaviors must be voluntary, be observed in a 'relaxed field,' not be functional in the observed context, and have elements that are exaggerated, segmented, and nonsequential in relation to the functional behavior" (Burghardt 2005 cited in Pellegrini 2009, p. 132).

Leisure time, and perhaps socialising in particular, are prime opportunities for playfulness of this kind. By definition, leisure is voluntary and should happen in a 'relaxed field'. But there is also the experience of leisure becoming more competitive and a feature of one's presentation in the world, which makes it less a 'relaxed field' than a vital arena for the crafting of the all-important personal identity and sense of personal worth (Rojek 2005). Professionalisation of sport and leisure activities continues at pace, and individuals are increasingly tracking their leisure performances with activity apps, 'Go Pro' cameras, cycling route apps, and many more commodified ways to quantify your leisure life and challenge you to improve it are markers for the modern middle class.

How much time is now truly left for the human animal to be at play awaits more research. The signs are not promising. Aspiration can have a patina of positive playfulness at times (the enjoyment of 'just doing it') but even on the playing field Adam Smith's whisper to become "the impartial spectators to our own character and conduct" is likely to make itself heard. If neither work nor play are havens for the production of a wellbeing free from the siren call of aspiration how shall we find wellbeing in this world?

# References

Berman, M. G., Kross, E., Krpan, K. M., Askren, M. K., Burson, A., Deldin, P. J., et al. (2012). Interacting with nature improves cognition and affect for individuals with depression. *Journal of Affective Disorders, 140,* 300–305.
Bock, J. (2004). Introduction: New evolutionary perspectives on play. *Human Nature, 15*(1), 1–3. https://doi.org/10.1007/s12110-004-1000-1.
Bollen, J., Gonçalves, B., van de Leemput, I., & Ruan, G. (2017). The happiness paradox: Your friends are happier than you. *EPJ Data Science, 6*(4), 1–10. https://doi.org/10.1140/epjds/s13688-017-0100-1.
Byers, J. A. (1998). The biology of human play. *Child Development, 69*(3), 599–600. https://doi.org/10.1111/j.1467-8624.1998.tb06227.x.

Cederström, C., & Spicer, A. (2015). *The wellness syndrome*. Cambridge: Polity.

Cropanzano, R., & Wright, T. A. (2001). When a 'happy' worker is really a 'productive' worker: A review and further refinement of the happy-productive worker thesis. *Consulting Psychology Journal: Practice and Research, 53*(3), 182–199.

Csikszentmihalyi, M. (1997). *Finding flow: The psychology of engagement with everyday life*. New York: HarperCollins.

Csikszentmihalyi, M., & Graef, R. (1980). The experience of freedom in daily life. *American Journal of Community Psychology, 8,* 401–414.

Csikszentmihalyi, M., & LeFevre, J. (1989). Optimal experience in work and leisure. *Journal of Personality and Social Psychology, 56*(5), 815–822.

Davies, W. (2015). *The happiness industry: How the government and big business sold us well-being*. London: Verso.

Diener, E., Ng, W., Harter, J., & Arora, R. (2010). Wealth and happiness across the world: Material prosperity predicts life evaluation, whereas psychosocial prosperity predicts positive feeling. *Journal of Personality and Social Psychology, 99*(1), 52–61. https://doi.org/10.1037/a0018066.

Fredrickson, B. L. (2004). The broaden-and-build theory of positive emotions. *Philosophical Transactions of the Royal Society of London. B. Biological Sciences, 359*(1449, September 29), 1367–1378.

Gowdy, J., & Krall, L. (2013). The ultrasocial origins of the Anthropocene. *Ecological Economics, 95,* 137–147.

Gray, P. (2011). The decline of play and the rise of psychopathology in children and adolescents. *American Journal of Play, 3*(4), 443–463.

Gray, P. (2013). *Free to learn: Why unleashing the instinct to play will make our children happier, more self-reliant, and better students for life*. New York: Basic Books.

Harré, R. (1983). *Personal being: A theory for individual psychology*. Oxford: Blackwell.

Harré, R. (1998). *The singular self: An introduction to the psychology of personhood*. London: Sage.

Harré, R. (2016). Hybrid psychology as a human science. *Theory and Psychology, 26*(5), 632–646.

Hollway, W. (1991). *Work psychology and organizational behaviour: Managing the individual at work*. London, UK: Sage.

Jackson, M. (2018). *Distracted: Reclaiming our focus in a world of lost attention*. New York: Prometheus Books.

Judge, T. A., Heller, D., & Klinger, R. (2008). The dispositional sources of job satisfaction: A comparative test. *Applied Psychology: An International Review, 57*(3), 361–372.

Judge, T. A., & Klinger, R. (2008). Job satisfaction: Subjective well-being at work. In M. Eid & R. J. Larsen (Eds.), *The science of subjective well-being* (pp. 393–413). New York: The Guildford Press.

Judge, T. A., Locke, E. A., & Durham, C. C. (1997). The dispositional causes of job satisfaction: A core evaluations approach. *Research in Organizational Behavior, 19,* 151–188.

Kahneman, D. (2011). *Thinking, fast and slow*. Australia: Penguin Group.

Kaplan, S. (2010). Directed attention as a common resource for executive functioning and self-regulation. *Perspectives on Psychological Science, 5,* 43–57. https://doi.org/10.1177/1745691609356784.

Kaplan, S., & Kaplan, R. (1983). *Cognition and environment: Functioning in an uncertain world*. Ann Arbor, MI: Ulrich's.

Killingsworth, M. A., & Gilbert, D. T. (2010). A wandering mind is an unhappy mind. *Science, 330*(6006), 932. https://doi.org/10.1126/science.1192439.

Lamblin, M., Murawski, C., Whittle, S., & Fornito, A. (2017). Social connectedness, mental health and the adolescent brain. *Neuroscience and Biobehavioral Review, 80,* 57–68.

Leahey, T. H. (2000). *A history of psychology: Main currents in psychological thought* (5th ed.). Upper Saddle River, NJ: Prentice Hall.

Lemire, D. (2013). A historiographical survey of Literacy in Britain between 1780 and 1830. *Constellations (University of Alberta Student Journal), 4*(1), 248–261.

Louv, R. (2008). *Last child in the woods: Saving our children from nature-deficit disorder*. Chapel Hill, NC: Algonquin Books of Chapel Hill.

Lyubomirsky, S. (2013). *The myths of happiness: What should make you happy, but doesn't, what shouldn't make you happy, but does*. New York: The Penguin Press.

McAdams, D. P. (2013). The psychological self as actor, agent, and author. *Perspectives on Psychological Science, 8*(3), 272–295. https://doi.org/10.1177/1745691612464657.

Pellegrini, A. D. (2006). Play as a paradigm case of behavioral development [Review]. *Human Development, 49*(3), 189–192. https://doi.org/10.1159/000091897.

Pellegrini, A. D. (2009). Research and policy on children's play. *Child Development Perspectives, 3*(2), 131–136.

Peterson, C., Ruch, W., Beermann, U., Park, N., & Seligman, M. E. P. (2007). Strengths of character, orientations to happiness, and life satisfaction. *The Journal of Positive Psychology, 2*(3), 149–156. https://doi.org/10.1080/17439760701228938.

Rogers, C. R. (1959). A theory of therapy, personality, and interpersonal relationships, as developed in the client-centered framework. In S. Koch (Ed.), *Psychology: A study of a science: Study 1* (Vol. 3, pp. 184–256). New York: McGraw-Hill.

Rojek, C. (2005). *Leisure theory: Principles and practice.* Basingstoke: Plagrave Macmillan.

Rojek, C. (2010). Leisure and emotional intelligence. *World Leisure Journal, 52*(4), 240–252.

Ryan, R. M., & Deci, E. L. (2017). *Self-determination theory: Basic psychological needs in motivation, development, and wellness.* New York: Guilford Press.

Sales, N. J. (2016). *American girls: Social media and the secret lives of teenagers.* New York: Alfred Knopf.

Schiffer, L. P., & Roberts, T.-A. (2018). The paradox of happiness: Why are we not doing what we know makes us happy? *The Journal of Positive Psychology, 13*(3), 252–259. https://doi.org/10.1080/17439760.2017.1279209.

Sennett, R. (Ed.). (2006). *The culture of the new capitalism.* New Haven: Yale University Press. Retrieved from https://ebookcentral.proquest.com.

Stokes, P. (2017). Temporal asymmetry and the self/person split. *Journal of Value Inquiry, 51*, 203–219. https://doi.org/10.1007/s10790-016-9563-8.

Twenge, J. M. (2013). Does online social media lead to social connection or social disconnection? *Journal of College and Character, 14*(1), 11–20. https://doi.org/10.1515/jcc-2013-0003.

Twenge, J. M., Joiner, T. E., Rogers, M. L., & Martin, G. N. (2018). Increases in depressive symptoms, suicide-related outcomes, and suicide rates among U.S. adolescents after 2010 and links to increased new media screen time. *Clinical Psychological Science, 6*(1), 3–17. https://doi.org/10.117/2167702617723376.

Twenge, J. M., & King, L. A. (2005). A good life is a personal life: Relationship fulfillment and work fulfillment in judgments of life quality. *Journal of Research in Personality, 39*(3), 336–353. https://doi.org/10.1016/j.jrp.2004.01.004.

Wyles, K. J., White, M. P., Hattam, C., Pahl, S., King, H., & Austen, M. (2019). Are some natural environments more psychologically beneficial than others? The importance of type and quality on connectedness to nature and psychological restoration. *Environment and Behavior, 51*(2), 111–143. https://doi.org/10.1177/0013916517738312.

# 8

# In Praise of Ordinariness: The Wisdom of Living

## Aspirational Culture, Persons, and Wellbeing

In his book *In Pursuit of Unhappiness*, philosopher Daniel Haybron (2008, p. 225) begins his chapter on 'The Pursuit of Unhappiness' with an apt homily:

> For most of the living world, the good life is mainly a matter of context. Given the right setting and a good dose of luck, most organisms tend to do well, or at least to succeed in their terms: that's basically how they're wired. Conversely, put a typical creature in the wrong setting and—good luck or no—it is lost, pretty much guaranteed a quick death.

Humans are adaptable, so a 'quick death' for the species was never on the cards. But we are now a "species out of context" and that has made 'the good life' difficult to experience. Through the long history of our species our adaptability to almost all the physical and ecological environments the earth could generate depended upon a cooperative social form that could re-adjust the coordination of the social group— sometimes within moments—in response to threats, ambiguities, and opportunities. Paradoxically, it was the *constancy* of this social form that

© The Author(s) 2019
K. Moore, *Wellbeing and Aspirational Culture*,
https://doi.org/10.1007/978-3-030-15643-5_8

allowed the *flexibility* in our adaptive responses to the unpredictability and uncertainty inherent in a complex natural and physical world. Survival did not depend upon the ingenuity of individuals but on the ability of the social group to harvest and 'sieve' individual contributions in ways that transformed and amplified the range of adaptive responses possible. As Daniel Dennett (1995) put it, our particular form of sociality proved to be a spectacular 'crane' that could 'winch' human adaptability to a level that far surpassed what was previously possible.

As a species we evolved to fit into this highly cooperative form of sociality. We became friendlier (facially and temperamentally); we increased our capacity to remember (e.g., others' faces and past behaviours); we were 'domesticated'; and most important of all, we became *persons*. Through their success at creating 'fit for purpose' cognitive 'gadgets' such as language and metacognition, human cultures could help us coordinate our activity with each other by virtue of discovering the 'good trick' (another of Dennett's phrases) of taking each other, and ourselves, as persons. Not only did this allow us to hunt and gather effectively together and to share the tasks of child-rearing within an egalitarian social structure but it also gave us the impressive and probably unique abilities to generate a near-infinite variety of shared meanings and practices in response to life's challenges. To become a person was, and is, the achievement of participation in those meanings and practices. To mix metaphors, that shared world is both the sea we all swim in and the soil that gives birth to us as persons.

The account of persons I have tried to outline in the previous chapters makes it clear that the 'context' that creates and sustains all of us as persons—and not simply as biological human beings—is itself an extraordinary feat of evolution. That context took a primate and turned it into a being that could see itself as a singularity and a unity, but also a being that had a coherence and continuity that did not just span minutes but could encompass decades—an entire life. It did this for the purposes of social regulation and because of the advantages that accrued from that regulation. To be a singular unity that also happens to be attached to a particular body makes it just the kind of being that is relatively easy to track and hold to account, and is able to be coordinated in a normative and moral manner—but only within the context of a group of other persons. What the same person did—yesterday, today, and tomorrow—could now not only be tagged or indexed to a particular organism but could also form narratives (lives). Creation of these narratives would, from the start, have involved a complex juggling of social roles, reputations, relationships, long-term commitments—and the reflexive possibilities that come from the opportunity to renegotiate and haggle over each of these. The adaptive possibilities and constraints that arose from these narratives—which is to say, from the lives of persons—was unprecedented in the animal kingdom. For the first time on earth, a world of responsibilities, duties, and rewards came into existence. Along with that new world came a new kind of wellbeing, one intimately connected to the standing of a person in such a world.

For millennia, this animal-turned-person endured. Fitted well for a small society of egalitarian but autonomous cooperators, it persisted even while the biological being it depended upon sometimes struggled to survive. Population levels remained static, at best. This unlikely bio-cultural hybrid was the glue that held the hunting and gathering way of life together by being the channel for cultural inheritance and training.

Then, something changed. Agriculture was adopted, food surpluses could be generated (at least periodically), and populations increased. Individual persons began to specialise in their daily activities, narrowing their skills and refining their work practices. As economies expanded so did social hierarchies. The ultrasocial experiment our species began some 12,000 years ago took us out of our environmental context by transforming the environment from a place in which we live (a home) into a site for the extraction of the resources we now need to live. Taken on its own, that ecological uprooting of our species is now having dire consequences in the shape of climate change, biodiversity and habitat loss, water quality, desertification, and a host of local environmental problems. But we also began to be taken out of another context, another 'home'—the form of sociality that gave us our personal being.

The evolutionary irony was that this ecological and social disembedding was possible for one reason—the entity of the 'person' had already evolved. Persons were well-designed—'pre-adapted'—for recruitment into the increasingly complex ultrasocial societies being generated. As sociocultural artefacts they had evolved to facilitate social regulation and cooperation making them perfect for the thoroughly interdependent lives that were being fashioned in the new ultrasocial economic arrangements.

My claim is that the whole enterprise of the last 10,000 years has been, at base, an 'aspirational' one. That is, human ultrasociality required an expansionary and exploitative dynamic and, on those dimensions at least, could be described as progressive, deeply innovative, and, therefore, 'aspirational'. Unfortunately, however, 'persons'—the particular beings that fueled this social form—were not doing well, which perhaps should not be all that surprising given their wellbeing was never a necessary part of the overall dynamic.

The Danes have a word that has been loosely translated as 'wellbeing' and which has become something of a fashionable preoccupation amongst educated people outside of Denmark. *Hygge*, apparently, refers to a sense of warmth and comfort in the world and, for Danes, brings to mind drinking hot drinks next to log fires. A recent blog post on the 'Jacobin' web page noted that *hygge* is more than just an individual 'preference' that can be skinned and on-sold to non-Danish westerners. It rests, instead, on the foundational social and economic structures associated with the social democratic Danish nation state. The sense of security and the feeling that, as a Dane, one has time to nurture friendships and savour what simply living as a human being has to offer does not arise from some hard to replicate cultural quirk. It is a direct emanation of a whole way of organising a society and, so, living.

This interpretation may seem romantic or even ideological but, as I have already established, personal wellbeing depends on the often unseen and unacknowledged collective commitments, social and economic institutions, and coordinating processes that form the background for our lives; it is these features of our world that enable and sustain our personhood. Ideally they provide us with a sense of personal continuity, coherence, and a 'unity of unities' as Rom Harré (1983) calls it. Our actions, our consciousness, and our lives (our biographies) are not only each united within themselves but form a unity together—they essentially create our life as a person.

There is an *ordinariness* to this achievement. It amounts to the peculiar kind of 'nature fulfillment' that eudaimonists from Aristotle onwards have seen as central to the wellbeing that comes from a 'good life'. Yet, it is not only the fulfillment of our biological 'nature' but also of our personal nature (i.e., our 'nature' as persons); a nature that exists in moral orders formed by the cultures within which people live. When the cultural evolution of personhood first began at the time humans still lived by hunting and gathering, those moral orders would have provided sparsely built but clear frames. Today, for many—even most— people, they create mazes of moral complexity from which there seems no way out and which, consequently, drive unprecedented levels of perfectionism and anxiety.

The newly invented self-monitoring 'Lockean self' has, in the twenty-first century, become a paradoxical caricature that simultaneously loudly asserts its own distinction, uniqueness and merit while privately cowering at the prospect of the judgment of others. It contorts itself in this way solely to meet the cultural demands of living in an aspirational culture.

It is true that our aspirational culture creates persons who orient their entire lives around the conscious efforts associated with aspiring in any number of ways, but there is nothing inherent in being a person that requires aspiration to become a way of life. Persons pre-existed the emergence of the sociocultural imperative for people, singly and as a collective, to aspire. Thus, it would be possible for our economic, social, and psychological 'aspirations' to simply focus on the continuation of the 'ordinariness' of living as persons.

The aim of a culture—to the extent that cultures have aims—is to survive, materially, in the present and to reproduce itself into the future. The means by which cultures have evolved to reproduce themselves is via the continuous creation of persons. Without persons there is no human culture, at least not in the sense that we usually mean. Creating and sustaining persons is the 'ordinary' function of a culture.

It is a feature of aspirational cultures that the 'ordinary' is often disparaged or at least viewed critically as something in need of constant innovation and improvement. Of course, there are times that the 'ordinary' can itself be a threat to the good life if the habitual practices individuals and societies engage in prevent adaptive responses to a new disruption. Challenges sometimes arise that cannot be overcome by doubling-down on what has always been done (i.e., by repeating the 'ordinary' way of going on).

But, if there are limits to the usefulness of ordinary practices there are also limits to the benefits of change. The principal limit to change for human cultures is the need to produce, sustain, and reproduce viable persons. Once that 'ordinary' process begins to fail a culture cannot hold itself together. Crucially, not every outcome of human development ends with a viable form of personhood. A person is not an infinitely variable cultural artefact. Just as, ultimately, there can be no such thing as a 'chair' if there are no objects that afford 'sitting on' (for humans) so too there can be no such thing as a person if there are no entities that can successfully coordinate themselves collectively (for the purposes of cultures).

Our species has evolved remarkable capacities to alter its niche and survive in all sorts of environments. But as I have shown, these altered niches often create considerable challenges for those same capacities. As P. E. King et al. (2018) argue, individuals—using their evolved capacities—need to 'mind the gap' between the variety of new niches humans are capable of constructing and the ability of their offspring to thrive in those new niches. They propose that this 'gap' is likely responsible for the difficulties humans have with thriving (at the individual, rather than the population, level).

The greatest such 'gap' that has arisen for humans is the one created by the adoption of agriculture and the way it transformed our sociality into ultrasociality. P. E. King et al. (2018), go on to argue that the same 'big brains' that helped create the 'human nature-niche' gap can help solve the problem of thriving in these new niches. They argue that our abilities at self-regulation, sociality, and informational learning (rather than learning directly by experience) also facilitate thriving and, in fact, appear in many accounts of human thriving.

I have gone a step further than King et al. in suggesting that this 'gap' has grown so large that it fundamentally threatens human thriving by undermining our culture's ability to create viable persons and, since it is persons whose thriving or wellbeing is of concern, it also fundamentally threatens our wellbeing as persons. Not coincidentally, the problems we are now experiencing are deeply connected to our capacities for self-regulation (now an omnipresent demand for an exhausting process of self-monitoring), sociality (the punishing effects of social monitoring, surveillance, 'fluid', weak and ephemeral social relationships, and the resulting problems of perfectionism), and informational learning (the rapid obsolescence of 'knowledge' and craft, the uncertainty over the validity and efficacy of 'knowledge', etc.).

But even critics of our aspirational culture rarely recommend the rejection of what that culture has produced. Anthony Giddens, for example, argued against rejection of reflexive modernity not least because of the economic dividends and innovations it had allowed. And while acknowledging how today's ultra-fragmented world has created income inequality, social instability, and deep fractures at the heart of most people's daily lives, Richard Sennett (2006) also advised against wishing it away.

According to Sennett (2006, p. 3), "[i]t would be irrational to believe that this economic explosion should never have happened". He suggests that global improvements in living standards and the surge in technological innovation arose partly from the same process of the dismantling of centralised mechanisms of control that generated the problems and anxieties people experience today. His hope was that different forms of social structures could arise that would make the inherent instability of the new social forms bearable for individuals and communities.

The three challenges that Sennett's (2006, pp. 3–5) "ideal man or woman" must face are products of the new economic and social arrangements. The first is the need for the individual, in the absence of institutional stability, to "improvise his or her life-narrative, or even do without any sustained sense of self". The second is the need for the individual to constantly develop new skills and "mine potential abilities, as reality's demands shift" (e.g., the shift from craftsmanship to supposed 'meritocracy' which "celebrates potential ability rather than past achievement").

The third and final challenge, according to Sennett (2006, p. 4), is to "let go of the past" since what is in the past counts for little in a society structurally focused on the immediate future and its supposed opportunities. A being who can meet these new challenges most resembles Stokes (2017) concept of the temporally asymmetric 'self' rather than the diachronic person. Such a 'self' values the past hardly at all but the present and immediate future greatly. So long as the situations and culture in which it operates allows it, this self will happily shed its past multiple times and reinvent itself anew to take advantage of the next opportunity.

As Sennett (2006, p. 5) notes, however, this particular kind of self "oriented to the short term, focused on potential ability, willing to abandon past experience is—to put a kindly face on the matter—an unusual sort of human being" and "[m]ost people are not like this". I would go further and assert that it is actually impossible to attempt to permanently be this kind of self.

The 'logically primitive', 'powerful particular' in the social world (to combine phrases borrowed from Strawson and Harré) is a person—and that is what we all are; inescapably. Only those who have never mastered the first-person pronouns, who have never developed a 'theory' or understanding of themselves, and who therefore have no sense of their own singularity could possibly succeed at being the kind of self that Sennett acknowledges is "an unusual sort of human being".

The flight into the self that supposedly constitutes the "ideal" man or woman in an aspirational culture is an impossible flight from personhood, with all the perils for our wellbeing that such flight entails. As Harré (1998) points out, we are able to have, and commonly do have, multiple versions of 'Self 2' (the theory we have of our own self) and 'Self 3' (the self that others take us to be) but there is only ever one Self 1 (which is a descriptor for our sense of singularity and unity). To challenge the singularity of Self 1, Harré claims, is to push at the borders of psychopathology and threaten a fundamental disruption to our sense of being a person.

I have highlighted this idea of disruption as a major threat to our wellbeing as persons throughout this book. The original and most fundamental disruption turned humans into a 'species out of context'. The embedded processes of ecological feedback were disrupted once agriculture was widely adopted. Feedback was not entirely absent—droughts, plagues of insects, infectious epidemics and famines ensured that—but, once agriculture became locked-in, the feedback became a problem requiring innovation to sustain the agricultural mode rather than an indication to ease back on production.

That fundamental disruption then led to other disruptions of the social world such as the establishment of hierarchies (including sex hierarchies) and the generation of roles for non-productive members of the group who benefitted from, and often enforced, the new hierarchies. Along with that broad social disruption came disruption of interpersonal, daily relationships which needed regulation in new and explicit ways. The 'civilising process' described by Norbert Elias' (2000) was the outcome of this. Refined and specified codes of acceptable, appropriate, and decent behaviour became influential in social regulation—initially amongst the elite but eventually fully 'democratised' via formation of the middle classes and their expansion.

The final disruption has been within each individual's life. Through the emergence and promotion of the self-monitoring 'Lockean self'—without which psychology would lack much of its current subject matter (Danziger 1997)—all of us have been split in two, creating a fundamental disruption at the heart of our personal being. This split, which strongly echoed the disruptive splits in our interpersonal lives and social worlds, did not arise out of nothing and no doubt had precursors in the more rudimentary senses of self that preceded it, but it had a crucial effect on both the potential for individual aspiration and for our individual wellbeing.

From that moment on, our selves—rather than simply our lives—could be regarded as objects to be worked upon for aspirational ends. To succeed at work we must attend to our motivation and mental energy; to become accepted by others we must focus on adjusting our personalities; to optimise our life chances we must work on our optimism and self-regulation; to gain a sense of self-worth we must nurture our self-esteem and learn to love ourselves. Each of us has essentially become our own aspirational project.

Today, it is not only our jobs, skills, and personal goals that are subject to disruption. Our social world is also subject to unprecedented turbulence. We are residentially mobile, which affects our friendship ties and sense of self (Oishi 2010) and the distance and frequency of these residential moves during childhood and adolescence is even implicated in incidence of psychosis (Price et al. 2018).

This repeated unhooking of persons from social environments creates its own, deeply personal, disruption. Persons, by definition, are adept at manufacturing, moment-by-moment, the coherence and unity required for personhood including a whole-of-life narrative. That narrative may need constant editing to maintain its integrity as a story of just *this* life of a person but, nevertheless, this is what persons are designed to do. In an aspirational culture, however, the threat to this ability of persons continually to narrate their own lives as the coherent lives of agentic persons subject to the prevailing moral orders it encounters is unprecedented.

Aspirational cultures put us all into an excruciating bind. On the one hand, these cultures encourage, reinforce, and even demand we become that "unusual sort of human being" described by Sennett (2006, p. 5), one who is "oriented to the short term, focused on potential ability, willing to abandon past experience". On the other hand, like all cultures such cultures also regulate us by assuming us to be 'persons'. Thus, though we may have to act day-by-day as if the past—our own past—does not matter, no society ever really relinquishes its right to hold us to account for that same past.

The most corrosive effects on our wellbeing arise out of this bind: we find ourselves acting in ways that—later or even at the time—we, as persons, would eschew or even despise. Self-worth and integrity become fundamentally elusive once we grasp what is needed to survive in such a culture—self-promotion, self-monitoring, and intense curation of our 'selves'. These are just the kinds of pressures that the research shows are being felt acutely by young people. To express it differently, the practical necessity of inauthenticity (e.g., on social media and even our increasingly fleeting face-to-face interactions) continually clashes with the ethic to be authentic and to act with integrity.

At the end of a long evolutionary and historical journey, persons now daily find themselves in just these sorts of moral and normative binds. We seek out ways to resolve them or, even, to dissolve them but the complexity of the social and economic machinery within which we make these attempts today overwhelms far too many of us. To put it in a nutshell, life, as a person, has just become too hard.

## Wellbeing and Persons: An Argument in Three Parts

In this book I have constructed an argument in three parts. First, I have claimed that the wellbeing we are concerned with is the wellbeing of persons. Persons, as I have been at pains to point out, are not, primarily, psychological beings or subjects; they are sociocultural artefacts formed by and through sociocultural activity. What we normally take to signify internal psychological complexity is in fact complexity in the actions of persons operating in the discursive and moral contexts of what Harré calls an ontology of persons.

Our personal psychology is constructed in real time and makes use of the materiality of our biological bodies, the physical settings we occupy and the social and discursive positions from which we act. The art of being a person in any particular culture is called personhood. The wellbeing of persons therefore amounts, in large part, to how successful persons are at practising this art. That success, in turn depends upon how we have been formed as persons and the 'fit' of what is required to enact our personhood with the demands of the culture that has formed us.

In the second part of my argument, I have suggested that what I have called 'aspiration'—defined as an organising principle that aligns all elements of a culture around imperatives for growth, expansion, improvement, progress, and exploitation—has been a prominent aspect of human cultures over the past 10,000 years or so. But while aspiration has been implicit and incipient in most cultures during that time period, it is now the dominant logic of a global culture and is increasingly open-ended in scope. It is characterised by mutually reinforcing economic, social, political, and personal elements each of which, in its own way, expresses that logic. Most human effort, directly or indirectly and individually or collectively, is now aspirational in focus and intent.

The third part of my argument makes the claim that the aspirational culture we are all locked into is fundamentally detrimental to the well-being of persons. This conclusion is itself composed of three broad claims. The first is that the economic, social, political, and interpersonal arrangements within aspirational cultures make the central tasks involved in enacting personhood particularly difficult to achieve. Those tasks concern the achievement of continuity, a coherent unity of consciousness, action, and biography, and a sense of agency. An aspirational culture repeatedly disrupts those fundamental activities of personhood.

The second claim is that aspirational cultures constitute persons (and personhood) in a form that compounds the difficulty in accomplishing those tasks. That is, aspirational cultures create persons who are ill-equipped to sustain personhood within those cultures. Specifically, persons are encouraged to acquire selves (that is, theories of themselves) understood as entirely fluid with little stability or essential continuity, ready to respond, adapt and morph at a moment's notice. At the same time, each person is also encouraged to pursue a unique, clearly-defined, and distinctive self and life in the midst of this unstable and uncertain world. In order to acquire this kind of self we also have to practice constant self-monitoring. That means we are trained to adopt a 'Lockean self' or what Adam Smith called "the great judge and arbiter of our conduct".

The third claim is that aspirational cultures, in multiple ways, do not support the acquisition of the personal, largely discursive, skills that might provide some defence against the difficulties of sustaining personhood. It is striking that the most educated people today are the ones who claim the greatest sense of meaning in their lives. That is, they have the skills to present—to themselves and others—some semblance of coherence about their life trajectories. Yet, it is also telling that those who possess such a sense of meaning also suffer from the most worry and stress and so can experience less positive affect. It is as if the skilled effort required to support and sustain a meaningful and defensible sense of personhood comes at the cost of a daily experience of happiness. The self-regulatory effort is too great and requires too constant a vigilance for the simple enjoyment of life.

## A Research Agenda

From this three-part argument the beginnings of a research framework and agenda become clear. Persons are formed by and act within a socio-cultural context. In the world of persons things are done. Doing things requires both tasks to perform and tools with which to perform them. A psychological study of wellbeing that is based on a theory of persons and personhood would therefore have three main areas of focus: Persons, tasks, and tools. Each focus area would suggest many potential research questions.

One focus would be on the cultural context and how it intersects with the creation of personhood. How does a particular cultural context form persons? That is, what kinds of social institutions are involved in the development (ontogeny) of persons and what are their main functions in relation to developing persons? For example, the education of children may be informal and integrated into the everyday activity of the community as it is in many hunter-gatherer groups, or it could be formalised around schools, disciplinary instruction, and bureaucratic assessment, monitoring, and management as in many nation states today. These different institutional arrangements are suited to quite different functions of persons within their respective cultures (e.g., the creation of more or less autonomous cooperators or of differentiated and disciplined contributors to an ultrasocial set of economic practices).

Further, what version of personhood does a culture favour? An obvious way to gain insight into how to answer this question would be to investigate the kinds of selves that are encouraged and adopted in a particular culture (Harré's Self 2 and Self 3) since they are modelled on the prevailing concept of a person. These notions of 'self' are the ready-made 'theories' or fictions that persons use to provide guidance and justification for their actions, and which are used by a local community to characterise individual persons. Selves, understood in this way, are derivative of a culture's favoured account of persons.

There is already a considerable amount of research postulating the existence of various forms of selves—independent, interdependent, relational, and collective selves are just some examples. Once current research on the 'self' is released from the assumption that the self is an internal individualised psychological entity or process, empirical findings could be reinterpreted and integrated into a person-based research agenda.

Such a research agenda could also focus on the extent to which persons in a particular culture make reference to these various selves and in what situations a focus on the self is greater or lesser. This would provide some measure of the extent to which a culture encourages its members to produce elaborate theories of self with which to guide themselves. That is, it would provide insight into how psychologised the notion of a person has become in any particular culture.

By 'psychologised' I mean the extent to which the psychological activity of persons has come to be reduced to individualised, internal, and sub-personal processes such as cognitive and neurophysiological processes. Are people encouraged, for example, to see memory as residing within their minds or brains, on the one hand, or within their activity as persons living a life? Is the mind or brain seen as a tool used to remember something, or are minds and brains instead seen as the mechanisms that, in fact, do the remembering? The psychology of a person is to be found in their activity, not in an interior world of unconscious psychological states and events. By contrast, the psychology of a 'self' is understood as the attributes or components of that self.

How persons are produced by a culture and the kinds of persons it produces are closely connected to the typical tasks required to be accomplished by persons in that culture. In today's society, for example, a typical life-task might be obtaining work sufficient to sustain oneself (or a family) independently of others. Other tasks include becoming literate to a certain standard, presenting as an open, friendly person with a fulfilling life and being a well-informed, hands-on and 'intensive' parent (Ishizuka 2018).[1]

Further research questions could include whether such tasks are carried out cooperatively or competitively, collectively or individually? Are these tasks tightly prescribed or only vaguely specified? Which tasks are seen as more central for persons to achieve and which are more optional? How extensive and effortful are the tasks and how time-consuming are they likely to be? That is, how much of one's time needs to be devoted to these culturally prescribed tasks? What other kinds and amounts of resources are needed (e.g., money, cultural capital, social connections)? How closely monitored are the tasks? Are the tasks mutually supportive or contradictory? That is, how feasible or practically possible is it to achieve the variety of tasks required of a person? Connected to the relative importance of tasks is the question of what sanctions or rewards, if any, accompany failure or success at a task?

A third area of focus for research into a person-based psychology of wellbeing would be what sort of 'tools' are typically required by persons in a particular culture to accomplish the required tasks. An important sub-set of these tools, of course, are the skills to deploy other tools effectively. These tools may include a fully developed set of neurocognitive mechanisms, including the culturally-derived 'cognitive gadgets' highlighted by Heyes (2018), or a body capable of the necessary physical acts for achievement of the tasks. They may also include the more abstract tools involved in mastery of the discursive skills necessary for personhood itself (e.g., mastery of personal pronouns) or for particular tasks, as well as physical tools and technologies.

Fundamental research questions would concern the number and variety of tools necessary for at least the central tasks a culture requires of persons. But there are also questions about access to the tools, how individual persons can acquire or develop the tools and the support, in the culture, for that acquisition and development to occur. Is development of the needed tools supported or undermined by the culture? How widespread and how equal is access to the necessary tools amongst persons in a culture? Do some tools have other uses—beyond the tasks required by a culture—and what consequences might those uses have for a person's ability to succeed at other tasks or for their wellbeing in general?

For example, does the set of discursive skills acquired through extended education have other uses such as perfecting discursive aggressiveness towards others in competitive contexts or even in undermining one's self; for example, the ability to construct strong arguments about one's lack of worth or the meaninglessness of one's life? And furthermore, what features of the cultural environment affect how these other uses impact the wellbeing of others or of the person with the tools?

# The Wellbeing Paradox Revisited

The research agenda and questions such an agenda generates may also help to deepen our understanding of what I have called the 'Wellbeing Paradox'. Most current explanations for why people have a negative view of the current state of the world invoke a version of false consciousness (see Chapter 1). We are victims of some combination of being overwhelmed by media focused on the negative aspects of life, ignorant of the facts that indicate widespread improvements in modern life, or unwitting dupes of our evolved cognitive biases that make us remember and pay particular attention to anything likely to be a threat.

Pessimism is, on this reading, an unfortunate but insistent tendency—propelled partly by human nature and partly by modern social institutions—that can only be avoided through a comprehensive commitment to rationality. There is, however, another explanation. People may be open to critical and pessimistic accounts of the world because that resonates with their daily experience of life. That is, judging by their own immediate experience people may intuit that something is awry with the world and so are more receptive to claims that the world in general is 'going to hell in a handbasket'. The sense that something is wrong or out of alignment in their own lives makes it easier to believe that something is wrong with the world as a whole. That is especially plausible if the feeling of wrongness amounts to an almost existential sense of the difficulty of simply being a person and living a life.

Persons are mainly concerned with the maintenance of their own personhood and their good standing through interactions with other persons in the prevailing local moral order. In a literal sense, this continuing normative interaction is the environment within which a person exists. It is also the environment that persons are reliant upon for their sense of continuity, unity, and the other attributes of personhood. This environment is the basis of the wellbeing of persons in exactly the same way that the wellbeing of polar bears requires maintenance of the habitat within which polar bears can be polar bears.

Being a person requires quite particular conditions that allow personhood to occur. Without those conditions, personhood would be difficult, even impossible, to achieve and maintain. As animals, humans can adapt to most of the physical and environmental conditions on earth, which is why humans can be found from the tropics to the Arctic. By contrast, personhood depends upon specific social and cultural conditions to develop and be maintained. These conditions presumably prevailed during the hundreds of thousands of years our species survived as hunter-gatherers and it was specifically these conditions which gave rise to the first versions of persons.

The central argument proposed in this book has been that, since the agrarian revolution, the aspirational logic that has underpinned economic, social, political, and interpersonal life has progressively taken its toll on the ability to establish and maintain personhood. Essentially this aspirational imperative has created a social and economic context that has increasingly compromised the conditions for the generation of personhood.

A sense of personal unity, continuity, agency, and even singularity— the hallmarks of personhood—all become significantly more difficult to accomplish in cultures geared towards aspiration at all levels and in all dimensions. From the point of view of persons, these difficulties amount to existential challenges. Some individuals will appear to surmount these challenges and become exemplars of what is needed to benefit from an aspirational culture. But even such apparently model persons can find their personal resources wanting or lacking when circumstances change—sometimes leading to a spectacular unravelling of their lives—and, in any event, they appear to form a smaller proportion of the population as time passes. It is a rare person who has a robust and persistent sense of being at home in her life.

Many of the mental health issues afflicting modern populations can be understood as attempted adaptive responses to these challenges to personhood. In the unstable and uncertain contexts of today's world, increased rates of perfectionism (Curran and Hill 2017), for example, can be seen as indications of the impact of aspirational imperatives on our attempts to maintain personhood and therefore being persons in good standing in the local moral order. At the population level, and significantly more than previously, we experience the world as demanding unrealistic levels of achievement. This experience is expressed in increased perceptions of social perfectionism—the feeling that others demand perfection from us.

In response to these demands (e.g., various modes of more or less obligatory success—financial, educational, social, relationship, self-care and other-care) we then demand better performances from ourselves leading to ever greater levels of self-oriented perfectionism. We also express other-oriented perfectionism (our demand that others be perfect) as we become less tolerant of the performance of others. After all, paradoxically, our ultrasocial interdependency means that others can affect our chances of success even in a world where, supposedly, we are solely responsible, as individuals, for both successes and failures. Intimate partners, for example, can be seen to fail to provide us with what we need to have fulfilling and successful relationships; the ineptness of other members of our sporting team is blamed for losing an important game; the laziness of a colleague is blamed for the loss of an important account, the incompetence of the slow driver in front of us is the reason we will be late for work. Blaming ourselves and blaming others are simply two sides of the same perfectionistic coin that we use to navigate our personal narrative in an aspirational world perceived as increasingly demanding of the perfect performance at every turn.

Seeing our lives as a series of attempts to be persons in a hostile environment also might explain the observed increases in hypomania, anxiety, depression, and perceived external locus of control, especially in young people (Twenge 2000; Twenge et al. 2004, 2010, 2018). For example, adoption of hypomanic attributes and behaviour is one obvious response to the high-energy demands for continuous striving. Similarly, anxiety can be understood as an exhausting adaptation to the need for constant self-monitoring that follows from the sense that the world is a malevolent 'tester' of our abilities to cope well enough to succeed at the tasks our culture sets for us.

Depression is the equally exhausting, embodied breakdown in the face of the demands to maintain functioning personhood in a hostile environment. A perceived external locus of control can be both a realistic response to the difficulties individual persons have in navigating life in the midst of the vicissitudes and uncertainties of an aspirational world and a strategy to deflect personally targeted judgments of one's worth that are inherent in that same culture.

Today, people struggle not because of a failure to appreciate and be grateful for the health and economic advances that have recently emerged from a history of aspirational effort. That is, they are not depressed because they are unaware that global poverty has decreased and so have too pessimistic a view of the state of the world. When it comes to the experience of psychological pain, it is not so much the state of the world that matters to them as the state of their lives.

Sociologist Ruut Veenhoven (2010), a 'new optimist' who claims things are getting better and better for human beings, suggests that "modern society provides a challenging environment that fits an innate human need for self-actualization" a need that arose because "the human species evolved in rather tough conditions and therefore typically thrives in modern society with its complexities, competition and choices" (Veenhoven 2010, p. 120). Life was never meant to be easy (in evolutionary terms) and so we fortunately evolved an innate need to 'self-actualise' to meet the challenges of 'tough' conditions—which happen to be replicated in modern societies. Our nature, that is, has fitted us well to the kind of society we have now created.

My conclusion is the opposite. Far from being well fitted to the modern world, our 'nature' *as persons* has made us susceptible to be involved in the creation of a culture and society that is a poor fit for that 'nature'. Further, that nature did not lead to the evolution of a 'need' to self-actualise. Its only 'need' is for the sociocultural conditions for the establishment and maintenance of viable personhood and so to be a person in good standing in its culture. To have such good standing requires that a person have the skills and capacities to fulfill the sociocultural tasks and demands required of persons in that culture.

What then of Veenhoven's (2010) finding that, at least in some European countries (though not in the United States or Japan), life satisfaction measures have increased and, along with increased life-expectancy, have therefore produced more 'well-being'? (Veenhoven uses the measure of 'Happy Life Years' for wellbeing or 'enjoyment'—calculated as the product of a nation's average life satisfaction scores and life-expectancy at any point in time.) When persons answer surveys and complete questionnaires they are responding to an invitation to be involved in a conversation (Harré 1998). A conversation about 'satisfaction with life' already presumes familiarity with an aspirational account of life and a desire-satisfaction theory of wellbeing. While Veenhoven claims that such measures must include some personal assessment of levels of enjoyment it is not clear that they do.

As Diener et al. (2010) found, life evaluations seem to be more associated with a material form of prosperity than with what they call 'psychosocial prosperity', which is more associated with positive affect. This chimes with the interesting finding discussed in Chapter 9 of the *World Happiness Report, 2018* (Helliwell et al. 2018) that South American countries, despite severe economic, political, and social difficulties, nevertheless have populations reporting some of the highest levels of positive affect in the world seemingly because of their strong family and social relationships. It seems likely that what Veenhoven reports as increased enjoyment is closer to a report on increased material prosperity or, perhaps, increased material security rather than increased affect or enjoyment of life.

Finally, it is telling that Veenhoven (2010) notes how challenging life in today's world is, arguing that it therefore matches life in hunter-gatherer times. As much of this book has argued, the challenges of life in today's aspirational culture are different in both type and degree than those complex, ecological challenges faced by hunter-gatherers (see Chapter 2). Ultrasociality, for example, introduces new social forms and associated social coercive pressures that are quite distinct from any challenges in the much flatter, egalitarian societies that apparently dominated in human prehistory.

## Final Thoughts

Shortly before his death in 1987 the comparative mythologist Joseph Campbell said that he did not think people were searching for meaning; rather, he believed that what they were really after was the feeling of being alive. That is, people seek an experience of living gained from an immediate and (psychologically) effortless activity that employs their entire being and that gives their acts a sense of clarity and certainty. If that is the 'cure' then the 'illness' is presumably a corresponding sense of always acting in the opposite way—with constant effort, hesitancy, distraction, and disruption. We have a sense, that is, of failing at our central task—being alive as a person.

A thorough-going aspirational world is one of fluid and unpredictable economic and social change, fragmentation of personal experience in time, space, and relationships, and an increase in the depth and breadth of demands for us to 'self-monitor' ourselves as we navigate its complicated and often contradictory ways. All these features compound to inflict the 'illness' of our time and to make its 'cure' ever more elusive. The tragedy of this world—and of the last 10,000 years or so of human history—is best summed up by a line from one of Shakespeare's great tragedies, *King Lear*. "Striving to better, oft we mar what's well".[2] We have unwittingly paid the price of the recent improvements in the human condition in the same coin that was minted by the long decline in the human condition after the agrarian revolution: our wellbeing as persons.

Wellbeing researchers verge on this sense of an unencumbered, unhesitating vitality when they speak of the importance to wellbeing of 'intrinsic motivation' (and associated degrees of motivation outlined in Self-Determination Theory), 'flow', and 'vitality' itself. But these concepts are limited to particular actions of individuals at particular moments in time. What is missing is an account of the much more fundamental basis of our wellbeing in the ongoing cultural activity—within the world of persons—that continues the project of our existence as persons.

There is a sense in which being a person is itself a work of fiction (Harré 1998). This might seem ludicrous since, for most people, it is their sense of being and acting in the world *as a person* that seems most real. It is as a person that we are born in a certain place to particular parents. It is our person that goes to certain schools, works at particular jobs, has specific friends, family members, hobbies, successes, failures, and any number of other unique biographical details. How can this bedrock of our experience, as persons, be said to be 'in a sense' fictional?

When Nick Chater (2018), in his book *The Mind Is Flat*, attempts to describe the psychological attributes of Anna Karenina he points out that we know as much about her inner life (the inner life of an entirely fictional character) as we do about our own (beyond our specific ability to perceive our own bodies). We do not infer our inner life, or in some other way know it; we *express* it. And we express it in our activity in the world- just as Anna Karenina does (or just as Leo Tolstoy does as he authors her actions).

The only thing, then, that provides our own reality in contrast to the reality of a fictional character in a novel is that, as actual persons, our fictionality—the meaningful activity we generate—is tied to a particular body and is therefore anchored by and enacted in the world and constrained by it, though this constraint ensures that we exist. Without bodies others would find it near impossible to respond to and take us as persons. Their ability to see us as individuals and so treat us as a person would be radically difficult.

This is closely related to Strawson's (1959, p. 340) insight that ascribing states of consciousness at all (which would include such states as being happy, satisfied, having a sense of meaning, etc.) depends upon the concept of 'person' in that "a necessary condition of states of consciousness being ascribed at all is that they should be ascribed to the *very same things* as certain corporeal [bodily] characteristics, a certain physical situation, etc." The 'very same thing' is the particular person who is, for example, both happy (a mental state) and sitting in the airport lounge (a physical-material situation). That is, states of consciousness and the situated activity of persons in the material world inevitably go together. If correct—and I think it is—all of this means that our wellbeing (and all the supposed psychological states it includes) fundamentally depends upon the ease of continuation of this kind of cultural activity.

We exist—as persons with minds, feelings, thoughts, motives, etc.—as part of what Harré (1983, p. 20) refers to as the "fundamental human reality", a "conversation, effectively without beginning or end, to which, from time to time, individuals may make contributions". It is the integrity of this 'conversation' that we depend upon. This is the 'flow' that is ultimately needed to maintain us as persons. Moments of 'flow' (Csikszentmihalyi 1990, 1997) in our life are desirable and contribute to our sense of wellbeing but, more fundamentally, it is the flow of this activity by, and between, persons that constitutes the basis for our wellbeing. The more this flow is disrupted the harder it is to maintain any form of wellbeing for persons. We can perhaps keep our bodies well, our minds 'sharp' and active, and even our 'selves' in a coherent form but these efforts will amount to little in terms of wellbeing if we struggle in the task of being a person, and in being a person of good standing in the world of other persons. The conclusion of this book is that it is the stability of this 'flow' that is under threat in an aspirational culture.

As noted in Chapter 6, from life's accidental discovery of the remarkable trick of replication, the hallmark of the living world has been to find more and more creative ways to maintain stability via evolved systems. That is still our task today. By understanding that we are, first and foremost, persons we can begin that task with some sense of the direction in which we must move.

We must, for a start, abandon the idea that we are, as persons, infinitely malleable because by its very 'nature' personhood is a form of stability and continuity. A person is the unit of coordination in human sociality. If it morphed constantly its principal sociocultural function would be impossible. It is a precarious creation at the best of times. While persons require 'selves' (their theories of who they are) they must not be understood as merely 'selves', either by themselves or by others. The prime focus of a person (because it is a sociocultural creation) is, and should be, the world, not itself. More to the point, a person is a continuous activity, or enactment, in that world. It is not an entity separate from that world (the only world there is) or in some self-referential way, independent of it.

A person is an outward-oriented being by 'nature' since its concern is interaction and coordination with other persons. It has taken 12,000 years to construct an increasingly pervasive and complex set of aspirational institutions sufficient to turn persons inward towards a fictional inner world. It has taken a few hundred years to convince persons that it is 'natural' to have a 'Lockean self' and to be dictated to by its needs for everything from fame and fortune, to personal growth and 'self-acceptance'. But none of these 'needs' are about inner states of the self. Their pursuit is activity in the world of persons. And it is this constant aspirational pursuit that results in the experiences of ill-being increasingly reported.

The wellbeing of persons depends upon surprisingly little. Their unity, singularity, and continuity emerge 'naturally' from direct and stable encounters with other persons when they are engaged in broadly cooperative activity. Such an ordinary world has sufficient resources to trigger most of the features of a life of wellbeing—autonomy, engagement, a sense of competence, positive affect, creativity, and deep satisfaction. Yet, this kind of ordinariness has been displaced by an 'ordinary life' that, in the long pre-history of our species, is far from ordinary. We have been coerced and cajoled to live lives far removed from those that suit either our biology or our sociocultural nature as persons.

The evolved fit that presumably obtained for so long between our physical bodies and physiology, on the one hand, and our social existence as individual persons, on the other, has now become a site of pain. As persons, we try to maintain our integrity—and good standing—by trying to conform to the imperatives that an aspirational culture demands of us, but which places our biology under chronic pressure.

As a fast growing body of research shows we are now having fundamental difficulties in carrying out the most basic of animal functions: eating, sleeping, physical movement—and these issues are compromising our bodily integrity, our health and our well-being. Indeed, our difficulties with accessing species appropriate nutrition, sleep and physical activity are even beginning to turn the much vaunted 'increased life expectancy' graphs in very much the wrong direction (e.g., Sachs 2018).

Our dependency upon ever-more complicated and unpredictable economic and social machinery and increasingly Kafka-esque bureaucratic technical systems has progressively enclosed our lives within tighter perimeters. The remarkable truth of our species is that, ever since the turn to ultrasociality, we have spent our time shedding the simple wisdom of living that every other animal enacts with little hesitation or effort in its life every day.

It is not that we are unaware of the importance of living wisely in this way, or of its relationship to wellbeing. King (2008), for example, has argued that, 'surprisingly', pursuing happiness can often lead to the development of maturity or 'wisdom'. By wisdom she means "the fundamental pragmatics of life permitting exceptional insight, judgment, and advice involving complex and uncertain matters of the human condition" (Baltes and Staudinger 1993, p. 76 cited in King 2008, p. 441). These 'fundamental pragmatics of life' are nothing other than the skills involved in living as a physically embodied person. An aspirational culture is now a strong current or headwind that is forever pushing us away from gaining and expressing these skills, thus making it harder to be wise in a simple, human way.

Our task in living is not to see ourselves as some psychologically complicated mechanism that needs constant monitoring, adjustment, and improvement in order to thrive and flourish—as our aspirational culture increasingly encourages us to see ourselves. Instead, we need see ourselves as nothing other than the persons that we already are, agents in a normative world of other persons—and demand a world that allows us to be that way.

There is an adage that has often been misattributed to the philosopher Bertrand Russell (and John Lennon, apparently) which, properly interpreted, could serve as a pocket antidote to the pressures of an aspirational world: 'Time you enjoy wasting is not wasted time'. With the usual caveat that people, especially today, claim they enjoy many things that actually harm them there is something true about the benefit of doing things that provide those often unexpected and, usually, effortless times we enjoy.

In an aspirational culture we are tempted to call these times 'wasted' simply because they seem to serve no clear aspirational end. But, every time they happen, they serve an end more important for our wellbeing than any aspirational end ever could. At those moments we are being ourselves, without hesitation or confusion. As a Buddhist monk supposedly once said, 'When I am hungry, I eat. When I am tired, I sleep.' Those are the moments when we are simply being the beings we are. There is nothing special about those experiences—as rare as they may be in our lives today. We are merely being human beings and, as a natural part of that, being persons.

But, of course, it is not true that this adage could ever serve as a complete 'antidote' to the pressures of an aspirational culture. It is no cure but more like a poultice we might apply to our pressured selves from time to time. The only real cure follows from the fact that persons are sociocultural artefacts. For those concerned about improving human wellbeing at its roots, the main task has to be challenging and changing the aspirational structures, practices, and institutions of today's world. Experiments to this end are already in motion (e.g., trials of a 'universal basic income', movements for 'simple living', 'downshifting', and 'slow living').

In the end, however, it is not just individuals who must cease to see aspiration as the point of their lives but our entire (and rapidly globalizing) culture which must find a way to restructure itself while still in accelerating motion. That is not an easy task but as Václav Havel famously said "hope is not the conviction that something will turn out well, but the certainty that something makes sense, regardless of how it turns out".

By understanding that, after all, we are persons who come into existence together and that we are not 'separate selves' striving independently, and aspirationally, to make something of our lives (and our 'selves') then perhaps we can see our way back home—and begin to construct a world in which it will no longer be so very hard simply to be a person.

## Notes

1. The survey carried out by Ishizuka (2018) in the United States found that the once elite practice of 'intensive parenting' has now been democratized. Intensive parenting is characterized by time- and resource-intensive parenting, with a focus on extracurricular activities, reasoning with children, eliciting their thoughts and feelings, and advocating for one's children with teachers and professionals. Fifty years ago, intensive parenting was considered an upper-middle class phenomenon with the lower classes favouring a more 'indulgent' or even 'neglectful' approach ('accomplishment of natural growth'). Today, however, parents subscribe to the value of intensive parenting (if not the expensive practice of it) irrespective of class or race, presumably in response to perceptions that life is now too difficult and competitive to leave a child's life outcomes to a natural process (i.e., to leave it to chance).

2. The quote comes from Act I, Scene IV when the character Albany (Goneril's husband) tries to caution Goneril (one of Lear's daughters) about making matters worse with her father. The rest of the play, being a tragedy, bears out the wisdom of Albany's instinctive cautiousness.

# References

Chater, N. (2018). *The mind is flat: The illusion of mental depth and the improvised mind*. London, UK: Allen Lane.

Csikszentmihalyi, M. (1990). *Flow: The psychology of optimal experience*. New York: Harper and Row.

Csikszentmihalyi, M. (1997). *Finding flow: The psychology of engagement with everyday life*. New York: HarperCollins.

Curran, T., & Hill, A. P. (2017). Perfectionism is increasing over time: A meta-analysis of birth cohort differences from 1989 to 2016. *Psychological Bulletin*. https://doi.org/10.1037/bul0000138.

Danziger, K. (1997). The historical formation of selves. In R. D. Ashmore & L. Jussim (Eds.), *Self and identity: Fundamental issues* (pp. 137–159). Oxford: Oxford University Press.

Dennett, D. C. (1995). *Darwin's dangerous idea: Evolution and the meanings of life*. London: Penguin Books.

Diener, E., Ng, W., Harter, J., & Arora, R. (2010). Wealth and happiness across the world: Material prosperity predicts life evaluation, whereas psychosocial prosperity predicts positive feeling. *Journal of Personality and Social Psychology, 99*(1), 52–61. https://doi.org/10.1037/a0018066.

Elias, N. (2000). *The civilizing process: Sociogenetic and psychogenetic investigations* (2nd ed.). Oxford: Wiley-Blackwell.

Harré, R. (1983). *Personal being: A theory for individual psychology*. Oxford: Blackwell.

Harré, R. (1998). *The singular self: An introduction to the psychology of personhood*. London: Sage.

Haybron, D. M. (2008). *The pursuit of unhappiness: The elusive psychology of well-being*. Oxford: Oxford University Press.

Helliwell, J. F., Layard, R., & Sachs, J. D. (2018). *World happiness report 2018*. New York: Sustainable Development Solutions Network.

Heyes, C. (2018). *Cultural gadgets: The cultural evolution of thinking*. Cambridge, MA: Harvard University Press.

Ishizuka, P. (2018). Social class, gender, and contemporary parenting standards in the United States: Evidence from a national survey experiment. *Social Forces, soy107*. https://doi.org/10.1093/sf/soy107.

King, L. A. (2008). Interventions for enhancing subjective well-being: Can we make people happier, and should we? In M. Eid & R. J. Larsen (Eds.), *The science of subjective well-being* (pp. 431–448). New York: The Guildford Press.

King, P. E., Barrett, J. L., Greenway, T. S., Schnitker, S. A., & Furrow, J. L. (2018). Mind the gap: Evolutionary psychological perspectives on human thriving. *The Journal of Positive Psychology, 13*(4), 336–345. https://doi.org/10.1080/17439760.2017.1291855.

Oishi, S. (2010). The psychology of residential mobility: Implications for the self, social relationships, and well-being. *Perspectives on Psychological Science, 5*(1), 5–21. https://doi.org/10.1177/1745691609356781.

Price, C., Dalman, C., Zammit, S., & Kirkbride, J. B. (2018). Association of residential mobility over the life course with nonaffective psychosis in 1.4 million young people in Sweden. *JAMA Psychiatry*, E1–E9. https://doi.org/10.1001/jamapsychiatry.2018.2233.

Sachs, J. D. (2018). America's health crisis and the Easterlin paradox. In J. F. Helliwell, R. Layard, & J. D. Sachs (Eds.), *World happiness report* (pp. 146–159). New York: United Nations Sustainable Development Solutions Network.

Sennett, R. (Ed.). (2006). *The culture of the new capitalism*. New Haven: Yale University Press.

Stokes, P. (2017). Temporal asymmetry and the self/person split. *Journal of Value Inquiry, 51*, 203–219. https://doi.org/10.1007/s10790-016-9563-8.

Strawson, P. F. (1959). *Individuals: An essay in descriptive metaphysics*. London: Methuen.

Twenge, J. M. (2000). The age of anxiety? Birth cohort change in anxiety and neuroticism, 1952–1993. *Journal of Personality and Social Psychology, 79*(6), 1007–1021. https://doi.org/10.1037//0022-3514.79.6.1007.

Twenge, J. M., Zhang, L., & Im, C. (2004). It's beyond my control: A cross-temporal meta-analysis of increasing externality in Locus of Control, 1960–2002. *Personality and Social Psychology Review, 8*(3), 308–319.

Twenge, J. M., Gentile, B., DeWall, C. N., Ma, D., Lacefield, K., & Schurtz, D. R. (2010). Birth cohort increases in psychopathology among young Americans, 1938–2007: A cross-temporal meta-analysis of the MMPI. *Clinical Psychology Review, 30,* 145–154. https://doi.org/10.117/2167702617723376.

Twenge, J. M., Joiner, T. E., Rogers, M. L., & Martin, G. N. (2018). Increases in depressive symptoms, suicide-related outcomes, and suicide rates among U.S. adolescents after 2010 and links to increased new media screen time. *Clinical Psychological Science, 6*(1), 3–17. https://doi.org/10.1177/2167702617723376.

Veenhoven, R. (2010). Life is getting better: Societal evolution and fit with human nature. *Social Indicators Research, 97*(1), 105–122.

# Index

© The Editor(s) (if applicable) and The Author(s) 2019
K. Moore, *Wellbeing and Aspirational Culture*,
https://doi.org/10.1007/978-3-030-15643-5

.